SANSKRIT & PRAKRIT
Sociolinguistic Issues

MLBD SERIES IN LINGUISTICS

General Editor
DHANESH JAIN

Volume VI

SANSKRIT & PRAKRIT
Sociolinguistic Issues

MADHAV M. DESHPANDE

MOTILAL BANARSIDASS PUBLISHERS
PRIVATE LIMITED • DELHI

First Edition: Delhi, 1993

ISBN : 81-208-1136-4

Also available at :

MOTILAL BANARSIDASS
41 U.A., Bungalow Road, Jawahar Nagar, Delhi 110 007
120 Royapettah High Road, Mylapore, Madras 600 004
16 St. Mark's Road, Bangalore 560 001
Ashok Rajpath, Patna 800 004
Chowk, Varanasi 221 001

PRINTED IN INDIA

BY JAINENDRA PRAKASH JAIN AT SHRI JAINENDRA PRESS, A-45 NARAINA INDUSTRIAL AREA, PHASE I, NEW DELHI 110 028 AND PUBLISHED BY NARENDRA PRAKASH JAIN FOR MOTILAL BANARSIDASS PUBLISHERS PVT. LTD., BUNGALOW ROAD, JAWAHAR NAGAR, DELHI 110 007

Dedicated
with love
to
my wife

SHUBHANGI

CONTENTS

AN APOLOGIA

By

Professor Ashok R. Kelkar

Those who know me know how much I hate to write Forewords and such. With the passing of time, an invitation to writing one only comes as a painful reminder as to how one is getting identified with the benign senior citizenry. So perhaps I owe it to my friends and to myself to say why I am making here an exception.

Professor Madhav M. Deshpande has fought his way into a no man's land, namely, the historical sociolinguistics of South Asia. Mainstream sociolinguists are largely busy with contemporary problems and have almost forgotten that one important way of understanding the present is finding out how the present has historically come to be what it is. Mainstream historical linguists in turn have preoccupied themselves with the bones and sinews of language (as Deshpande himself has done in chapter VIII) almost to the exclusion of the ethology and ecology of this animal — or rather the linguistic ethology and ecology of the human animal. A senior citizen could perhaps offer to the present venture some air cover.

A valuable asset in historical reconstruction is the imaginative ability to think of the persons involved not as shadowy venerable (or despicable) figures, but as human beings of the same flesh and blood as us. Consider the way Deshpande (in chapter V) accounts for Pāṇini's neutrality as between geographical regions: "Pāṇini's region was on the margins of bigger political entities [like the Persian and the Magadhan empires]. ... Pāṇini [himself an Udīcya] perhaps chose not to recognize openly the political superiority of the Prācyas, nor could he proclaim the Udīcyas to be superior, since they were politically the dominated region rather than being the dominant one." How very human of him to be diplomatically neutral! And yet Deshpande does not forget to insert the scholarly qualification of 'perhaps'.

This brings me to another positive aspect of Deshpande's work. His is the middle ground between the meticulous, text-oriented scholar and assumptions. Scholarly caution does not tie him down to the certain detail away from the hurly-burly of the traffic of language; speculative theory does not allow him to fly in the face of contrary or totally absent evidence. While he is quick to note the implications of the "melting-pot" demography for language variation, he is quick to note the anachronism of Chatterji's speculations on Manu's "use" of history (in chapter VII). Fortunately this middle ground is no longer a no man's land that it once used to be. More and more people today are choosing to be both humanists and human scientists at the same time.

But this has perforce pushed Deshpande into a really difficult domain. It is to his credit (as when he speaks in chapters II, III, and IV of the doctrine of the *nityatva* of the Sanskrit language as opposed to the mutability and variability of the other modes of speech) that he has realized the need for the risky enterprise of insinuating oneself under the skin of the ancient Indians, the need to take an insider's view of their world. One of the first Indologists to become aware of this problem was the great editor of the critical edition of *Mahābhārata*, V.S. Sukthankar. He argued that categories borrowed from Western textual criticism probably fail to do justice to the *Mahābhārata* phenomenon. Those who inherited and in turn transmitted the work probably thought of it as shared ancestral property. What they were doing to it was not seen as distortion, insertion, or excision doing violence to the integrity of a past text. The very ontology of the text was differently conceived by them. In reconstructing the ontology of the Sanskrit language as presupposed by Patañjali and others, we have to realize that their answer to the question, when is the language identical with itself, was quite different, for, while Sanskrit is *a* language for us, it is *the* language for them. I call this demand for taking an insider's view of the *Mahābhārata* transmission or of the transmission and the study of the Sanskrit language a demand for the endocentric perspective.

But of course having placed ourselves in a time machine and having walked into the past we must not forget to come back! The endocentric perspective must be supplemented by the exocentric perspective, the outsider's view. If we fail to do this, we are also likely to fail to realize that the ancient Indian past was not an unchanging past. Commentaries are fine and certainly cannot be ignored. But we mustn't lose sight of the fact that a commentator may be as much separated from the original author in perspective as we are from either of them. If a modern scholar can fail to grasp what Pāṇini was about, so can a Patañjali or a Nāgeśa.

I am happy to find that Deshpande does not forget to come back just as he does not forget to leave our company from time to time.

Turning around, I realize that I need not write that foreword after all. Rather I can best leave the job of introducing to the reader the studies gathered here together with their underlying methodology to the author himself.

Pune, 19 June 1990 ASHOK R. KELKAR

PREFACE

Madhav M. Deshpande

In this volume, eight contributions having bearing on socio-linguistics of Sanskrit and Prakrit are brought together. These represent some of my work in this area stretching for a period of about fifteen years. Of these eight contributions, six are revised versions of earlier publications [Chapter I = Deshpande 1987, Chapter IV = Deshpande 1985c, Chapter V = Deshpande 1985b, Chapter VI = Deshpande 1982b, Chapter VII = Deshpande 1983a, and Chapter VIII = Deshpande 1979b], while the articles *Loka: The Linguistic World of Patañjali* and *On Vernacular Sanskrit: The Gīrvāṇavāṅmañjarī of Dhuṇḍirāja Kavi* are published here for the first time. The first three articles represent revised versions of lectures presented at the Centre of Advanced Study in Sanskrit at the University of Poona, India, during the summer of 1987. Apart from these three initial articles, all the other articles were conceived of independently at different times and appeared in different publications. Thus, they read more like independent articles, rather than as chapters of a single book. I have made some revisions in these articles, but little to hamper their independent character. The price I have to pay in maintaining their independent readability is to tolerate a certain amount of overlap of topics. However, I have reduced the degree of repetition by consolidating the bibliography and the notes.

While these are more or less independent articles, they are all permeated with a common approach to the subject matter. In these articles, issues of language history and interaction in South Asia are placed not only within the context of what we know about the society, culture, religion and the political structures of those ancient times, a deliberate effort is made to uncover the attitudes of the ancient Indians themselves. I began studies of Indian linguistic history with this multivalent approach more than a decade ago, and it has yielded many important results. The main thrust of my studies has been an investigation of language-data and linguistic theory within the context of the socio-cultural world of ancient India. As we know from extensive studies of many regions of the world, language-use and ideas about language in the modern world are deeply nomic factors. It stands to reason that the situation in ancient and classical India could not have been different in this respect. The studies presented here, each in its way, attempt to uncover these complicated networks of influences.

A general outline of my investigation of the Indian approaches to "history" was presented in my article "History, Change and Permanence: A Classical Indian Perspective" (= Deshpande 1979), and a discussion of the importance of studying the total context within which ancient Indian grammarians functioned appears in the introduction to my book *Sociolinguistic Attitudes in India: An Historical Reconstruction* (= Deshpande 1979a). Since these discussions form the basis of most of the ensuing studies, it may be useful to briefly summarize the main themes.

While working on ancient texts, such as the works of Sanskrit grammarians in ancient India, one needs to recognize that these texts do not share the same perspective on history as a modern historian does. In looking for "history" in these texts from our modern perspective on history, we need to keep in mind that we are perhaps creating a picture of a world which was unknown to the texts and their authors themselves. While we can argue, and with good justification, that facts of history as we see them did influence the works of these ancient authors, we must not overlook the more obvious point that these authors were actually more influenced by the history of the world as they knew it. Thus, we need to make a deliberate effort to see how the ancients saw their world, so that we may be able to better explain the questions concerning the motivations behind the statements in ancient works. We need not agree with the ancient view of the world, or share their admiration or disdain for certain social structures. However, we must make every effort to comprehend the ancient world-views and attitudes.

In general, the ancient classical Indian tradition believes in mythical versions of Indian history in which the entire caste-system, and those world populations which were outside of it, were ultimately born from the same act of creation. The ideal structure of the society, as enshrined in the law-books, was believed to go back to the first acts of creation. The peoples outside the caste-system were believed to be those, who, for some reason or another, left it and ceased to practice their caste duties. Thus, the increasing diversity of the world was deemed to be a result of a kind of fall from grace. At the core of this ancient and classical perspective of history is the notion that cycles of the existence of the world begin with creation and end in its destruction. Within these cycles, however, there is an inevitable progression from an initial golden age of purity and truth (*satya-yuga*) to the final age of universal strife (*kali-yuga*), which ends in the destruction of the world. Thus, change is generally considered to be degenerative - going from a state of relative purity to a state of decay. These ideas about history then manifest differently in different philosophical and religious systems. For the Sanskrit grammarians, the eternally pure Sanskrit language degenerated into Prakrits when used by inferior people, and, according to the Sāṃkhyas,the original pure state of Primal Matter (*prakṛti*) undergoes degenerative transformations (*vikṛti*) in the evolution of the world, a process which a philosopher needs to undo, as it were, in the course of reaching a state of equilibrium. These are different manifestations of the same underlying attitude toward history as a degenerative transformation. In order to maintain a certain level of purity in the world, one needs to at least freeze certain stages of history and guard them against further change, if one cannot ideally reverse the direction of the inevitable degenerative transformation. The law-books, the grammars of Sanskrit, the various practices of Yoga etc. all seem to fulfill the same general purpose. In this fashion, the ancient Indian world-views became determining factors for the decisions made by ancient Indians. This is one side of the story.

The other side of the story lies in the modern uncovering of the periods of ancient Indian history or pre-history which were inaccessible to the classical mind. The epoch of the Indus-Valley Civilization, and the migrations of the Austro-Asiatics, Dravidians and Aryans, and their conflicts and convergences over millennia are essentially unknown to the world of classical India. For this world, there is no history or pre-history to Sanskrit going back to the Indo-European past, but only a degenerative history leading to the emergence of the "fallen" vernaculars. Thus, the classical mind, being unaware of this pre-history, could not have consciously taken it into consideration in formulating its world-view. In fact, it is the ignorance of this pre-history that allows the emergence of the classical world-view. How would one explain the facts of Sanskrit, if one believed that it had no history, and that it was an eternal language? Thus, the lack of knowledge of pre-history and history itself presented an intellectual challenge to those who were working within the classical world-view, and they had to create functionally viable thought-structures within the limits of this paradigm. This they did admirably well.

I perceive my task as that of a mediator between the ancient world-views and our own world-view at present. Ultimately, for us, our understanding of ancient India must be situated firmly within our modern perspective on human history. However, in order to be able to do this task, it is important to incorporate into our modern perspective a fuller comprehension of how the ancient Indians saw their world. We can neither disregard the ancient perspectives and be engrossed merely in our own evaluation of the material remains of ancient India, nor can we be carried away by the ancient perspectives and forsake our independent judgment based on historical evidence unknown to or disregarded by the ancient Indian texts. We must give due importance to both of these dimensions.

I believe the foregoing paragraphs sufficiently explain the nature of my concerns and illustrate my approach to the study of ancient India in general, and its linguistic history in particular. To say anything more is to take away something from the studies presented here. I hope that these studies, in this consolidated form, will reach a wider audience and will stimulate further research in socio-linguistics of Sanskrit and Prakrit.

I would like to express my gratitude to Professor Ashok R. Kelkar for having written *An Apologia* for this book. I want to thank all those friends and colleagues who have over the years encouraged me to follow this particular line of investigation. While a good deal of conclusions reached in these studies are inherently hypothetical, and are bound to remain hypothetical, I feel that the historical reconstruction that I have pursued has given me a better sense of Indian linguistic and sociolinguistic history, than simply be in possession of disconnected statements scattered through hundreds of texts. I would not deny the possibility of other alternative reconstructions and would welcome further efforts in that direction.

I am dedicating this book to Shubhangi, my wife, who has stood by me all these years, and, as a true *saha-dharma-cāriṇī*, shared with me the struggles of life. I am grateful to her for all her love and patience.

** NOTE: In this book, the character "*ḷ*" is used to represent the vocalic "l" of Sanskrit, while the character "*Ḷ*" is used to represent the retroflex consonant which replaces the intervocalic "*ḍ*" in the *Ṛgveda*, and which occurs in languages like Marathi.

I

SANSKRIT AND PRAKRIT: SOME SOCIOLINGUISTIC ISSUES

1. Introduction

1.1. In my 1979 monograph *Sociolinguistic Attitudes in India: An Historical Reconstruction,* I discussed in detail several questions relating to the social attitudes connected with the use of various Indo-Aryan languages in their historical development. In his foreword to this monograph, M.B. Emeneau says (Deshpande, 1979a, foreword, p. 1):

> In the earliest period, speakers of Indo-Aryan - Vedic and living Sanskrit - were concerned with neighboring languages, whether they were other varieties of Indo-Aryan or were non-Indo-Aryan; the historical dimension had hardly yet come into play. Thereafter, when Sanskrit was no longer a living language but was a language of high prestige that had ceased to be anyone's first language, the concern was essentially an evaluation of various vernaculars as against the classical language. The situation was complicated by the circumstance that some 'protestant' communities combined an adversary position on the language with an adversary stance against the religious and social doctrines and practices of Hinduism.

In my monograph, I attempted to disentangle the complicated results and attitudes involved in these phases of the Indian linguistic history. In this chapter I propose to continue some of the same discussion, but extend it further with additional evidence and conclusions. In the following discussion, I may inevitably have to repeat some of the material which I have discussed in the above mentioned monograph, but I hope this transgression will be of use for those who have not had the opportunity to read my previous work.[1]

2. Sociolinguistic Attitudes in Vedic India

2.1. We will briefly review the sociolinguistic situation prior to the emergence of Jainism and Buddhism in ancient India. The literary record of India begins with the *Ṛgveda*, a collection of hymns in praise of Aryan gods composed by various priests who served different Aryan clans and their kings. Certain Aryan clans gradually moved into India from the northwest around the middle of the second millennium B.C. At the time they entered India and confronted the indigenous peoples whom they called Dāsas and Dasyus, their sociolinguistic attitudes were fairly simple. Though they had already confronted and perhaps partially converged with non-Aryan peoples in Iran and elsewhere, they had a pervasive notion of their own ethnic identity. They glorified their language as being divine and produced by the gods themselves.

2.2. The Aryans generally looked at the mass of non-Aryans as substandard human beings, godless non-sacrificers, worshippers of dummy gods and phallic gods, and those whose language was obscure and unintelligible. The non-Aryan languages could not have pleased the Aryan gods, and hence were held to be ritually inferior. As the Vedic Aryans gradually moved into the interior of India, they began adjusting themselves to the local scene. Through contacts and convergence with non-Aryan languages and through internal propensities of its own, the old Indo-Aryan language of the Vedic texts was slowly becoming archaic, and was being replaced by new vernacular forms of the Indo-Aryan languages. This probably forced the Aryans to look at the sacred old Aryan language and their own current form of language more carefully. The end of this stage is marked by the great grammarian Pāṇini (about 500 B.C.). Pāṇini calls what we call Sanskrit simply *bhāṣā* "language". A distinction is made in his grammar between *bhāṣā* "the colloquial language" and *chandas* "the language of the Vedic texts". To be more specific, these two are viewed as being distinct subdomains of a unified Sanskrit language. While literally the term *bhāṣā* stands for "language"; in fact, it actually refers to the upper-class language, in relation to which other forms of Indo-Aryan and non-Aryan languages were viewed as being substandard, as those peoples themselves were placed lower in the social hierarchy.

2.3 According to the Purāṇic records, Pāṇini was contemporary of a king, named Mahāpadma, who is described as a Śūdra who destroyed all true Kṣatriyas, members of the warrior and kingly class, who according to Brahmanical notions are alone fit to be rulers. To speak of Kṣatriyas being destroyed by Śūdra chieftains probably refers to their mixed origin and / or their anti-Brahmanical attitudes. At any rate, as the Śūdra rulers became very powerful, their "substandard" dialects must also have gained in prestige. This period roughly corresponds to the rise of Buddhism and Jainism, and the insistence of these two faiths in using the local vernacular languages in preference to Sanskrit may be related to changes of this kind. The founders of these two faiths, Buddha and Mahāvīra, both came from the eastern Kṣatriya clans that lie outside the Brahmanical region of Āryāvarta. The Maurya dynasty, which arose in this region, showed distinct preference for Buddhism and Jainism; during the reign of Aśoka Maurya, Buddhism received royal patronage and spread all over India and Sri Lanka.

3. Alternative Sociolinguistic Perspectives in India

3.1. I would like to discuss the question of the relative prestige of Sanskrit and Prakrit in some greater depth. The standard Brahmanical view of Prakrits is too well known. As Daṇḍin says in his *Kāvyādarśa*:[2] "In literature, the languages of Ābhīras etc. are considered to be *Apabhraṃśa* (i.e. the term is not applied to Prakrits). On the other hand, in the (Brahmanical) sciences (such as Sanskrit grammar), anything other than Sanskrit is labeled *Apabhraṃśa*." Here we have a clear statement of the difference between the view held by grammarians like Kātyāyana and Patañjali on the one hand, and that held by the poeticians on the other. There is obviously a greater degree of puritanism among Sanskrit grammarians. But would it be appropriate to assume that the low prestige for Prakrits was a universally acknowledged fact in ancient India? This is analogous to the question concerning the relative prestige of Brāhmaṇas and Kṣatriyas. Would it be appropriate to say that the higher status of the Brāhmaṇas was universally acknowledged by the Kṣatriyas of ancient India? I would like to argue that there are at least two contending views held by the Brāhmaṇas and the Kṣatriyas, each group creating a parallel but opposite hierarchy. This is why we must look at the testimony coming from various Brahmanical and non-

Brahmanical texts as representing not the absolute standards of social prestige, but as representing dissenting views on social prestige. For instance, even in a Brahmanical text such as the *Śatapatha-Brāhmaṇa*, there is evidence for such a dual perception:[3] "Brahman, verily, was all this in the beginning. It being alone was not powerful enough. It created forth Kṣatra of an excellent form, i.e. these Kṣatras among the gods, Indra, Varuṇa, Soma, Rudra, Parjanya, Yama, Mṛtyu and Īśāna. Therefore, there is nothing beyond the Kṣatra. Therefore a Brāhmaṇa takes his seat below the Kṣatriya at the Rājasūya sacrifice. He (the Brāhmaṇa) bestows that glory upon Kṣatra alone. This Brahman is the birth-place of Kṣatra." One can clearly see in this passage two concurrent images fused together. The physical fact is that the Brāhmaṇa priest sat below the king in the ceremony of Rājasūya, as he also obviously sat below the king at his court. This shows the true political hierarchy. However, the Brāhmaṇa priest, in his own theological speculation, raises himself above the king and derives the essence of kingship from his own essence. It is not clear from the Brahmanical texts whether the kings themselves actually ever accepted this reverse order of prestige, in spite of such occasional assertions in texts like the *Bṛhadāraṇyaka-Upaniṣad*:[4] "(The king) Ajātaśatru said (to the Brahmaṇa Gārgya) - 'It seems to be reverse of the normal order that a Brāhmaṇa should approach a Kṣatriya hoping that he may teach him about Brahman'." The authors of Brahmanical texts are Brāhmaṇas and not Kṣatriyas, and they represent the Brahmanical views of social prestige, even through the words of a Kṣatriya character.

3.2. Buddhist and Jaina texts of the early period provide us a counterbalance to this Brahmanical perspective. They provide us the Kṣatriya perspective. A close study of these sources can give us a better sense of the differing perspectives held by the various social groups in ancient India, and this may help us explain certain aspects of their language use and attitudes as well. In what follows, I shall discuss some of these alternative social perspectives in greater detail.

4. Sociolinguistic Attitudes in Buddhism

4.1. All evidence points to the fact that Buddha used his own Prakrit dialect to teach his doctrine. One of the obvious reasons is that he wanted to reach the masses, and this he could have done only by using the local dialect. He claims that his doctrine is for the benefit of the masses (*bahu-jana-hitāya bahu-jana-sukhāya*). B.C. Law (1933, p. xvi) cites the *Araṇavibhaṅgasutta* of the *Majjhimanikāya:* "Now a man of a particular locality, when he is in other localities where different names of the same thing are in vogue, knowing that in different localities different names of the same thing are used conventionally by the gentlemen, uses different names in different localities without any attachment to his own local form." This suggests Buddha's preference for local dialects. However, this does not mean and should not be interpreted to mean that Buddha used "lower" languages, which he would not have used otherwise, simply to reach the lower classes. Such a view would be quite misleading.

4.2. Buddha claimed to represent the Aryan way of life, as can be seen from dozens of expressions in the Buddhist canonical texts. For example, *ariya dhamma* "the Aryan doctrine", *ariya magga* "the Aryan path" etc. In all these cases the word Aryan may be generally translated as "noble", but it is a loaded word. It represents an attempt on the part of Buddha to create and assert a new conception of Aryanhood, to combat the conservative concept held in the Brahmanical circles. On the higher philosophical plane, Buddha totally rejected hereditary caste rank. But on the lower social plane, Buddha asserted a social hierarchy different from that of the Brahmanical belief. He clearly asserts that Kṣatriyas are superior to Brāhmaṇas. Thus, far from its being an inferior dialect, Buddha must have considered his own dialect to be superior to that of the Brāhmaṇas, as he considered his own Kṣatriya rank superior to theirs.

4.3. We may look at the evidence for this conclusion in greater depth. There is clear evidence in the canonical Pali texts to show that there was great tension between Brāhmaṇas and Kṣatriyas and that they held essentially opposing conceptions about each other's social status. At the beginning of the famous *Mahāparinibbānasutta*, the Magadhan king Ajātaśatru is depicted as being desirous of attacking and destroying the Vajjins. He calls his Brāhmaṇa minister and says:[5] "Come, O Brāhmaṇa, and go where the lord (Buddha) is. Having approached the lord, salute the feet of the lord with my words, and then say: 'O lord, the Magadhan king Ajātasatru, the son of the princess of Videha, is desirous of attacking the Vajjins." In the original passage, the use of language is quite noteworthy. The king uses the second person singular forms *tvam, upasaṅkama, vadehi* etc. for his Brāhmaṇa minister Vassakāra, and uses the respectful words such as *bhagavat* for Buddha. The Brāhmaṇa minister having accepted the king's command then approaches Buddha and twists the king's words into his own words:[6] "O Gotama, the king Ajātasattu ..." Here, the Brāhmaṇa minister, instead of using the appellation *bhagavat* for Buddha simply calls him "O Gotama". At the end of the interview, the Brāhmaṇa minister says:[7] "Now, O Gotama, we must go. We are very busy and we have a lot of work to do." The Brāhmaṇa uses a second person singular form for Buddha and uses a first person plural form for himself. Then watch Buddha's response:[8] "O you Brāhmaṇa, (do) whatever you think the time is appropriate for." Buddha uses a second person singular form for the Brāhmaṇa minister. While such passages are clearly no recordings of actual conversations between these historical individuals, they show a great deal of sociolinguistic understanding on the part of the compilers of the Buddhist canon. The Brāhmaṇa and Buddha clearly held opposing perspectives of respect for each other. The *Ambaṭṭhasutta* of the *Dīghanikāya* contains Buddha's dialectic which argues that socially the Brāhmaṇas are lower than the Kṣatriyas. Buddha argues that if there is a son born of a Kṣatriya man and a Brāhmaṇa woman, the Brāhmaṇas would accept him as an equal and teach him the Vedas etc., but the Kṣatriyas would never make him a king. According to him the same would happen to a son born of a Brāhmaṇa man and a Kṣatriya woman.[9] In conclusion of this argument, Buddha says:[10] "O Ambaṭṭha, thus even when a Kṣatriya reaches an extremely fallen state, even then Kṣatriyas alone are superior and Brāhmaṇas are inferior. Among people who are concerned about birth, the Kṣatriya is superior."

4.4. This idea of Kṣatriyas being superior to Brāhmaṇas is maintained in the canonical Buddhist literature even in irrelevant contexts to a textually ridiculous extent. In the same *Ambaṭṭhasutta*, the Brāhmaṇa Ambaṭṭha is complaining to Buddha that Brāhmaṇas alone are superior to the rest of the Varṇas, and yet the Śākyas do not respect them. One would expect that in the mouth of this irate Brāhmaṇa, the list of the four castes would have Brāhmaṇas at the top. However, the monastic compilers of the Buddhist canon inserted the standard Buddhist list of the four castes as: Kṣatriya, Brāhmaṇa, Vaiśya and Śūdra.[11] The *Poṭṭhapādasutta* of *Dīghanikāya* contains a passage where Buddha talks about a person who is in love with a girl but does not know whether she is Kṣatriya, Brāhmaṇa, Vaiśya or Śūdra.[12] In the *Mahāparinibbānasutta,* Buddha lists eight assemblies, and the list begins with *khattiya-parisā* and *brāhmaṇa-parisā* in this very order.[13] Interestingly, at the concluding event of Buddha's life, his cremation, his followers and the assembled folks quarrel for his remains citing the fact that they were Kṣatriyas and that he was a Kṣatriya and that therefore they had a greater claim to his remains.[14] Ironically, it is the Brāhmaṇa Doṇa who is called upon to mediate in this conflict among the assembled Kṣatriyas.

4.5. From the above evidence, which can be multiplied considerably if one combs through the entire Buddhist canonical literature, one may confidently claim that the early Buddhists held a view of social hierarchy which was opposite of the view held by the Brāhmaṇas. The same may then be extended to the language used by Buddha. The Prakrit which he used to preach was in all probability no lowly language in his own view. It must have been, in his own estimation superior to the Sanskrit of the Brāhmaṇas.

4.6. Buddha advises his monks that they should teach the doctrine in their own language (*sakāya niruttiyā*). It is reported in different Buddhist texts that monks who were of Brahmanical origin showed concern that the Prakrit-speaking monks of diverse origins will corrupt the sayings of Buddha, and that they asked his permission to render his words into Sanskrit.[15] The Brāhmaṇa monks were worried that the non-Brāhmaṇa monks who made "mistakes" in the use of genders, numbers and tenses, and in pronunciation, were sure to corrupt the words of Buddha. If such pleas are historically true, they certainly indicate that Brāhmaṇas, even those who had been converted to Buddhism, could not leave behind many of their Brahmanical sociolinguistic attitudes. It is likely that this story is constructed by the early Buddhist monks who thereby wanted to emphasize their fear that any attempts to render Buddha's words into Sanskrit originate in Brahmanical intentions to subvert the Buddhist faith from within. Buddha is said to have rejected these pleas and to have ordained that everyone should use his own particular dialect in reciting the sacred texts.

4.7. We may contrast this situation with the late traditions of Sanskritic Buddhism. These viewed Buddha as a Sanskrit speaker, and their canon is in mixed or pure Sanskrit. This shift may be explained on the background of the sociolinguistic factor that almost all the major Mahāyāna teachers are Brāhmaṇas converted to Buddhism. Perhaps their labeling of some other Buddhist sects as Hīnayāna "lower path" may have a sociolinguistic reason, i.e. the Brahmanical contempt for Prakrits, in addition to doctrinal reasons. Thus, in terms of language use and linguistic attitudes, one may safely conclude that the early Buddhism represented a distinct point of view of Kṣatriya superiority over Brāhmaṇas, while the late Buddhism of Sanskrit Hīnayāna and Mahāyāna texts represents importation of Brahmanical linguistic attitudes into Buddhist traditions. For this later Sanskrit Buddhism, Buddha's Kṣatriya status has a somewhat different value. Interestingly, according to the later Buddhist traditions, which being in Sanskrit represent a different sociolinguistic point of view akin to that of the Brāhmaṇas, the Bodhisattvas are born either in Brāhmaṇa or Kṣatriya families, but never in Cāṇḍāla, Veṇukāra, Rathakāra or Puṣkasa families. The *Lalitavistara* says that when Brāhmaṇas are prominent in the world, the Bodhisattva is born in a Brāhmaṇa family, and when the Kṣatriyas are prominent in the world, the Bodhisattva is born in a Kṣatriya family. But the Bodhisattva is never born in a *hīna* "lower" family. According to this text, the world was dominated by Kṣatriyas at the time of Buddha's birth and hence he was born in a Kṣatriya family. In theory at least, our text can conceive of Brāhmaṇas being prominent in the world at some other time, but even in theory it cannot conceive of anyone other than these two being prominent in the world.[16] This text rejects for instance the lineage of Kosalas as being inappropriate for the Bodhisattva by claiming that they were Mātaṅgas in their previous lives.[17] In ancient India, when Brāhmaṇas and Kṣatriyas vied with each other for superior status, they both seem to agree on the lower rank of the Vaiśyas and Śūdras. The *Lalitavistara* passage may represent a concession granted by the Brāhmaṇa converts to Buddhism to themselves. This is probably a mid point in shifting sociolinguistic attitudes in Buddhist traditions, which are later fully dominated by converted Brāhmaṇas. The *Lalitavistara* itself shows the place the Brāhmaṇas have acquired in Buddhist social thinking. For instance, when the Bodhisattva was waiting in the *Tuṣita* heaven, considering how he should be born on the earth, according to *Lalitavistara*, a Devaputra named Ugratejas said: "The Bodhisattva must enter his mother's womb in that very form which has been described in the *Mantra-veda-śāstra* of the Brāhmaṇas."[18] I am offering this evidence in order to show the probable link between the direction toward Sanskritization of Buddhism and the increasing prominence of Brahmanical elements within the Buddhist traditions.

5. Sociolinguistic Attitudes in Jainism

5.1. In choosing Prakrits for religious discourse, the Jainas had a motive quite similar to that of the early Buddhists. Mahāvīra was born in a Kṣatriya family, which from the Brahmanical point of view belonged to the mixed Aryanized population of northeastern India. His conflicts with the Brahmanical order were quite similar to Buddha's. Just as everything Buddhist is emphatically labeled Aryan in the Buddhist canon, similarly the Jaina canon presents a distinctive notion of Aryanhood. It will be apparent by now that conceptions of the Aryan as a social entity vary widely and are heavily laden with hierarchical values.

5.2. The *Paṇṇavaṇāsutta*, about the first century B.C., has a long section (p. 35-37) describing the Jaina conceptions of "Aryan" and "Mleccha" or non-Aryan. I will discuss these notions in detail to bring out their significance as an alternative social conception contrasting in every way with the corresponding Brahmanical conception. Here the discussion begins with a list of peoples whom the Jainas considered non-Aryan or Mleccha. The list includes: Saga, Javaṇa, Cilāya, Babbara, Kāya, Muruṇḍa, Uḍḍa, Bhadaga, Niṇṇaga, Pakkaṇiya, Kulakkha, Goṇḍa, Siṃhala, Pārasa, Gondhoḍamba, Damila, Cillala, Pulinda, Meya, Palhava, Mālava, Gaggara, Ābhāsiya, Ṇakka, Cīna, Lhasiya, Khasa, Khāsiya Neḍura, Maṇḍha, Ḍombilaga, Laüsa, Baüsa, Kekkaya, Aravāga, Hūṇa, Romaga, Bharuga, Ruya, Gandhāhāraga, Ajjala, Pāsa, Malaya, and Mūyali. If we compare this list with the lists of Mlecchas from the Brahmanical literature, we do find some agreement between the Jainas and Brāhmaṇas as to who the Mlecchas are, but the Brahmanical conception excludes several communities which are considered to be Aryan by the Jainas.

5.3. Who are the Aryans? According to the *Paṇṇavaṇāsutta*, there are two kinds of Aryans: a) *iddhipattāriya* = *ṛddhiprāptārya* "Exalted

Aryans", and b) *aniḍḍhipattāriya = anṛddhiprāptārya* "Non-exalted Aryans", or perhaps "Normal Aryans". The Exalted Aryans, according to this text, include Arahanta, Cakkavaṭṭi, Baladeva, Vāsudeva, Cāraṇa and Vijjāhara. Interestingly, it excludes Brāhmaṇas, and also Vaiśya and Śūdra groups. It includes Kṣatriya characters and religious figures. The conception of normal Aryans provides even more fascinating information. They are subdivided into nine different categories:

Khettāriya	*(kṣetrārya)*	"Aryan by Region"
Jātiāriya	*(jātyārya)*	"Aryan by birth"
Kulāriya	*(kulārya)*	"Aryan by clan"
Kammāriya	*(karmārya)*	"Aryan by function"
Sippāriya	*(Śilpārya)*	"Aryan by profession"
Bhāsāriya	*(bhāṣārya)*	"Aryan by language"
Nāṇāriya	*(jñānārya)*	"Aryan by wisdom"
Daṃsaṇāriya	*(darśanārya)*	"Aryan by realization"
Carittāriya	*(caritrārya)*	"Aryan by conduct"

The Jainas, at this stage, seem to claim that the peoples listed as Mlecchas were not Aryan, but on the other hand, there is an implicit claim that whoever is Aryan in terms of the listed features is Aryan. In short, those who are Aryanized are Aryans. Thus there must have been a large population which was Aryan from the Jaina point of view, and which regarded itself as Aryan, but whose claims to Aryanhood were denied by the Brāhmaṇas.

5.4. The first category of Aryans is "Aryan by region". Our text lists regions which are Aryan in its opinion, and says that the Exalted Aryans are born in these regions. The Jaina Aryan regions are: Magadha, Aṅga, Vaṅga, Kaliṅga, Kāsī, Kosala, Kuru, Kusaṭṭa, Pañcāla, Jaṅgala, Suraṭṭha, Videha, Kosambī, Saṇḍilla, Malaya, Vaccha, Accha, Dasaṇṇa, Cedī, Sindhusovīra, Sūraseṇa, Bhaṅgī, Vaṭṭa, Kuṇāla, Lāḍhā, and Keyaïäḍḍha. This conception of Jaina Aryan lands must be closely compared and contrasted with the Brahmanical conception of Aryan lands. The Brahmanical conception as seen in Patañjali's *Mahābhāṣya* and in *Dharmaśāstra* texts[19] claim that the Aryans mainly reside in the region of Āryāvarta, which lies to the east of the Ādarśa mountains, to the west of the Kālaka forest, to the south of the Himalayas and to the north of the Vindhyas. The

Baudhāyanadharmaśāstra (1.1.32-33) gives us a clear idea of how the Aryas of Āryāvarta viewed the mixed populations of the "outer regions": "The inhabitants of Ānarta, of Aṅga, of Magadha, of Surāṣṭra, of the Deccan, of Upavṛt, of Sindhu and Sauvīra, are of mixed origins. He who has visited the countries of the Āraṭṭas, Kāraskaras, Puṇḍras, Sauvīras, Vaṅgas, Kaliṅgas, or Pranūnas shall offer a Punastoma or a Sarvapṛṣṭhī sacrifice for purification." It is extremely important to note that seven of the eight regions here listed as "impure" are included in the Jaina list of Aryan lands. Many more of the Jaina Aryan regions would not be acknowledged as such by the Brahmanical Dharmaśāstras. This is indicated on the accompanying map. Thus there was considerable tension between Brahmanical Aryans and the Jaina and Buddhist Aryans.

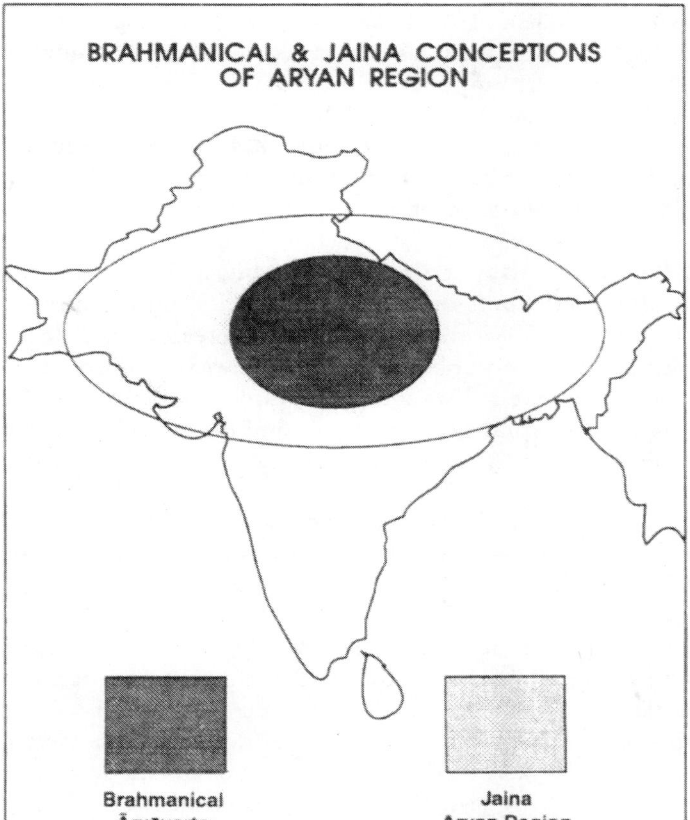

5.5. The *Paṇṇavaṇāsutta* lists six *jāti-ariyas* "Aryans by birth": Ambaṭṭha, Kalinda, Videha, Vedaga, Hariya and Cuṃcuṇa. The Brāhmaṇas are not listed here at all. According to the Brahmanical sources, however, one of these six; the Ambaṭṭhas, are born of a Vaiśya mother and a Brāhmaṇa father (*Manusmṛti*, 10.8); another, the Videhas, are born of a Brāhmaṇa mother and a Vaiśya father (*Manusmṛti*, 10.10). The other four are not even heard of in the Brahmanical lists. This may indicate that the early Jainas defined their social prestige in terms which were markedly non-Brahmanical.

5.6. As for the Aryans by clan, the *Paṇṇavaṇāsutta* lists six Aryan clans: Ugga (Ugra), Bhoga, Rāiṇṇa (Rājanya), Ikkhāga (Ikṣvāku), Ṇāta (Jñāta) and Koravva (Kauravya). Mahāvīra was born in one of these, the Ṇāta. Buddha's Śākya clan is traditionally believed to be part of the Okkāka (= Ikkhāga, Ikṣvāku) line and is therefore included here. This includes a few clans which were of probably very low status from the Brahmanical point of view. Thus, the *Manusmṛti* (10.9) says: "From a Kṣatriya and the daughter of a Śūdra springs a being, called Ugra, resembling both a Kṣatriya and a Śūdra, ferocious in his manners, and delighting in cruelty." The conflict between these two conceptions is quite obvious.

5.7. Who are Aryans by their work? According to the *Paṇṇavaṇāsutta*, there are many kinds of such Aryans, including merchants, pot sellers, bards and bearers. The Aryans by profession include tailors, weavers, makers of woolen and straw footwear, makers of books, vehicles and painters. If we compare these lists with the Brahmanical notions of castes and professions, we find that all of these must be subsumed in the two lower caste ranks, i.e. Vaiśyas and Śūdras. The agricultural profession is not included in the Jaina list. This Jaina constituency interestingly is affirmed also by the *Nāṭyaśāstra* (17.50) which says that Ardhamāgadhī is the language of Ceṭas, Rājaputras and merchants.

5.8. According to the *Paṇṇavaṇāsutta*, the Aryans by language are those who speak Ardhamāgadhī and use the Brāhmī script. The Brahmanical tradition would of course regard any non-Sanskrit language as "degenerate", though they do admit that Aryan languages were spoken by those who were not Aryans socially. The *Manusmṛti* (10.45) says: "All those tribes in this world, which are excluded from the community of those born from the mouth, the arms, the thighs, and the feet of Brahman, are called Dasyus, whether they speak the language of the Mlecchas or that of the Aryans." In the accompanying diagrams I have presented the two differing conceptions of Aryanhood and the areas of conflict.

Brahmanical Conception

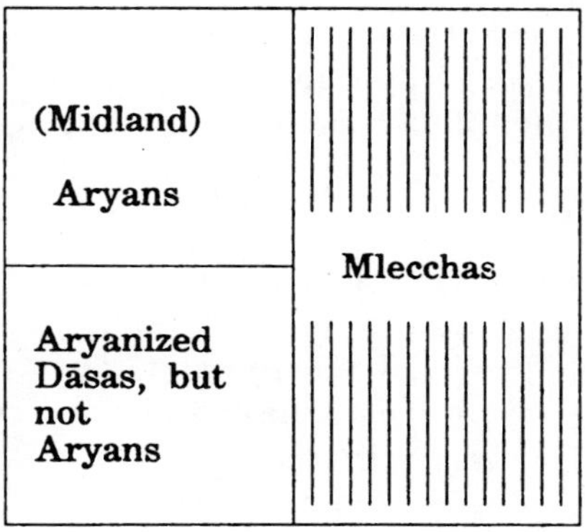

Jaina Conception

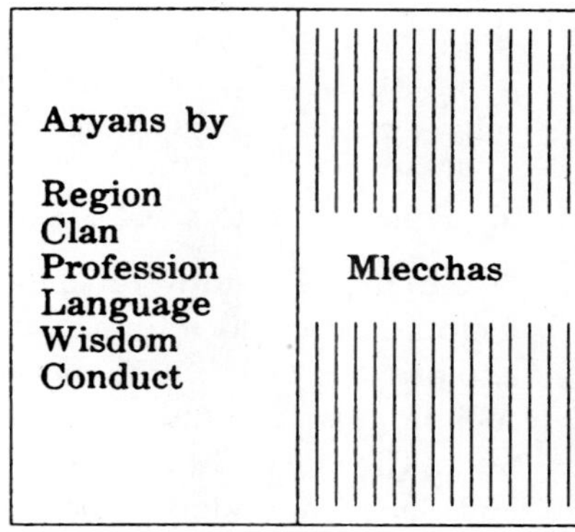

Tripartite Result

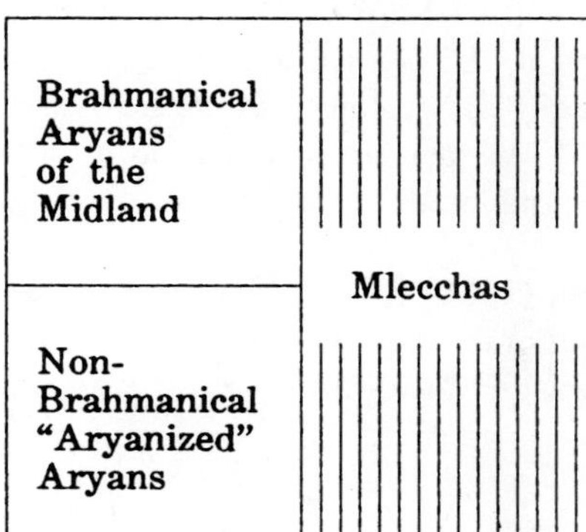

5.9. With the above background, we can better appreciate the self-assertion of the Jaina texts, both socially and linguistically. The *Samavāyaṅgasutta* says[20] that Mahāvīra expounded his doctrines in the Ardhamāgadhī language. While he was speaking Ardhamāgadhī, it was automatically transformed into different languages which were pleasant, wholesome and beneficial to all the Aryans, non-Aryans, animals, birds and snakes. The *Ovavāïyasutta* reports that Mahāvīra had conversations with the king Kūṇiya (= Ajātaśatru) in Ardhamāgadhī.[21] The *Bhagavaïsutta* raises a question about the language of the gods:[22] "O Lord, in which language do the gods speak? Which language is the distinguished language? O Gotama, gods speak in this Ardhamāgadhī language. This Ardhamāgadhī language is the most distinguished language." For the ancient Jainas, those who speak the Ardhamāgadhī language are linguistically Aryan, speakers of the most distinguished language.

6. Political Factors and Sociolinguistic Attitudes

6.1. In my 1979 study, I had discussed in many places how political factors do affect sociolinguistic attitudes. Here I would like to briefly explore the connection between the political factors and the sociolinguistic attitudes expressed in the early Buddhist and Jaina texts. The Pali tradition calls the Pāli language by the name Māgadhī and claims that Buddha spoke this language and that this language is the original language of all beings (*sabbasattānaṃ mūlabhāsā*). As quoted above, the Jaina texts make a similar claim on behalf of Ardhamāgadhī. Both of these are indeed varieties of Magadhan Prakrit and make the highest claims of prestige. We are not concerned here with the purely linguistic question of whether Pāli and Ardhamāgadhī as we know them now are truly Magadhan dialects or not. We are concerned about the origins of the sociolinguistic claims made on behalf of these languages.

6.2. K.R. Norman (1980) has extensively discussed these Buddhist and Jaina passages making a claim for Pāli and Ardhamāgadhī to be the original language of the canon and the original language of all beings. He suggests (p. 67):

> I would suggest that the idea of languages developing from Māgadhī is a clear indication of the state of affairs in North India during the time of the Mauryan empire in the fourth and third centuries B.C., and I think that the idea of language development expressed in the Buddhist and Jain texts must have been arising during, and very probably because of, that empire. During the

> Mauryan period Māgadhī, the language of Aśoka's capital Pāṭaliputra, was the administrative language of North India, and it, or a modified form of it, was inscribed all over India to make Aśoka's decrees known to his subjects. I would, therefore, suggest that Māgadhī *sabbasattānaṃ mūlabhāsā* was a (fairly) correct statement as far as North India was concerned in the fourth and third centuries B.C., and it was natural that a statement which Aśoka might have made about his administrative language should be adopted by the Buddhist missionaries when they went to Ceylon. A similar use for missionary purposes would doubtless account for the Jain adoption of the same phrase."

I fully agree with the political motivation which Norman finds in these Buddhist and Jaina assertions. However, as I have pointed out there are much deeper social reasons for the adoption of Prakrit, instead of Sanskrit, by these traditions, and the initial blossoming of these traditions obviously occurred in the region where Māgadhī was the dominant Prakrit.

6.3. Since the fall of the Mauryan empire, however, things gradually changed, and Māgadhī, which was once the most prestigious language, later became a low class language in Sanskrit dramas. This has to do with the loss of power to the region of Magadha and the rise of empires in other regions of India, more to the west and south of Magadha. Thus the rise in the prestige of Mahārāṣṭrī Prakrit may indeed be connected with the rise of the Sātavāhana power. In later centuries, the overall political prestige of Sanskrit rose continuously in such a way that it eclipsed the prestige of Prakrit which it had in the Mauryan days. As Romila Thapar (1973: 51) points out, "the earliest Sanskrit inscription of any importance is that of the Śaka ruler Rudradāman, and dates to the second century A.D., the previous inscriptions having been composed in the Prakrits and the local languages, such as Aramaic and Tamil." The rise in the prestige of Sanskrit must have begun slowly after the fall of the Mauryas at the hands of the Brāhmaṇa Puṣyamitra Śuṅga, and it gradually continued to rise in such a way that the royal inscriptions in India gradually changed from Prakrit to Sanskrit. The Śaka rulers began using Sanskrit, which was also used extensively by the Gupta kings. While the early Vākāṭaka inscriptions are in Prakrit, region by region they gradually change to Sanskrit. Also while the early Pallava inscriptions are in Prakrit, the late Pallava inscriptions are in Sanskrit. Nowhere do we see a shift from Sanskrit to Prakrit in the history of Indian inscriptions.

6.4. This directionality is quite instructive. This loss of prestige for Prakrit resulted in a very remarkably different picture in Sanskrit dramas where the king always speaks Sanskrit, while the thieves and rogues are given Māgadhī as their speech. It is not always clear whether those kings whose inscriptions are in Sanskrit ever spoke Sanskrit themselves, but certainly the ideal was a Sanskrit-speaking king, as can be seen from the anguish of the Prakrit-speaking Sātavāhana, insulted by his Sanskrit-speaking wife, depicted in the famous story about the origins of the Kātantra grammar.[23] Interestingly, while the later Prakrit poets and Jaina authors continued to defend Prakrit against Sanskrit, as I have shown in detail in my (1979a) study, these later defenses were based more on aesthetic grounds than that of social prestige. Even a poet such as Rājaśekhara who clearly has a soft corner for Prakrits, insists in his *Kāvyamīmāṃsā* (p. 50) that a good poet should have servants fluent in Apabhraṃśa, and maidservants fluent in languages like Māgadhī. His wives should be fluent in Sanskrit and Prakrit. It is important to note that Prakrit for Rājaśekhara refers not to Māgadhī, but to Mahārāṣṭrī. Thus, even those who loved Prakrits in later centuries could not defend their social prestige in terms of the then current state of affairs. This is what may have forced the reluctant Jaina traditions to use Sanskrit in later periods.

II

LOKA: THE LINGUISTIC WORLD OF PATAÑJALI

1. Introduction

1.1. In my 1979 monograph *Sociolinguistic Attitudes in India: An Historical Reconstruction*, I had discussed the evidence for language attitudes in Patañjali's *Mahābhāṣya*. In his review of this monograph, Franklin C. Southworth raised some valuable questions which make it necessary to re-analyze the *Mahābhāṣya* evidence in greater details. Since it is his comments which made me reconsider the textual evidence from the *Mahābhāṣya*, I would like to begin this discussion by quoting his comments fully. Southworth (1981: 934) says:

> It is difficult to follow D's presentation of the chronological relationship between Sanskrit and Prakrit. By the time of Kātyāyana (ca. 300 B.C.) and Patañjali (ca. 100 B.C.), D states, 'even Brahmins have begun using Prakrits as their first language, while Sanskrit is retained in the ritual and scholastic contexts.' Yet on the grounds that later grammarians 'consider the first three sages of Sanskrit grammar to be *lakṣyaikacakṣuṣka* "those whose sole attention is fixed on the linguistic usage to be described" '(in contrast to the grammarians following Patañjali, who were considered '*lakṣaṇaikacakṣuṣka* "those whose sole attention is fixed on the grammatical rules"'), D would like to claim that 'up to the time of Patañjali, Sanskrit was a living language in some sense.' What sense can he possibly have in mind? D wonders if Patañjali himself did not have a Prakrit language as his mother tongue, Sanskrit being his second language.' If so, are we to assume that his second language was learned from people who spoke it as a first language? D points out that 'even the upper-class women were using Prakrit languages at this time, and did not and could not speak Sanskrit.' ... And if Brahmin women of that period did not know Sanskrit, they

could hardly teach it to their children. So where did the native speakers come from? Admittedly, archaic and evolved forms of a language can co-exist in the same speech community, especially a community which possesses highly developed rituals which value the use of the older forms. But how long can the older forms remain alive without special efforts? By Pāṇini's time (about 500 B.C.), 'the Aryan language of the early Vedic texts was fast becoming archaic'; and this was very likely an important stimulus to the development of the study of Sanskrit grammar. One might even go so far as to suggest that the very act of fixing the forms of the Vedic hymns (1000 B.C.) may have been a response to an awareness of change. The use of Prakrit by the Buddha and other religious reformers of his time may well have reflected a separate, and less conservative, segment of the speech community than that in which Pāṇini was raised; but if we find 'sufficient evidence of Prakritisms even in Vedic literature,' then it is stretching things a bit to speak of Sanskrit as a 'living language' (in ANY sense) as late as 100 B.C. Sanskrit was presumably used as a language of scholarly and religious discourse by priests and others, and learned from them as a 'second language' by young Brahmins (as is the case today). Kātyāyana and Patañjali may have regarded the Sanskrit of these Pandits as some kind of 'living' language (in any case, it was the language of the gods); but I question whether we can do so today.

1.2. While I disagree with some of Southworth's comments, I think that his criticisms bring up historical and terminological questions which are extremely important, and in this paper I propose to take a closer look at the evidence presented by Patañjali's *Mahābhāṣya* keeping in mind these criticisms. The basic questions raised by Southworth may be restated as follows. Was Sanskrit a 'living' language at the time of Patañjali? What would the word 'living' mean in such a context? Does a language have to be a 'first language' in order to be a living language, or can a 'second language' be a living language as well? If Sanskrit was a learned second language at the time of Patañjali, how could there be any grammar-independent usage of Sanskrit? If there was no grammar-independent usage of Sanskrit at that time, i.e. if all Sanskrit was learned from traditional grammars such as that of Pāṇini, then how could Patañjali argue that grammar is dependent upon the usage of social élites (*śiṣṭa*)? For grammar to be dependent upon the linguistic usage of social élites, that linguistic usage must be independent of the pressure of a prescriptive grammar. Such are the questions which must be dealt with in order to properly benefit from Southworth's criticisms. As we shall see, part of the problem lies in interfacing the objective approach of a modern linguist with the partly objective and partly culture-conditioned approach of a traditional grammarian such as Patañjali. While Patañjali lacked the modern terminology and ideology of historical linguistics, second language acquisition, diglossia, bilingual communication etc., the modern linguist lacks Patañjali's theology and transcendent cosmography of Eternal Sanskrit, his unflinching adherence to Brahmanical puritanism and his sociolinguistic concern for the well-being and the survival of Brahmanical ideals. Thus, there is clearly a need for a terminological and conceptual translation from Patañjali to modern linguistics. In the following analysis, I shall attempt this task, without losing track of the textual and historical evidence.

2. *Loka* and *Veda* in Patañjali

2.1. Pāṇini's grammar deals primarily with two varieties of Sanskrit, i.e. Vedic Sanskrit and colloquial Sanskrit. To refer to the first, Pāṇini uses the generic term *chandasi,* while to refer to the latter, he uses the term *bhāṣāyām.* His unqualified rules refer to the common factor of all domains, while his qualified rules specifically refer to the particular domain with which they are qualified. (For details, Deshpande, 1985) In the beginning of his *Mahābhāṣya,* Patañjali says that Pāṇini's science of grammar deals with words belonging to both *loka* 'the world' as well as *Veda* 'the Vedic scriptures' and he cites examples of these two kinds of words.[24] On this passage, Kaiyaṭa offers two interesting interpretations of the term *laukika* 'worldly'.[25] In the first interpretation, the Vedic scriptures are also part of the world, and hence their language is also *laukika,* but it is mentioned separately to indicate its special importance. In the second interpretation, the term *laukika* is equivalent to the term *bhāṣā* 'colloquial usage' used by Pāṇini, and hence the terms *laukika* and *vaidika* refer to two separate domains.

2.2. In his very first *Vārttika,* Kātyāyana seems to be using the word *loka* in both the wider and the narrower meanings. The *Vārttika* says: "Given that the relationship between words and meanings is established on the basis of (the usage of language in) the world (*lokataḥ*) to communicate meaning, the science of grammar makes a restriction concerning merit, as is done (by other legal and ritual systems) in worldly (*laukika*) and

Vedic matters."[26] In the first expression *lokataḥ*, we must read this wider meaning for the notion of "world", while the terms *laukika* and *vaidika* seem to have been used in the narrower sense. While it is difficult to decide as to which interpretation Patañjali himself may have had in his mind, it is certain that he included the geographical and mythological *loka* 'worlds' such as the seven continents of the earth, the heaven and the netherworld, along with hundreds of known and unknown branches of the four Vedas as subdomains in his conception of the total field of usage of Sanskrit (*śabdasya prayogaviṣayaḥ*), and he illustrates geographically restricted usages as well as usages which are found only in Vedic texts. After citing these vast sub-domains, he remarks that it would indeed be hazardous to assert the non-existence of certain words without checking this vast field of usage.[27] Thus there is this vast panchronic field of usage as conceived by Patañjali, where the conventional "world" and "scriptures" are simply subdomains, along with the more exotic subdomains such as heavens and netherworlds. Thus, the usage of Sanskrit is not conceived in terms of a changing history of a normal language, but in terms of the eternal existence of a non-changing language. However, this eternal language has varieties of manifestations in different domains of a vast cosmology. Thus, one could say that Patañjali's notion of the vast field of usage of language (*mahān śabdasya prayoga-viṣayaḥ*) corresponds to the wider meaning of *loka* in Kātyāyana's *Vārttika*, while the terms *laukika* and *vaidika* refer to exclusive subdomains of this large field.

2.3. Patañjali admits that some of these domains of Sanskrit usage, similar to the practice of hundred or thousand-year long sacrifices, are not contemporary (*na cādyatve kaścid api vyavaharati*), and yet he asserts that, like the ritual traditions of ancient sages, these non-contemporary domains of Sanskrit usage must still be described by the science of grammar, since they do form part of the eternal dharma.[28] Thus the eternality of language as a religious dogma is balanced by a recognition that many fields of Sanskrit usage are not strictly contemporary. But clearly the religious motivation of preserving all the ancient textual traditions is so strong and so much part of the endeavor of a genuine Sanskrit grammarian, that Patañjali regards this commitment to describe all known Vedic textual traditions as a reason for many of Pāṇini's rules containing option-terms such as *bahulam, anyatarasyām, ubhayathā, vā* and *ekeṣām*.[29] While Patañjali would admit that the Vedic texts are not strictly speaking contemporary (*na cādyatve kaścid api vyavaharati*), still he is quite emphatic about their eternal nature or constant presence (*nityatva*).[30]

2.4. Kātyāyana and Patañjali make an interesting distinction between the domain of Vedic texts and contemporary usage. In Vedic texts, the corpus is fixed and hence the description of Vedic usage must precisely follow what one actually finds in Vedic texts. In contrast with the finiteness and fixed textual nature of the Vedic usage, the contemporary usage is more flexible.[31] The commentators have a somewhat difficult time with this statement. Kaiyaṭa says that even with reference to contemporary usage a grammarian must describe only what he finds, and hence this could not be a peculiarity of Vedic usage.[32] On the other hand, Nāgeśabhaṭṭa is more forthright in admitting that while the Vedic texts represent a fixed corpus, the non-Vedic colloquial usage, even if it is not observed by a grammarian in his own contemporary times, could still be recorded on the basis of other ancient traditions of grammar and learning and hence the contemporary usage is not as finite as the Vedic texts.[33] In general, it would seem that when it came to describing Vedic texts, the Sanskrit grammarians were not describing the language of the Vedic speakers as such, but language as attested in existing texts, while in describing the colloquial usage of Sanskrit, they were describing not a fixed corpus, but a somewhat flexible usage of speakers known to the grammarians. This is a significant distinction made by Sanskrit grammarians themselves. Thus, while *vaidika* refers to this non-contemporary textual material, *laukika* refers to the flexible contemporary usage of Sanskrit with which the grammarians were either personally acquainted or which was known to them through other prior descriptions.

2.5. Kātyāyana and Patañjali invoke the notion of *loka* in many places as an authority both for linguistic facts and also for interpretive logic. This brings out a very important aspect of their conception of *loka*. They rely on their observation of the surrounding world for information on language and culture.[34] But these observations can only be synchronic. Since the Vedic texts were handed down orally, the knowledge about these Vedic texts which the Sanskrit grammarians possessed was in large measure based upon their acquaintance with contemporary traditions of recitation, and hence their information about Vedic texts also has a strong synchronic dimension. Patañjali says that the sound *a* with open pronunciation is found neither in the *loka* nor in the Veda.[35] Similarly, he says that short *e* and *o* are found only in the Sāmaveda-recitation of the Sātyamugri and

Rāṇāyanīya traditions, but they are not found in the *loka* or in any other Vedic tradition.[36] In such contexts, *loka*, as clearly distinct from *Veda*, seems to refer to the contemporary usage of Sanskrit as known to the grammarians.

3. Motivations for Studying Sanskrit Grammar

3.1. Patañjali's discussion of the purposes for studying Sanskrit grammar brings out many aspects of the usage of Sanskrit in his days as well as his own perception of the position of Sanskrit. We will discuss some of the major passages. At the outset, Patañjali points out that there are five reasons for studying Sanskrit grammar. These are preservation of the Vedas, linguistic recontextualization of Vedic ritual formulas (*ūha*), religious commitment based on scriptural injunctions, economy of effort in attaining mastery of the language and removal of interpretational doubts.[37] Patañjali feels that it was absolutely necessary for a grammarian to explain these purposes for studying Sanskrit grammar, because in his days there were people who did not believe in the necessity of studying Sanskrit grammar. Patañjali says that in ancient days people first studied the science of grammar (including phonetics), and then they learned the Vedic texts. However, he claims, his contemporaries learn the Vedic texts without learning the science of grammar, and then they are quick to say: "Vedic language is known to us from the Vedic texts and the colloquial language is known to us from the linguistic usage of the world. Therefore, the study of grammar is purposeless."[38] From such passages in the *Mahābhāṣya*, it is clear that there was a dispute between grammarians on the one hand and some priestly Brāhmaṇas on the other concerning the necessity of acquiring Sanskrit through the study of Sanskrit grammar. The priestly Brāhmaṇas could acquire a knowledge of the Vedic texts through memorization of these texts and they could acquire the knowledge about the ritual application of these texts through some kind of ritual apprenticeship. Similarly they could acquire some sort of knowledge of priestly Sanskrit through the same avenue, while they could acquire Prakrit as their mother tongue. These priests saw no reason to study Sanskrit grammar for any of these skills, and this attitude is later continued in the traditions of Mīmāṃsā and Nyāya which reject the necessity of studying Sanskrit grammar for these same reasons.[39] This attitude may also be linked with an earlier debate concerning the meaningfulness of Vedas recorded in Yāska's *Nirukta* (1.15-16). This debate occurring about the middle of the first millennium B.C. shows that while the oral traditions designed to preserve the Vedic texts were successful in preserving the surface form of these texts with a relatively small amount of change, there was no such corresponding high success in preserving the meaning of the Vedic texts, which in the course of time naturally became partially unintelligible. Yāska reports that there was a school headed by Kautsa which believed that the Vedic texts had no meaning whatsoever, and that presumably their efficacy consisted *purely* in their proper recitation in ritual. Yāska on the other hand defends meaningfulness of the Vedic texts, but insists that without the science of etymology one may not be able to discover their meaning. Thus a section of the priestly class was satisfied simply with the recitational (and magical) value of the sounds of the Vedic texts, while there was another section which insisted on academic efforts to make sense of these ancient texts. Patañjali's discussion is a continuation of this theme, and many of the arguments found in the *Mahābhāṣya* are identical with arguments in the *Nirukta*. Thus it is clear that by the time of Patañjali, the Vedic texts were understood more as texts rather than as "living" language-usage, and the priests had little interest in understanding the meaning of these texts. The etymologists and grammarians on the other hand probably represented a minority of Brāhmaṇas who insisted on academic efforts to understand the meaning of the Vedic texts. This may help us understand why Patañjali insists again and again that without acquiring the science of grammar one cannot "properly" deal with Vedic ritual.

3.2. It would be interesting to analyze the contexts where Patañjali feels that the knowledge of grammar is absolutely essential. While there is clearly an attitudinal element involved in Patañjali's assertions, which are not shared by others, these assertions help us understand the situation of Sanskrit as perceived by Patañjali.

a) In the context of Vedic ritual, often one is required to take a mantra given in reference to a certain deity and use it with reference to another deity. Such recontextualization of Vedic mantras requires substitution of many words, changes of case-endings, verb-endings etc. This linguistic recontextualization of Vedic mantras is called *ūha*. Patañjali says that a person who does not know grammar cannot properly make the requisite changes.[40]

b) Grammar should be studied for an economical access to Sanskrit. A Brāhmaṇa must learn Sanskrit and, without studying grammar, there is no other economical way of acquiring Sanskrit.[41]

c) One should study grammar also for the purpose of clearing doubts concerning the interpretation of accented texts. The priests prescribe that a *sthūla-pṛṣatī* cow be sacrificed for Agni and Varuṇa. Here there is a doubt whether they mean a cow with big spots (*sthūlá-pṛṣatī*) or a big cow with spots (*sthūla-pṛṣatí*). A person who does not know grammar cannot differentiate between the two accented variants. If the first member retains its original accent, then it is a *bahuvrīhi* compound (i.e. "a cow with big spots"). If the final vowel of the compound is accented, then it must be a *tatpuruṣa* compound (i.e. "a big cow with spots").[42] The same theme is brought up again by citing the example of Vṛtra's misuse of the expression *indraśatrú*. Vṛtra performed a sacrifice to obtain a son who would be Indra's killer (*indrasya śatruḥ, indraśatrúḥ*, a *tatpuruṣa* compound with the final vowel accented). However, he wrongly accented the word and pronounced it as *índraśatruḥ* with the first member accented, which became a *bahuvrīhi* compound meaning "he whose killer is Indra". After citing this example, Patañjali says that one must study grammar so that one would not use wrong accents.[43] This story indicates that accents as features of normal spoken Sanskrit were no longer prevalent in Patañjali's time and that they had to be academically learned in the context of studying the recitation of the Vedas. He points out that in his contemporary world (*loka*), if a student reciting the Vedas pronounced an *anudātta* vowel in the place of an *udātta* vowel, the teacher slapped him and told him that he was altering the accents.[44]

d) Patañjali asserts that without the science of grammar one cannot understand the meaning of Vedic texts and that Vedic texts which are purely memorized and recited without an understanding of their meaning are like fuel without fire.[45]

e) In responding to a student's salutation, a teacher is supposed to use a *pluta* "extra-long" vowel. A person who does not know grammar would not know how to use such a *pluta* vowel, and such an ignorant person should be spoken to not with the respect due to a teacher, but should be treated like a woman who would be expected not to know such things.[46] Patañjali says that we must study grammar so that we will not be treated like women. This shows Patañjali's belief that women in his days could not pronounce the *pluta* vowels etc. in a proper way. In another context he suggests that for most people, it was difficult to predict where the *pluta* vowels occur and that a person desirous of not being too adventurous should treat all *pluta* vowels as optional.[47]

f) The priests say that on the tenth day, one should name a newborn son. This name should have a voiced consonant at the beginning, a semivowel in its interior, its first vowel should not be a *vṛddhi* (= *ā*, *ai*, *au*) vowel, and it should have either two or four syllables. It should be a verbal derivative (*kṛt*) but not a secondary noun (*taddhita*). Patañjali argues that without studying grammar, it is not possible to know such distinctions, and hence it is not possible to follow the priestly injunctions.[48]

g) If a sacrificer who has embarked upon a sacrifice uses a non-standard expression (*apaśabda*), then he must perform an expiatory sacrifice for Sarasvatī. Patañjali takes the word *apaśabda* to mean a non-standard or a non-Sanskrit expression, and says that we must study grammar to avoid being liable for such expiatory rites.[49] It seems more likely that the word *apaśabda* in this context means "a vulgar expression" rather than "an ungrammatical expression", but Patañjali gives us his own view as a grammarian.

From all these discussions in the *Mahābhāṣya*, it is clear that at least in the opinion of Patañjali a number of features of Sanskrit, such as accents, prolated vowels, and the meaningfulness of archaic words, were already problematic in his times. Such features could not be understood purely from *loka*. They had to be academically acquired. Here, the grammarians claimed that they could be acquired only through the study of grammar, while others from the priestly profession claimed that such features could be acquired directly from the study of the Vedas (*vedān no vaidikā śabdāḥ siddhāḥ lokāc ca laukikāḥ*).[50]

4. Patañjali on the Interaction between Sanskrit and Prakrit

4.1. From even a casual reading of the *Mahābhāṣya*, a fact clearly emerges, namely that there was a fierce competition between Sanskrit and Prakrit, and that in this competition the Prakrit had already surpassed Sanskrit as the language of the world (*loka*). Under these circumstances, the Sanskrit grammarians defended Sanskrit as the language of *dharma*, rather than as a language of worldly communication. The grammarians openly acknowledge that the function of communicating meaning is done equally well by Sanskrit and Prakrit. However, the grammarians stipulate that one *should* communicate by using Sanskrit rather than by using Prakrit. Such a restriction is called a *dharmaniyama* "a religious restriction", and further Patañjali admitted that such a restriction applied only in the context of sacrificial performances (*yājñe karmaṇi sa niyamaḥ*).[51] Patañjali tells us the story of sages called Yarvāṇastarvāṇaḥ. These sages were so named because they spoke a vernacular language with expressions like *yarvāṇa* and *tarvāṇa*, in stead of speaking the standard Sanskrit forms *yad vā naḥ* and *tad vā naḥ*. However, they spoke the proper Sanskrit forms during ritual performances.[52] By ascribing this linguistic pattern to these so-called sages, Patañjali implies that such was the linguistic behavior of even the most learned men of his times. They spoke Prakrits in all normal non-ritual contexts, while they maintained Sanskrit in ritual and academic contexts. Patañjali points out that even Brāhmaṇa girls and women did not and could not generally speak Sanskrit, and they were prone to mispronouncing Sanskrit words like *ṛtaka* as *ḷtaka*.[53] This mispronunciation ascribed to Brāhmaṇa women reflects a characteristic of the Magadhan Prakrit where Sanskrit *r* was reduced to *l*. A similar Prakritized pronunciation *helayo helayo* for a supposedly proper Sanskrit *he arayaḥ he arayaḥ* is ascribed by Patañjali to the so-called Asuras, who spoke Prakrits not only in normal contexts, but also in ritual contexts.[54] Patañjali disapprovingly says that that was why they were defeated.[55] This points to the fact that a very large segment of the population was a monolingual Prakrit-speaking community, who had no ability to switch to Sanskrit in any context. On the other hand, Sanskrit grammarians expected Brāhmaṇas to regard Prakrits as defilements (*apaśabda*) and barbaric usages (*mleccha*), and avoid using them as far as possible. But the pressure of Prakrits was very considerable. Patañjali says that corresponding to a proper Sanskrit word such as *go* 'cow', there are numerous substandard fallen usages such as *gāvī, goṇī, gotā, gopotalikā* etc.[56] While the Brahmanical élites studiously insisted on using forms like *ājñāpayati, vartate* and *vardhate*, the world (*loka*) predominantly used *āṇapayati, vaṭṭati* and *vaḍḍhati*.[57] The world (*loka*) also used forms like *kassati* and *dissati* for the proper Sanskrit words *kṛṣati* and *dṛśyate*.[58] It is thus quite obvious that Brāhmaṇas who insisted on maintaining Sanskrit lived in a thoroughly Prakrit-speaking world.

4.2. Patañjali's *Mahābhāṣya* provides ample evidence to reconstruct the social situation of the Brāhmaṇa communities who maintained the knowledge of Sanskrit. The Brāhmaṇas lived in close contact with other castes. Even those villages which could be called Brāhmaṇa villages were said to have at least five artisan castes.[59] Patañjali informs us that occasionally two Brāhmaṇa residences may be separated by the residence belonging to a Śūdra.[60] The Brāhmaṇa communities in Āryāvarta were surrounded by various non-Brāhmaṇa and non-Aryan communities. Patañjali says that peoples like Kiṣkindhas, Gandhikas, Śakas, Yavanas and others were outside the limits of Āryāvarta. Within the region of Āryāvarta, in Aryan towns and settlements, there were Śūdras like Cāṇḍālas and Mṛtapas, but they were excluded from sacrificial activities. Carpenters, blacksmiths, washermen etc. were also excluded from sacrificial activities. However, while the Caṇḍālas and Mṛtapas were excluded from sharing pots and pans, the utensils used by others mentioned above could be purified with some ritual cleansing.[61] Thus, the Brāhmaṇas came in contact daily with a variety of non-Brāhmaṇa peoples who obviously did not speak Sanskrit. It is unlikely that Brāhmaṇas spoke Sanskrit to these people. The situation of Brāhmaṇa women was also, generally speaking, similar to that of the non-Brāhmaṇas. Patañjali does refer to Brāhmaṇa women who in exceptional circumstances studied the grammar of Āpiśali or the Mīmāṃsā taught by Kāśakṛtsna.[62] However, generally speaking, women were not expected to appear in learned assemblies.[63] Elsewhere, Patañjali refers to Brāhmaṇa women not being able to pronounce Sanskrit properly. Thus, the Brāhmaṇas who spoke Prakrit with all these monolingual Prakrit speakers attempted to preserve and perpetuate Sanskrit within the confines of their ritual and academic activity.

4.3. For a community which was thus trying to preserve an academically acquired and maintained second language, some impact of the first language was inevitable. The grammarians recognized such influences and tried to ward them off. Even the *Prātiśākhya*s contain long lists of possible mispronunciations to be avoided, and at least some of these mispronunciations can be traced to the influence of the reciters' mother tongues.[64] Some of the mistakes occurred when a person attempted a hyper-correction. Patañjali says that one of the purposes of providing oral listings of nouns in *Gaṇapāṭha*s is to instruct students in proper pronunciation. Without such explicit instruction, students might wrongly pronounce *śaśa* as *ṣaṣa*, *palāśa* as *palāṣa* and *mañcaka* as *mañjaka*.[65] Some of these are Prakritic mispronunciations, while others are hyper-corrections.

5. Varieties of Sanskrit Evidenced in the Mahābhāṣya

5.1. It is quite clear that basically Patañjali defines standard Sanskrit and Pāṇinian Sanskrit as equivalents. However, this equivalence has some qualifications. It is recognized that the élites who spoke standard Sanskrit at the time of Patañjali had introduced certain innovations, and these had to be recognized as standard Sanskrit. Patañjali's discussion of how to decide the question of standard Sanskrit and its connection with Pāṇini's authority is very instructive:[66]

Q: Who are the *śiṣṭas*?

A: They are the grammarians.

Q: How is it?

A: Correct usage of language presupposes the science of grammar and grammarians know the science of grammar.

Q: But if the correct usage of language presupposes the science of grammar, and if the science of grammar presupposes the correct usage of language, then this definition becomes circular. Circular arguments do not stand valid.

A: Then we will define *śiṣṭas* by their way of life and place of residence. That particular way of life is found only in the region of Āryāvarta.

Q: Which province is Āryāvarta?

A: It lies to the east of the Ādarśa region, to the west of the Kālaka forest, to the south of the Himālayas and to the north of the Vindhya mountains. Those selfless Brāhmaṇas who live in this Āryāvarta, the land of the Āryas, who just store a basketful of grain, and have attained the highest wisdom in some branch of learning for its own sake, they are the *śiṣṭas* 'the normative speakers of Sanskrit'.

Q: If these *śiṣṭas* are the decisive standard for (the correctness of) words, what then is the function of the *Aṣṭādhyāyī*?

A: The *Aṣṭādhyāyī* aims at helping one recognize the *śiṣṭas*.

Q: How can the *śiṣṭas* be recognized by means of the *Aṣṭādhyāyī*?

A: One who studies the *Aṣṭādhyāyī* observes another person who is not studying it, but (nevertheless) is using words taught in it. He (i.e. the observer) then reflects: It must be either his born nature or divine grace that he does not study the *Aṣṭādhyāyī* and yet uses the correct words taught in it. He must also know other (correct) forms (which are not directly taught by the *Aṣṭādhyāyī*). Thus the *Aṣṭādhyāyī* aims at helping one recognize the *śiṣṭas*.

This discussion brings up some important issues. The relationship between "standard usage" and "Pāṇinian usage" is thus not isomorphic, but a dynamic one. Even as we agree with F.C. Southworth's assessment that Sanskrit by Patañjali's time was not a first language, the fact is clear that the standard for deciding "standard usage" was at this time external to the grammar itself. While the "standard usage" was generally in accord with Pāṇini's grammar, it did occasionally deviate from it. On such occasions, the latter-day grammarian was advised to take heed of the changed standard usage, and revise the grammar accordingly. Such revisions were either made in terms of reinterpretations of Pāṇini's rules or in terms of explicit addenda. Patañjali advises a grammarian not to be a *prāptijña* "one who knows what the rules of grammar will generate", but to be an *iṣṭijña* "one who knows the actual desired standard usage of the élites".[67]

5.2. This brings up a very interesting distinction between two types of historically un-Pāṇinian usages. Some of the latter-day Sanskrit usages were historically un-Pāṇinian, and yet they were part of the contemporary standard usage. A grammarian was supposed to accept these and revise his grammar. On the other hand, some non-Pāṇinian usages were not considered standard and the grammarian was supposed to reject them. Both types of these non-Pāṇinian usages may have been influenced by Prakrit mother tongues of the Sanskrit speakers. For instance, we are told that by Pāṇini's rules we get the forms *tvatkapitṛka* and *matkapitṛka*, while according to Gonardīya (who is identified with Patañjali by the tradition) the forms should be *tvakatpitṛka* and *makatpitṛka*.[68] Patañjali prefers the latter forms. It would seem that the latter forms like *tvakat* and *makat* are similar to forms like *hage* in Ardhamāgadhi, and the preponderance of forms like *ahakaṃ* in Jaina Sanskrit[69] would also indicate some closer connection with Prakrits. However, Patañjali regards these forms to be part of standard Sanskrit usage of his times. On the other hand, he cites certain usages as substandard Sanskrit usages which must be rejected. For instance, he cites *akṣīṇi me darśanīyāni* and *pādā me sukumārāḥ*.[70] The first usage means "my eyes are beautiful", and the second one means "my feet are delicate". However, in both cases, the speaker uses plural, instead of the expected dual. Kaiyaṭa says that such usages are seen in the world (*loka*), but Nāgeśabhaṭṭa adds that these are incorrect usages.[71] One can clearly see the Prakrit influence in these usages. The category of dual was lost in all the Prakrits, and hence for a Prakrit speaker using Sanskrit as his second language, the category of dual was difficult to cope with. Thus, these instances point to the existence of a sort of **Vernacular Sanskrit.**

6. Sanskrit as a Second Language: Living or Dead?

6.1. From the above discussion, it is thus quite clear that Patañjali would agree with F.C. Southworth in calling the contemporary Sanskrit a second language. In all likelihood, no one learned it from his or her mother at this point in time. However, the question of whether Sanskrit as a second language was a living language or a dead language is not totally closed in favor of Southworth. Patañjali's discussion shows in great detail the grammar-independent existence of Sanskrit as a second language. While the grammarians, as partisans of their science, argued that one needs to learn grammar in order to become proficient in this second language, they had to admit that there were others who spoke standard Sanskrit without acquiring it from a grammar book. The grammarians not only had to accept this grammar-independent usage of Sanskrit, they had to modify their rules in order to accommodate it. Revisions in and additions to Pāṇini's grammar proposed by Kātyāyana and Patañjali were often based not on some other grammar books, but upon their own usage of Sanskrit as *śiṣṭas*. Hence, such additions are called *iṣṭi* "statements of desired usages (which cannot be derived from pre-existing traditional rules)". This factor of independence from the rules of traditional grammar was reflected both in the newer forms of standard Sanskrit, as well as in newer forms of non-standard vernacular Sanskrit. Patañjali's assertion that Sanskrit was predominantly spoken in the region of Āryāvarta receives support from an unexpected area of modern research. Damsteegt (1978: 208) in his study of the Inscriptional Hybrid Sanskrit observes:

> There is greater Sanskritization ... in the Ma*hurā inscriptions. This is probably the geographical situation of Mathurā, in the Āryāvarta. It is this region where ... the classical Indian culture was formed. In Patañjali's *Mahābhāṣya,* it is described as the native country of the ideal Brāhmaṇas who can speak the classical language without having studied its grammar. This clearly indicates that in the age of Patañjali (i.e. about the end of the first millennium B.C.) this region was considered to be a stronghold of classical, brahmanical culture, and that Sanskrit had an important place in it. It is not at all improbable that the Buddhists and Jains, penetrating into the Āryāvarta from more eastern parts of the country, gradually came under the influence of this brahmanical culture and its characteris-

> tic language, Sanskrit, as a result of frequent intercourse with the Brāhmaṇas.

It is thus obvious that the question of whether Sanskrit was a first language or a second language must be differentiated from whether or not there was grammar-independent usage of Sanskrit in the days of Patañjali. Later the traditions of Mīmāṃsā and Nyāya also argue right down to the Middle Ages that there is no need to study grammar in order to learn Sanskrit and that Sanskrit can be learned simply by observing the linguistic usage of those who use it. The reality was most probably somewhere in the middle. It is this grammar-independent existence of Sanskrit usage which led me to call it a "living" language in some sense. It was not a living language in every sense like a first language, nor was it a totally dead language surviving only in frozen texts. It was a living second language whose usage went on changing at the margins and the grammarians had to adjust their rules to accommodate this marginal change. Since this change was only marginal, and not substantial, there was no need to force a clear break from the Pāṇinian description of Sanskrit. Therefore, the tradition appropriately found marginal means to tune Pāṇini's grammar to take care of this marginal change. It is a surprising fact that while the Sanskrit grammarians raise post-Vedic Sanskrit to the same religious status held by Vedic texts in terms of its merit-producing ability,[72] the Sanskrit usage, even within such narrow confines, did keep on changing at the margins and the grammarians were sensitive to this change. While the bulk of the Sanskrit usage was indeed a continuation of frozen structures, its edges were still fluid.

7. Conclusion

7.1. I hope the above discussion has clarified some of the important issues raised by F.C. Southworth. The terms Pāṇinian Sanskrit and standard (*śiṣṭa*) Sanskrit must be distinguished from each other from a historical perspective. This allows us to understand how Sanskrit grammarians took care of linguistic change, even when they did not openly admit the fact of change. Some historically Pāṇinian usages became totally obsolete and hence in some sense ceased being *śiṣṭa-prayoga*s. On the other hand many new un-Pāṇinian usages developed. Some of these were part of the contemporary *śiṣṭa* usage, while others were viewed as being substandard and were rejected. This provides us a way of analyzing different strands in the usage of Sanskrit ranging from the historically Pāṇinian Sanskrit to the rejected vernacular Sanskrit. Beyond these varieties of Sanskrit was the world of Prakrit languages, which were spoken by most, if not all, people as their mother tongues. The most outer layer was that of the so-called *mleccha* "barbarian" languages. These languages were obviously viewed as *apaśabdas*, and while their use on non-ritual occasions was acceptable, they were not allowed in the sphere of ritual. The general picture of the linguistic world of Patañjali is presented below in a convenient diagram:

Loka: The linguistic world of Patañjali

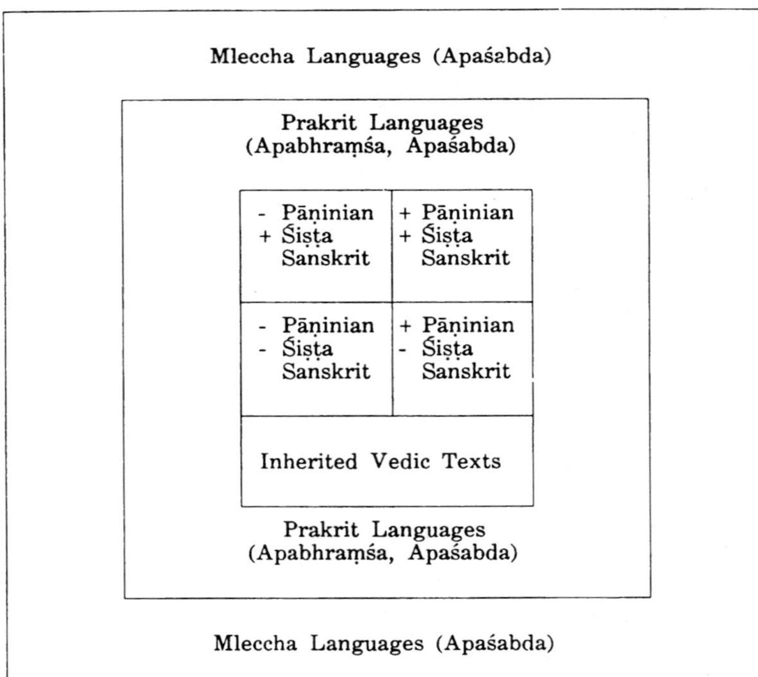

III

ON VERNACULAR SANSKRIT: THE GĪRVĀṆAVĀṄMAÑJARĪ OF DHUṆḌIRĀJA KAVI

1. Vernacular Sanskrit

1.1. In the last two papers, I have provided sufficient data relating to general sociolinguistic and linguistic issues concerning the relationship between Sanskrit and Prakrit. There is clear evidence in Patañjali that even the most learned speakers of Sanskrit spoke Prakrits as their first languages and used Sanskrit only in the context of learning and ritual. Quite clearly the same situation continued in later centuries; the only difference being the changing nature of the first languages of the speakers of Sanskrit. It is also clear from Patañjali's discussion that there existed forms of non-standard Sanskrit or vernacular Sanskrit which were influenced in some way by the features of the first languages of the speakers or users of Sanskrit. The Sanskrit grammarians, as orthodox protectors of the sacred language, never consciously accepted such an influence and certainly they did not look upon any such influence in a positive light. The grammatical tradition makes a distinction between two types of grammarians: *lakṣyaikacakṣuṣka* and *lakṣaṇaikacakṣuṣka* grammarians. Pāṇini, Kātyāyana and Patañjali are said to be grammarians of the first type, *lakṣyaikacakṣuṣka,* those whose attention is solely fixed on the Sanskrit usage to be described, i.e. those who could genuinely modify the rules of grammar by looking at the usage of Sanskrit which existed independently of these rules. All later grammarians belong to the second type, *lakṣaṇaikacakṣuṣka,* those whose attention is solely fixed upon the rules of grammar, i.e., they derive their idea of correct Sanskrit exclusively from the rules of grammar.

1.2. The tradition of Sanskrit grammar being part of the overall Hindu theological tradition, it obviously takes pride in believing that it was able to preserve the Sanskrit language and Pāṇini's grammar without the slightest change. Such a belief is not unique to Indian religious traditions. This is a general feature of all religious traditions. This belief is also similar to the belief of the parents of a child that they have transmitted their language exactly to their child. The common belief is that a child derives the grammar of his language from the grammar of his parents. Andersen (1973: 767) presents a model of linguistic change as follows:

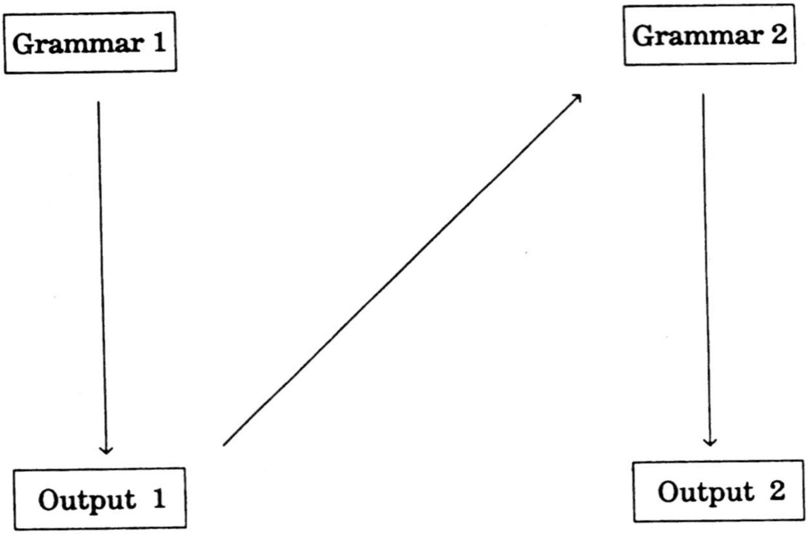

Andersen states that the common belief is that a child's grammar (GRAMMAR 2) is directly derived from a parent's grammar (GRAMMAR 1), and that a child's linguistic output (OUTPUT 2) is directly derived from a parent's linguistic output (OUTPUT 1). In contrast with this common belief, Andersen argues that GRAMMAR 1 leads to OUTPUT 1. This linguistic output of the parent is re-analyzed by a child and this re-analysis of OUTPUT 1 leads to the formation of GRAMMAR 2 which in turn leads to OUTPUT 2. In reality, a child hears the linguistic output of not only his parents, but of numerous people and then his re-analysis of this multiple output of others leads to the formulation of his grammar. Thus, the grammar of a child is inevitably different from that of his parents, though this difference need not be very great in a single generation.

1.3. In an analogous fashion, while the Sanskrit grammarians claim that the whole of the later tradition is *lakṣaṇaikacakṣuṣka*, i.e. they derive their knowledge of Sanskrit exclusively from the rules of grammar, the actual facts did not match this expectation. The grammar of Sanskrit in the minds of its users was not derived exclusively from a study of Pāṇini's grammar, but there were various different inputs which led to the formation of this user-grammar. Pāṇini's grammar was only one of the many inputs. A study of the existing traditional literature was an important factor. Similarly, the mother-tongue of the user was a very powerful factor. While the grammarians despised any such extraneous influences, the literary tradition often welcomed them. Vākpatirāja says in his *Gaüḍavaho* (verse 65):

> *ummilaï lāyaṇṇaṃ payayacchāyāe sakkaya-vayāṇaṃ /*
> *sakkaya-sakkārukkarisaṇeṇa payayassa vi pahāvo //*
>
> The beauty of Sanskrit words blossoms with a tinge of Prakrit. The effectiveness of Prakrit also increases by the elevating process of Sanskritization.

A tinge of Prakrit added to Sanskrit brought Sanskrit closer to the language of the home, while a judicious Sanskritization made Prakrit into a language of a higher cultural status. Both of these processes were simultaneous and worked at conscious as well as unconscious levels. Thus, while a latter-day Pandit claimed that his Sanskrit derived exclusively from his study of Pāṇini, in point of fact his output was unavoidably influenced by all these other factors. The more conscious a person was of the traditional rules of grammar and of the traditional high literary usage, the more his Sanskrit output looked like the traditional high classical language. But the more a person tried to be colloquial, the more his usage became influenced by the non-traditional factors.

1.4. Thus, within the usage of Sanskrit, one must conceive of a range of varieties more or less influenced by the non-traditional factors. It must also be kept in mind that there is no unique form of language which we can designate as **the vernacular Sanskrit**. We must carefully distinguish between the various kinds of non-standard Sanskrit, only some of which can be explained in terms of the influence of the substratum. Different usages exhibit totally different processes of de-standardization. Sometimes metrical necessity may force a poet to launch into a grammatically less desirable alternative. For instance, in a verse popular in Maharashtra describing various Gaṇeśa temples, the author says: *grāme rāṃjaṇa-*

saṃsthito gaṇapatiḥ kuryāt sadā maṅgalam, "May Gaṇapati residing in the village of Ranjangaon always bring about auspicious results". This is supposed to describe Gaṇeśa in Ranjangaon, Sanskritized as *rāṃjaṇa-grāma*. Grammatically speaking, one should say *rāṃjaṇa-grāme saṃsthito gaṇapatiḥ*, but that would violate the meter *Śārdūlavikrīḍita*. Thus the author chooses to violate grammar, but maintain the meter. Contrary to this preference, I found in a booklet named *Prātaḥ Smaraṇa* edited by Jagannatha Bharamarao Kesharkar (5th edition, Pune, 1936, Hind Sevak Chhapkhana) the following lines:

a) *ādau śrī-rāma-tapo-vanādhigamanaṃ hatvā mṛgaṃ kāñcanam* /, and

b) *ādau śrī-devaki-devi-garbha-jananaṃ gopī-gṛhe vardhanam* /

These lines are the initial lines of verses which depict the whole story of *Rāmāyaṇa* and *Bhāgavata* in one stanza each. These verses are in the meter *Śārdūlavikrīḍita*. Someone felt that he could not have the names *rāma* and *devakī* without the honorific *śrī* and thus this honorific was inserted in spite of the fact that it violated the meter. At the same time, the original composer of the verses took liberties with grammar in order to fit the meter. For instance, he split the word *kāñcana-mṛgam* into *mṛgaṃ kāñcanam* as if the word *kāñcana* were an adjective, which it is not. Similarly, in the second line, the author shortened the words *devakī* and *devī* into *devaki* and *devi* in order to fit the meter. Thus, violations of various norms seem to have come about for different reasons, and seem to have been helped by the flexibility of vowel length in metrical compositions in vernaculars like Marathi.

1.5. In other instances, one may see over-generalizations from within Sanskrit itself. For example, consider the following instance. During my visit to the Sri Venkateshwara Temple in Pittsburgh, Pennsylvania, I heard this conversation. The priest was blessing devotees at the temple. He asked a lady her name. She replied that her name was Kamalā. Then the priest uttered the blessing: *kamalāsya sukhaṃ bhavatu*. The priest overgeneralized the genitive affix *-sya* and extended it to the feminine stem *kamalā-*. In this example, one may not read any Prakrit influence, for the simple reason that the Tamilian priest had absolutely no knowledge of Prakrit. He was simply producing new instances of Sanskrit by extending the patterns he had heard and used in ritual. These are analogical formations.

1.6. In other instances, the influence of the substratum Prakrit may be justifiably suggested. Such is the example cited by Patañjali: *akṣīṇi me darśanīyāni pādā me sukumārāḥ*, "My eyes are beautiful and my feet are delicate" (*Mahābhāṣya* (K), Vol. I, p. 322). In this example, the use of plural instead of the expected dual may be most likely due to the influence of Prakrit which had no dual forms. However, it is basically a Sanskrit sentence. On the other hand, consider the following line from a Bhajana ascribed to Tulasīdās: *śrī-rāmacandra kṛpālu bhaja manaharaṇa bhava-bhaya-dāruṇam*. Here we find some forms declined properly, while others left undeclined. Such a language is hard to be described, except as a form of deliberately mixed Hindi-Sanskrit. This is used widely in Tulasidās's works for poetic effects. In many cases, the errors made by the users of Sanskrit reveal what is going on in their mind. For instance, many Pandits in Banaras start a sentence with *ahaṃ vadāmi*, and then follows a direct discourse preceded by the Hindi connective *ki*. If the Pandit is careful, he will use *yad* rather than *ki*. Such interference from the mother-tongue can be observed in every province of India. This kind of intrusion of the mother-tongue indicates that the person basically thinks in the mother-tongue and then puts the cloak of Sanskrit on his thoughts. In a sense, in such cases, the **deep structure** of this Sanskrit usage is not configured in Sanskrit, but in the mother-tongue of the user, and the Sanskrit which one sees or hears is only the **surface structure**. A person makes the minimal necessary changes to produce this Sanskrit surface structure. The more learned a user of Sanskrit, the more classical-like this surface structure becomes. The less learned a user of Sanskrit, the more mother tongue-like this surface structure becomes.

1.7. Among the many different varieties of non-standard Sanskrit which are attested in Sanskrit literature, there are some varieties which are distinctly influenced by the regional substratum languages. These varieties must be distinguished from non-standard varieties such as the Epic Sanskrit. Among the regionalized vernacular forms of Sanskrit, those attested in texts like the *Sekasubhodaya* from Bengal, the *Bharaṭakadvātriṃśikā* from Gujarat, and the *Gīrvāṇavāṅmañjarī* of Dhuṇḍirāja Kavi from Banaras may be cited as important instances. The editors of these nonstandard Sanskrit texts were not always cognizant of the linguistic value of these texts as indicators of a real vernacular usage of Sanskrit. Sukumar Sen, the editor of *Sekasubhodaya*, says in his introduction: "The book as we have it now is the result of handling of old material by person or persons not knowing much Sanskrit, whose main purpose appears to have been popularizing the Pir cult through interesting stories. The language of *Sekasubhodaya*, therefore, is not a kind of deliberate Mixed or Dog Sanskrit but is miswritten Sanskrit, i.e. Sanskrit written in the Bengali manner as is now quite well known in examination scripts." (*Sekasubhodaya*, Introduction, p. xi). In his notes, Sen points to a large number of Bengali traits in the Sanskrit of this text.

1.8. Johannes Hertel's *On the Literature of the Shvetāmbaras of Gujarat* (Leipzig, 1922) contains perhaps the best available discussion of problems posed by texts in Vernacular Sanskrit. So far this discussion has not received sufficient attention in the current approaches to this subject. Responding to Bühler who contended that the Jaina authors did not use correct Sanskrit, Hertel elaborated his idea of the continued existence of a kind of vernacular or spoken Sanskrit, which differed from the strict rules of the grammarians, but which was widely prevalent in many parts of India. Let me quote some of Hertel's significant observations:

> Now there are a great many words which occur in the Sanskrit current in Gujarāt, but which are unknown in other countries of India. (Hertel, 1922: 16)
>
> Sanskrit, however, was not only the language of the clergy and of the scholars, it was also the language of the courts and of diplomacy, and it was a spoken language down to comparatively recent times. It was understood even by a considerable part of the population which did not use it itself. The same Bilhaṇa whose nindā of the Gujarātīs we have quoted above, says, that in this country even the women of every house speak Sanskrit and Prakrit as fluently as their mother tongue: *yatra strīṇām api kim aparaṃ janma-bhāṣāvad eva / pratyāvāsaṃ vilasati vacaḥ saṃskṛtaṃ prākṛtaṃ ca//*, (*Vikramāṅkadevacarita*, XVIII, 6). (Hertel, 1922: 17)
>
> In Gujarat, Sanskrit must have been very generally understood even in the 17th and 18th centuries, at least by the higher classes of the population. ... On the other hand the modern vernaculars bear witness of the general prevalence of Sanskrit in a comparatively recent time. They are really crammed with Sanskrit words, and that is not only true of the actual literary languages, but also of the popular languages of by-gone centuries. (Hertel, 1922: 17)
>
> Of course, the Sanskrit spoken or understood by those who were no scholars, was a popular and colloquial one, not the highly

artificial language of kāvya verse and prose. The speakers of this colloquial Sanskrit did not study Pāṇini or Hemacandra, but such books as the *Muktāvabodhamauktika*. The Śvetāmbara authors of Gujarat used this colloquial Sanskrit in their stories in order to make them intelligible to their public, and the Kathānaka literature is an unmistakable testimony of the general use of this popular Sanskrit, but not, as it has been taken to be by European scholars, of the incapacity of Jaina authors. (Hertel, 1922: 17-18)

The wider the circles were to which the Sanskrit authors of Gujarat addressed, the more words they borrowed and adapted from the vernacular language. Part of such adaptations have become the common property of all Sanskrit writers of Gujarat. Hence a certain knowledge of the Gujarati language is absolutely necessary for every scholar who wishes to read Sanskrit works written in Gujarat. (Hertel, 1922: 18)

Indology must proceed to get rid of the tutelage of the Indian grammarians, who wrote in order to establish rules *to be observed* by the śiṣṭas, and especially by the poets, whereas truly scientific grammarians must collect, and discuss, and draw conclusions from the rules which the population - not only the śiṣṭas -, and the authors *really observed*, or else, *did not care about*. (Hertel, 1922: 20)

We must, moreover, cease to confound grammar with language, and must no longer allow the fact that Sanskrit words are spelled as in Pāṇini's time, to mislead us in our conclusions. Even Sanskrit phonetics have changed in the course of time, as Sanskrit is, and has been for many centuries, differently pronounced in the different countries of India. Much more evident are the changes which Sanskrit has undergone in other respects. Whole paradigms have become obsolete, and the very structure of the language has been altered in the course of the many centuries which followed Pāṇini. The same fact must be stated with regard to its vocabulary. There are the most remarkable differences between the varieties of even the Sanskrit written by the different court poets, or kavis; and popular Sanskrit, whose study has quite unduly been neglected by the scholars, widely differs from that of the classical authors. (Hertel, 1922: 21)

There is no such thing as standard Sanskrit even from the kavi point of view, and much less so from the standpoint of the truly scientific

> philologist; but there is a language, spread over a huge area, and used, through more than 2000 years after Pāṇini, orally as well as in writing, for literary as well as for everyday life purposes, by millions and millions of speakers and writers, belonging to entirely different climates, and countries, and races, and more or less influenced, in all these cases, by the vernaculars of the respective speakers and writers. (Hertel, 1922: 21)

> In all her different parts, India is a polyglot country. In Gujarat, e.g., Sanskrit, Mahārāṣṭrī, Apabhraṃśa, Hindi, and the different dialects of Old Gujarātī were spoken and written at the same time by the Hindus, and Urdū as well as Persian by the Mohammedans. All these languages could not possibly avoid to be influenced by one another. But similar influences must, as matter of course, have operated, and continue to operate, in any other Indian country, and especially strong must always be the influence which the respective vernacular exercises on the other languages. This fact which is of the highest importance not only for the development of Sanskrit, but also for the history of Sanskrit literature, has not yet found with Sanskrit scholars the attention which it deserves. When we shall have succeeded in making out, for all the different parts of India, the mutual relations which, of necessity, must everywhere exist between the Sanskrit and the respective vernaculars and especially between the vocabularies of these languages, it will not only be easy to fix the original country of any Sanskrit text, but also the provenience of more extensive interpolations. (Hertel, 1922: 22-23)

I have quoted Hertel's observations extensively because they are quite significant and because this publication is not easily available today. These remarks are as much applicable today as they were when he published his book. One may not agree with Hertel in every respect, and yet his comments are very instructive in pushing us toward a true understanding of the reality of the Sanskrit language as it existed, rather than that of the Sanskrit language as it is expected to be.

2. The *Gīrvāṇavāṅmañjarī* of Dhuṇḍirāja Kavi

2.1. U.P. Shah edited and published the texts titled *Gīrvāṇapadamañjarī* and *Gīrvāṇavāṅmañjarī* from Baroda in 1960 (*The M.S. University Oriental Series, No. 4*). Originally, these texts appeared in the *Journal of the Oriental Institute*, Vol. VII, No. 4, June 1958. The *Gīrvāṇapadamañjarī* is a work of Varadarāja, while the *Gīrvāṇavāṅmañjarī* is a work of Dhuṇḍirāja. Both of these texts were composed to teach Sanskrit by direct conversational method, and were supposed to provide an example of conversational Sanskrit. P.K. Gode dates Varadarāja to c. 1600-1650 A.D., and assigns Dhuṇḍirāja to c. 1702-1704 A.D. (Gode, 1954: 316-329; Gode, 1956: 161-171). Dhuṇḍirāja, as far as one can guess from his work, seems to have been a Marathi Brāhmaṇa settled in Banaras. He shows a detailed acquaintance with the street geography of Banaras, but is at the same time clear in his preference for the most pure Brāhmaṇas of Maharashtra belonging to the tradition of Madhvācārya. The text of the *Gīrvāṇavāṅmañjarī* presents to us a conversation between several characters, a Brāhmaṇa, his wife, sons and a Sannyāsin. The text describes a Brāhmaṇa doing his daily routine, inviting a Sannyāsin to dinner, the dinner itself, a conversation between the host and the Sannyāsin etc. Through these conversations, which are very humorous and entertaining, the author aims at teaching conversational Sanskrit in a painless manner. In his notes, U.P. Shah deals with the cultural contents of the text extensively. Here we will look at the linguistic make-up of the language of the text. This text is in what I would call vernacular Sanskrit. It extensively borrows vocabulary from Marathi and certain Hindi dialects of Banaras. The editor has tried to correct the forms which he perceived were incorrect, and yet a number of vernacular features of the text have survived in the existing edition. In what follows, I have noted down several instances of parallelisms between the language of the *Gīrvāṇavāṅmañjarī* and Marathi, Hindi, Gujarati, Bengali and Punjabi. The Marathi parallels are based on my own knowledge of Marathi as a native speaker, while my information about other languages mentioned above is based on my personal consultations with speakers of these languages. I would also like to thank my colleague Prof. Peter Hook for going over these instances.

3. Linguistic Parallelisms:

1. *ayi mayā dīrgha-śaṅkārthaṃ gamyate* /, (p. 19)
   "Hey! I have to go for (taking care) of the long danger."

The expressions *dīrgha-śaṅkā* "long danger" and *laghu-śaṅkā* "short danger" as euphemisms for defecation and urination occur in Brāhmaṇa Marathi. The words literally mean "great fear" and "small fear". These meanings are also known to exist in Hindi and Gujarati usage.

2. *āḥ, tasya arbhakasya kim / tan-nimittaṃ kiṃ viśiṣṭaṃ kartavyaṃ bhaviṣyati // sarveṣāṃ madhye so 'py ekaḥ āyāsyati /*, (p. 20) "Well, why worry about that little kid? What special thing would have to be done for him? Along with all others, he too - just a single child - will come."

Compare Marathi: *are tyā porāce kāy? tyācyā sāṭhī kāy khās karāyalā pāhije? sagaḶyāñcyā madhe tohī ek yeīl.*

3. *yan manasi āyāsyati tat kuru /*, (p. 20) "Do what comes to your mind."

Compare Marathi: *je manālā yeīl te kar.* In Hindi, one can say *jo man cāhe vah karo*, but not **jo man mẽ āegā.*

4. *rāṇḍeyaṃ śīghram utthāpaya / ... sa tu bhavat-pradeśe eva tiṣṭhati /*, (p. 20) "Wake up quickly this son-of-a-bitch. ... But he is (sleeping) right close to you."

Compare Marathi: *rāṇḍecyālā lavkar uṭhav. ... to tar tumcyā pāśīc āhe.* Also Hindi: *vah to āp ke pās hī hai.* Hindi *pās* or Marathi *pāśī* may have been interpreted as Sanskrit *pradeśe*, while the most likely Sanskrit candidate, from a historical point of view would be *pārśve*. The word *rāṇḍeya* "son-of-a-bitch, son-of-a-prostitute" has no parallel in Hindi, but there is an expression *raṇḍave* in Bihar. Marathi has the expression *rāṇḍecyā.*

5. *are balīvarda! śīghram uttiṣṭha.* (p. 20) "Hey you bullock! Get up quickly."

Compare Marathi: *are bailā, lavkar ūṭh. ṭ ahāṭ jhālī.* Hindi too has the expression *abe bail.* Hindi has *arī*, while Maithili uses *are.* Hindi also has the expression *pau phūṭī.*

6. *are adya gṛhe mahat prayojanaṃ tiṣṭhati tvam āpaṇe gaccha /* (p. 21) "Hey, today there is a big feast at home. You go to the bazaar."

Compare Marathi: *are āj gharī moṭhe prayojan āhe. tū bājārāt jā.* The word *prayojan* in the meaning of a celebration or feast is known only in Marathi.

7. *bhoḥ pitaḥ, kiṃ kiṃ gṛhṇāmi tad vadadhvam* /, (p. 21)
"O father, Tell (2nd plural) me what (repeated twice) I should buy."

Compare Marathi: *kāy kāy gheū te sāṅgā*. Note the use of *vadadhvam* implying the agent of the verb to be *yūyam* (= *tumhī*, 2nd plural in Marathi) rather than *bhavān* (= *āp* in Hindi). The use of second person plural as honorific is common in Marathi.

8. *uśīro grāhyaḥ tasyāparaṃ nāma sugandha-vāḶā ity udīrayanti janāḥ* /, (p. 21)
"You should buy Uśīra "*Andropogon Muricatus*". People call it by another name, i.e. *Sugandha-VāḶā*".

Note the reference to Marathi *Vāḷā* as an explanation for a Sanskrit word, indicating that Marathi was a more basic language than Sanskrit in the daily discourse of the author.

9. *kān kān gṛhṇāmi tad brūta* /, (p. 21)
"Tell (2nd pl.) me what (repeated twice) I should buy."

Compare Marathi: *kāy kāy āṇū te sāṅgā*. The use of *brūta* again implies the agent to be *yūyam* (= *tumhī* in Marathi). Also the expected classical Sanskrit would be *yān yān ... tān*. The use of interrogatives as relatives is widely prevalent in Indo-Aryan languages.

10. *vana-kāravellāni miliṣyanti ced gṛhāṇa* /, (p. 22)
"If you come across wild Kāravellas, buy them."

Compare Marathi: *rānaṭī kāralī miḶālī tar ghe*. Hindi also has the verb *mil* in this sense. Classical Sanskrit does not use this verb in this sense.

11. *ekasmin kāgade sarvam ālikha* /, (p.22)
"Write down everything on a (piece of) paper."

Compare Marathi: *ekā kāgadāvar sagaḶe lihī*. While Hindi uses the Persian loan *kāgaz*, Marathi uses *kāgad*. The author opts for the Marathi, rather than for the Hindi word. Also note the use of *eka* "one" as the indefinite-marker. This is similar to Hindi and Marathi.

12. *daṇḍavat praṇamya vākyam uvāca* /, (p. 22)
"Having prostrated like a staff, he said these words."

Compare the Marathi use of *daṇḍavat ghālaṇe.* This usage of *daṇḍavat* to refer to a prostration is found also in Hindi, Bengali, and Gujarati. This meaning is also known among Tamil Brāhmaṇas.

13. *are paraṃ tu tvaṃ gauḍavad bhāsase re* /, (p. 23)
"Hey, however, you look like a Gauḍa."

Compare Marathi: *are paṇ tū gauḍāsārkhā distos re.* The use of *re* at the end of sentences is common in Marathi.

14. *na hi re, tava sambandha-yogyā bhavati* /, (p. 23)
"Hey, that is not the case. She is fit for marriage into your (family)."

Compare Marathi *nāhī re.*

15. *svāminaḥ, bhavantaḥ agre bhavantu* /, (p. 24)
"My master, please you walk ahead (of me)."

Compare Marathi: *svāmī, āpaṇ puḍhe vhā.* The text seems to generally make a distinction between *bhavat* (= *āpaṇ* in Marathi) and *yūyam* (= *tumhī* in Marathi). The first is used as a formal honorific, while the other is used as the normal honorific. Hindi would be normally *āp āge caliye* but not *hoiye.* However, Bihari usage is *āge holiye.*

16. The text seems to use *are* with respect to male addressees and *ayi* with respect to female addressees. This matches nicely with the distinction between *are* and *aga* in Marathi, while it does not match with the Sanskrit usage of *are* and *ayi.* Consider for example: *na vā are* with reference to Maitreyī in *Bṛhadāraṇyaka-Upaniṣad* (4.5).

Ayi used consistently with reference to females:

ayi mayā dīrgha-śaṅkārthaṃ gamyate /, (p. 19)
"Hey, I am going to take care of the long danger."

ayi śṛṇoṣi /, (p. 20)
"Hey, will you listen?"

ayi adya mahat parva tiṣṭhati /, (p. 20)
"Hey, there is a major holy day today."

ayi ādau ghṛtena sarveṣāṃ patrāṇy abhighārya śīghraṃ pariveṣaya /, (p. 25)

"Hey, first having sprinkled all pots with clarified butter, then serve (the food) quickly."

Aye seems to be a variant of *ayi* in this text, restricted with reference to females:

aye tvaṃ śīghram upary āgaccha /, (p. 37)
"Hey, come upstairs quickly."

Are used consistently with reference to males:

are balīvarda, śīghram uttiṣṭha /, (p. 20)
"Hey, you bull, get up quickly."

are adya gṛhe mahat prayojanaṃ tiṣṭhati /, (p. 21)
"Hey, today at our house there is a big feast."

are antaḥpure gaccha /, (p. 21)
"Hey, go into the inner room."

are ādau vaṇijāpaṇe gatvā ... /, (p. 21)
"Hey, having first gone to the grocery-market ..."

are ādau sūraṇo grāhyaḥ /, (p. 21)
"Hey, first you should buy Sūraṇa."

are tintiṇīṃ mā vismara /, (p. 22)
"Hey, do not forget *Tintiṇī*".

are mūrkha tvaṃ kevalaṃ gardabha-prāyo 'si /, (p. 22)
"Hey you fool, you are simply like an ass."

are tava kā vā jñātiḥ /, (p. 23)
"Hey, what is your caste?"

are paraṃ tu tvaṃ gauḍavad bhāsase re /, (p. 23)
"Hey, however, you do look like a Gauḍa."

are tava gṛhaṃ kiyad dūraṃ tiṣṭhati /, (p. 24)
"Hey, how far is your house?"

are meṣāśrama /, (p. 24)
"Hey, you lazy goat..."

are kiṃ vadasi /, (p. 24)
"Hey, what do you say?"

are prabhākara śīghram ehi /, (p. 24)
"Hey, Prabhākara, come quickly."

are iyaṃ tava gṛhiṇī kim /, (p. 26)
"Hey, is this your wife?"

are tava kati apatyāni tiṣṭhanti /, (p. 27)
"Hey, how many children do you have?"

are tvaṃ paraṃ bhāgyavān asi /, (p. 27)
"Hey, you are truly lucky."

are etasyāḥ pariṇetā sa eva vā /, (p. 28)
"Hey, is that person her husband?"

are tava kaniṣṭha-kumārasya lagnaṃ kadā bhaviṣyati /, (p. 28)
"Hey, when will your younger son get married?"

are paraṃ tu mayā tava bhāryayā samā kāpi yoṣin na dṛṣṭā /, (p. 29)
"Hey, however, I have not yet seen a woman like your wife."

are śṛṇu /, (p. 29)
"Hey, listen."

are tava pitā vārāṇasīṃ tyaktvā gauḍadeśe bahu-varṣa-paryantaṃ kimarthaṃ sthitaḥ /, (p. 29)
"Hey, why did your father leave Banaras and go and stay in Bengal for such a long time?"

are tava gauḍadeśe kāni kāni tīrthāni vartante /, (p. 31)
"Hey, in your Bengal, what kind of holy places are there?"

are pūrvāśrame' smākaṃ karṇāṭaka-deśe cañjī-grāmaḥ /, (p. 34)
"Hey, in my previous state (of being a householder), my village in Karṇāṭaka was called Canjī."

are tat kim api mā pṛccha /, (p. 35)
"Hey, do not ask any of that."

are mayā pūrvāśrame vyavasāya-vṛttyā sthitam /, (p. 35)
"Hey, in the previous state of my life, I had a job."

are pūrvaṃ mama nikaṭe katiśo vārāṅganāḥ sthitāḥ /, (p. 35)
"Hey, previously how many courtsans stayed with me (what can I say?)"

are mama dvādaśa-varṣāṇi jātāni /, (p. 36)
"Hey, it has been twelve years for me."

are mayā ataḥ paraṃ maṭhaṃ prati gamyate /, (p. 36)
"Hey, now I will go to my monastery."

are tvaṃ tūṣṇīm āstaraṇaṃ vidhehi /, (p. 37)
"Hey, you must quietly spread my bed."

are adhunā kim api mā pṛccha /, (p. 37)
"Hey, now do not ask anything."

17. *svāminaḥ, adya param ati-kālo jātaḥ / sāvakāśatayā bhoktavyam* /, (p. 26)
"O Master, today it has been very late. Please eat at ease."

Compare Marathi: *svāmī, āj phārac veḶ jhālā.* Hindi does not have *sāvakāśa* in this sense of "at ease" which it has in Marathi. This meaning is not known in any of the other languages I investigated.

18. *paraṃ sādhvī bhavati* / ... *tvaṃ paraṃ bhāgyavān asi* /, (p. 27)
"(Your wife) is extremely good natured. You are extremely lucky."

Compare Marathi: *phār sādhvī āhe. ... tū phār bhāgyavān āhes.* The word *param* is used adverbially in this text in the same sense as Marathi *phār* "extremely".

19. *paraṃ lāvaṇyavatī vartate* /, (p. 27)
"She is very beautiful."

Compare Marathi: *phār lāvaṇyavatī āhe.* Again note the usage of *param.*

20. *param kuśalā vartate* /, (p. 28)
"She is exceedingly skillful."

Compare Marathi: *phār kuśal āhe.*

21. *tava paraṃ sukhadātrī bhavatu* /, (p. 29)
"May she give you a lot of happiness."

Compare Marathi: *tulā phār sukh deṇārī hovo.* Note the usage of *param.*

22. *ho, svāminaḥ* /, (p. 28)
"Yes, Master."

Compare Marathi: *ho svāmī.* Hindi uses *hā̃* but not *ho* for "yes".

23. *draṣṭavyam, svāminaḥ, yadā bhaviṣyati tadā khalu* /, (p. 28)
"We will see, Master. When it happens, then it truly happens."

Compare Marathi: *pahāyace svāmī. jevhā hoīl tevhā khare.* The Sanskrit *khalu* seems to have been used in the place of Marathi *khare* "true, truly". There is no parallel to Marathi *khare* in Hindi.

24. *tena dāsyāmīty uktaṃ vartate* / *param ṛṇānubandho balavattaraḥ* /, (p. 28)
"He has said that (he) will give (his daughter). However, fate is ultimately powerful."

Compare the Marathi expression *ṛṇānubandha* which refers to some pre-destined relationship. This meaning is also common in Gujarati.

25. *etāvān udyogaḥ* / *anyāsāṃ strīṇām āyāsyati* /, (p. 29)
"So much work! (Do you think) other women can do it?"

Compare Marathi: *itar bāykānnā yeīl kā̃?* Hindi also has a similar construction, and the late Classical Sanskrit has the construction *na vaktum āyāti* "X cannot speak".

26. *evaṃ vā tarhi samyak, na hi, mayā śrūyate, vaṅga-deśīyā brāhmaṇā veda-bāhyā bhavanti* /, (p. 30).

"If that is the case, then it is alright. (I do) not (wish to say, but) I have heard that Brāhmaṇas from Bengal are outside the Vedic tradition."

Compare Marathi: *ase asel tar ṭhīk. nāhi mhaṇje mī ase aikale āhe kī baṅgālī brāmhaṇ ved-bāhya astāt.*

27. *svāminaḥ, no ced anṛtam ucyate kim* /, (p. 31)
"Master, if (you do) not (trust me), (do you think) I am telling a lie?"

Compare Marathi: *svāmī, nāhī tar khoṭe sāṅgitle kāy*? Hindi also has the construction *nahī to.*

28. *evaṃ tarhi śrīmatāṃ kā vā vṛttiḥ sthitā, bhikṣuka-vṛttiḥ sthitā vā vyavasāya-vṛttiḥ sthitā* /, (p. 35)
"Thus then, Sir, what kind of livelihood did you have? Did you make your living as a priest, or did you have a job?"

In Marathi, the word *bhikṣuk* is used in the sense of a priest rather than a monk or a beggar. Similarly the word *vyavasāya* is used in Marathi in the sense of occupation rather than determination.

29. *adhunāpi yadā tasyāḥ smaraṇaṃ jāyate tadā mama manaḥ kutrāpi na lagati* /, (p. 35)
"Even now when I remember her, I cannot concentrate my mind on anything else."

Compare Marathi: *man kuṭhe hī lāgat nāhī.* Also Hindi: *man nahī lagatā.* One finds in late classical usage: *tasya tad eva hi madhuraṃ yasya mano yatra saṃlagnam* "With whatever a person's mind is enchanted, that alone appears sweet to him."

30. *mām api caturbhujaṃ vidhāya nītam* /, (p. 36)
"They took me away after capturing me."

Compare Marathi: *malā hī caturbhuj karūn nele.* The word *caturbhuj* occurs in Marathi in the meaning of 'captured'. This meaning is not found in Hindi, Gujarati and Bengali. Similarly, it is hard to explain the accusative *mām* except as an influence from a construction such as Marathi *malā nele.* In Sanskrit, an impersonal passive usage such as *nītam* occurs only under the condition that the sentence be intransitive. It could be argued that *mām* is the object of *vidhāya.*

31. *tadā tena tasyāḥ pāṇim avalambya tāṃ kroḍe upāveśayat* /, (p. 38)
"Then, holding her hand, he made her sit on his lap."

Compare Marathi: *tevhā tyāne ticā hāt dharūn tilā māṇḍīvar basavile.* Also Hindi: *tab usne uskā hāth pakaḍkar usko god mẽ biṭhāyā.* Only on the basis of some such interference from the vernacular can one explain the beginning of the sentence with *tena* in spite of the final active voice verb *upāveśayat.*

4. Conclusions

From the above evidence, one can draw several conclusions. It is quite obvious that the Sanskrit used by Dhuṇḍirāja is heavily influenced by Marathi and Hindi dialects of Banaras. This dual influence is one of the most interesting features of this text. In this respect, one may contrast this text with Sanskrit literary productions of recent times coming from Maharashtra which are studied by Usha R. Bhise (1980). The influence of Marathi and Hindi dialects on the language of the *Gīrvāṇavāṅmañjarī* is seen in its vocabulary, idioms and sometimes even in the syntactic errors made by the author. In many cases, the Marathi and the Hindi structures closely parallel the Sanskrit structure. However, in a few cases where Marathi differs from Hindi, the Sanskrit shows Marathi influence. This is a significant feature, indicating that Marathi was most probably the first language of the author, some form of Hindi his second language, and Sanskrit the third. The influence of the first language outweighs that of the second language. This pattern is seen in the Marathi families residing in Banaras even now. These families speak Marathi at home, Hindi to communicate with their neighbors, and then some of them may acquire Sanskrit as a third language. Thus the nonstandard aspects of this text are clearly very significant indicators of how the diglossic spectrum involving Sanskrit, Marathi and Hindi affected the nature of the linguistic output.

One can also draw another conclusion from the data given above. Many of the non-standard features of vernacular Sanskrit are shared in common by a large number of Indo-Aryan languages, while some features are found only in specific substratum languages. This points to a possible difference in the history of the different non-standard features of vernacular Sanskrit. Some of these features probably date back to a much older period when they were a common property of vernacular Sanskrit and Prakrit, while other features were acquired in particular regions of India.

IV

HISTORICAL CHANGE AND THE THEOLOGY OF ETERNAL (NITYA) SANSKRIT

1. According to the main stream of Hindu religious philosophy, the Vedic scriptures, and by extension the Sanskrit language are eternal entities. Depending on which particular school of philosophy one looks at, these entities were either created by some divine agency, or were always there, uncreated and eternally self-existent. It was always assumed in the tradition that man's knowledge of these entities was ever incomplete and as such could always be improved. The *Taittirīya-Brāhmaṇa* (3.10.11.4) says:

> God Indra showed the sage Bharadvāja three mountainlike masses. From each of these He took a handful. He called Bharadvāja and said: "These are the Vedas. Infinite indeed are the Vedas (*anantā vai vedāḥ*)."

The Hindu legal system always took advantage of this notion of eternal and infinite Vedas. Wherever no actual Vedic statement was available to justify a current practice or belief, the lawmakers of ancient India said that such a statement must have existed in the "original" Vedas, but that it was now lost. The existence of such a "lost" Vedic statement was reasoned on the basis of the tradition (*smṛti*) and from the practice and beliefs of the contemporary *śiṣṭa*s 'social élites', because it was generally held that they only continue to manifest in their behavior what was already there in the original eternal Vedas.

2. Sanskrit grammarians and etymologists in ancient India grew up in this kind of ideological framework and they extended the notion of eternal scriptures to the Sanskrit language at large. They did this both implicitly and explicitly. Yāska, the etymologist, says in his *Nirukta* (1.16):

> Vedic stanzas are (still) meaningful because their words are identical with those of the currently spoken Sanskrit.

Here Yāska assumes the linguistic identity of the Vedas and his contemporary Sanskrit about the middle of the first millennium B.C. This is also seen elsewhere in the *Nirukta* and in the works of Mīmāṃsakas.[73] Kātyāyana, the first extant commentator on Pāṇini, says:[74]

> Correct usage of Sanskrit leads to prosperity. This is similar to the correct use of the Vedic expressions.

Kātyāyana is clearly claiming the same religious status for contemporary Sanskrit which was unanimously ascribed to the Vedic scriptures and their language. However, while thus espousing the doctrine of eternal Sanskrit, both Yāska and Kātyāyana were also aware of the contemporary usage of this eternal language. Yāska, while explaining Vedic verses, often paraphrases Vedic expressions with contemporary expressions. Kātyāyana attempts to modify Pāṇini's rules in light of what he knows about Sanskrit usage in his own time. Thus there is clearly an awareness of the contemporary state of Sanskrit, and of the fact of its being somewhat different from the other states of Sanskrit seen either in the Vedas or in Pāṇini. This raises some important theoretical and substantive questions concerning the practice of linguistic science in ancient India. At this stage, I propose to discuss the relationship between the reality of historical change, the doctrine of eternal Sanskrit and linguistic theory in ancient India.

3. In his *Aṣṭādhyāyī*, Pāṇini deals with all diachronic and synchronic facts of Sanskrit which were known to him and which were accepted by the social and linguistic élites of his time as being *sādhu* "correct" usages. This mass of linguistic facts was roughly divided between two main domains, i.e. *bhāṣā* "contemporary standard language" and *chandas* "language of the Vedic texts". Pāṇini's general rules are applicable to both of these domains of Sanskrit usage. Those rules which applied only to the language of the Vedic texts were accordingly specified by stating the specific Vedic sub-domains. The domain of the contemporary spoken standard Sanskrit was also then sub-divided into domains of regional and scholastic dialects. Prakrits or vernacular languges obviously existed alongside Sanskrit when Pāṇini wrote his *Aṣṭādhyāyī*, but like most other Sanskrit grammarians, he gave no consideration to Prakrits. Theoretically speaking, Pāṇini's conception of Sanskrit is that of a *panchronistic*

flatland. It is neither purely diachronic nor purely synchronic. It includes all known diachronic and synchronic facts of Sanskrit.

Pāṇini attempts to describe the known facts of Sanskrit in all their colorfulness. He describes optional usages, marginal and preferred usages, and dialectal usages.[75] We observe various patterns in these descriptions which give us a picture of a living language.[76] Some of these major patterns are briefly stated below.

Pattern A:	Colloquial Usage Form X	Vedic Usage Form Y
Pattern B:	Colloquial Usage Form X	Vedic Usage Form X or Y
Pattern C:	Colloquial Usage Form X or Y	
Pattern D:	Colloquial Usage Form X preferred over form Y	

These patterns are significantly different from each other and they show us that the panchronic flatland of Sanskrit in Pāṇini has markedly different sub-domains. Thus there is an interesting balance in Pāṇini's grammar between the theology of eternal Sanskrit which would not ideally allow any such sub-distinctions, and the practical observation of a keen grammarian of marked distinctions of usage in different sub-domains.

4. This balance is gradually disturbed in the works of later grammarians in the tradition of Pāṇini. The marked distinctions of variation and dialectal usages made by Pāṇini are ignored and rejected by Kātyāyana and Patañjali. They consider Pāṇini's references to various different regions and teachers not as indications of dialectal usages, which is what they must have been, but as simple expressions of respect having no grammatical value. Thus, all these references are turned into pure options. Explaining the logic of this phenomenon, Kaiyaṭa says:[77]

> In view of the eternality of linguistic usage, it has no beginning in time, and hence there can be no restriction placed on the speakers. Teachers such as Gālava are mentioned by Pāṇini (purely) as persons who recorded that usage to show their authority as grammarians. Hence a reference to a teacher is only to pay him respect (and not to indicate a dialectally restricted usage).

5. This poses a difficulty in the understanding of the historical develop-

ment of Sanskrit, and of the exact reasons behind the altered interpretations of Pāṇini's rules in the works of these later commentators. Are we justified in accusing Kātyāyana and Pāṇini of being ignorant of Pāṇini's grammar? Siddheshwar Varma does exactly that:[78]

> Kātyāyana here failed (on P.5.3.92 (*ekāc ca prācām*)) to appreciate Pāṇini's specification of the option here, viz. its location in the eastern part of the country. So a historical fact was victimized at the altar of formal consistency.

This raises many interesting questions. Was the language itself changing or was it static? Was linguistic theory changing, or was it static? Perhaps what was happening to the language may explain to some extent what was happening to the linguistic theory. As far as we know, at this early phase of the Pāṇinian tradition, the usage of Sanskrit was not dependent on the rules of the grammarians, but the grammarians were sensitive to usage. Thus, for this early phase, we need not worry about the impact of grammar on the language.

6. Elsewhere (Deshpande, 1978: 90ff) I have dealt with the controversy among modern scholars concerning this issue about the possibility of language change and its connection (or non-connection) with the vissicitudes of linguistic theory in ancient India. In general, Bhandarkar, Devasthali and Laddu accepted the notion that there was linguistic change from Pāṇini to Kātyāyana and Patañjali, and Devasthali made the case that the differences of description among these grammarians are not an indication of differences in linguistic theory, but are indications of adjustments made in the rules to accommodate later developments in the language. Rosane Rocher in her earlier work held the view that the ancient grammarians of India had no notion of historical linguistics, and hence they were dealing with the same stage of the same language. The differences in their descriptions, according to Rosane Rocher, were not because of linguistic change, but because they chose different ways to describe the same stage of the same language. Joshi and Roodbergen totally rejected the possibility of detecting linguistic change from the works of Sanskrit grammarians, while George Cardona assumed a more moderate position in this debate.

The questions of fact and ideology must be distinguished clearly at every stage of this debate. Was it actually the same stage of the same language that these grammarians dealt with, or was it the case that they merely believed that it was the same stage of the same language? It is important to distinguish between the facts of language as we see them, and the question of whether the Sanskrit grammarians knew about these changes or whether they truly believed that there were no changes. A mixed position may also be considered as a possibility, i.e. that the grammarians were actually aware of the facts of linguistic changes, historical or otherwise, and yet, for reasons other than grammatical, they maintained the doctrine of eternal Sanskrit, and then tried as best as they could to accommodate the facts of linguistic change within the parameters of this dominant paradigm. A more judicious statement may be made concerning this situation that the language actually did change somewhat, and the grammarians were aware of some changes, and they did make some modifications in their linguistic theory. But they did not change their basic paradigm. They only added new epicycles to the old paradigm to accommodate the newly emerging situation.

7. While many of the scholars who have taken part in the debate mentioned above have important ideas to contribute, here I shall particularly focus my attention on some remarks by George Cardona (1977: 222-3):

> Whether we say that historical changes or dialectal differences are involved, the fact remains that there were differences; and Kātyāyana and Patañjali not only realized that these existed, but also suggested additions and and modifications to the *Aṣṭādhyāyī* in order to account for them. ... Kātyāyana and Patañjali subjected Pāṇini's rules to scrutiny, one criterion of which was completeness. The grammar had to account for all correct Sanskrit usage. Moreover, they viewed differences in usage as mere options, and they insisted that Pāṇini's rules account equally for features of Sanskrit which arose after him. This I consider a sensible position - justified by what Kātyāyana and Patañjali actually say, and in harmony with the view of all later Pāṇinīyas.

I concur with the substance of Cardona's remarks, but there are some parts of these remarks which need amplification. It certainly needs to be clarified whether or not we are claiming that Kātyāyana and Patañjali expect Pāṇini's grammar to account for features of Sanskrit which *we* believe arose after Pāṇini, or that Kātyāyana and Patañjali themselves believe that certain features of Sanskrit arose after Pāṇini and that they want Pāṇini's grammar to account for what they themselves know to be post-Pāṇinian usages. In terms of what Kātyāyana and Patañjali actually say, all the evidence supports the view that in their eyes Sanskrit was an eternal language.

The evidence shows that, very much like Pāṇini, they were willing to consider variation and differences between different domains of Sanskrit usage, such as the regional and scholastic dialects and the domain of *chandas,* but they never espoused the notion of historical change. This would have undermined their theological position. Thus the questions for modern researchers are very complex. How can we deduce historical change from the works of these writers who themselves did not subscribe to the notion of historical change? It would also be instructive to investigate how these writers, who themselves did not subscribe to the notion of historical change, account for features of Sanskrit which we believe are a result of historical change. It thus becomes increasingly evident that neither of these questions can be fully answered before we have a greater insight into the nature of the theoretical framework and the ideology of these grammarians. This is very much like trying to understand the actions of the nineteenth century British officers in India who believed firmly in what a modern historian now calls "the illusion of permanence" of the British Indian empire.[79] To a modern historian, the notion of eternal Sanskrit may very well seem to be like an illusion of permanence, and yet that was the basic paradigm of Sanskrit grammarians. I fully agree with Cardona that we must try to understand the works of Sanskrit grammarians in terms of their own belief-system. For this reason, an understanding of their cultural framework is essential to an understanding of their grammatical activity. We will take a closer look at the paradigm of eternal Sanskrit adopted by Sanskrit grammarians and then examine how the facts of what we call history are accounted for in this ahistorical paradigm.

8. Someone argues that a particular word is not found in usage (*aprayukta*), and Patañjali replies to him in the following manner (*Mahābhāṣya* (K), Vol. I, p. 9):

> Effort should be made (to search for the usage of a particular word). The domain of the usage of words is very extensive. The earth has seven continents. There are the three worlds. There are the four Vedas along with their ancillary texts and commentaries, and these (Vedas are) variously split. There are one hundred schools of Yajurveda, one thousand ways of Sāmaveda, the twentyone schools of Ṛgveda, the nine schools of Atharvaveda, debate texts, historical narratives, mythologies and medicine. All this is the domain of the usage of words. Without having heard this entire domain of the usage of words, it would indeed be risky to say that certain words are not found in usage.

In this passage, we see Patañjali's panchronic conception of the domain of the usage of Sanskrit which a grammar was supposed to describe. This domain has no reference to time or history. But all the known states and stages of the Sanskrit language were included in this atemporal domain. However, it is also clear that Patañjali was aware of the fact that certain usages were restricted to certain domains. He says (*Mahābhāṣya* (K), Vol. I, pp. 9-10):

> In this very wide domain of linguistic usage, certain words are seen to be restricted to certain domains. For instance, the verb *śavati* in the sense of going is used only in the province of Kamboja. The Āryas use only the nominal form *śava* 'dead, gone, dead body'. The verb *hammati* is used among the Surāṣṭras, the verb *raṃhati* is used among the mid-eastern regions, while the Āryas use only the verb *gam* 'to go'. The easterners use the finite verb *dāti* 'to cut', while the northerners use only the nominal form *dātra* 'cutter'.

This passage also occurs in Yāska's *Nirukta* (Vol. I, pp. 127-8) which dates to a period close to that of Pāṇini.

9. The conception of *prayoga-viṣaya* "field or domain of usage" as explained by Patañjali is a truly fascinating conception with many historical and descriptive implications. The diagram below provides a graphic rendering of this conception:

DIAGRAM A

PRAYOGA-VIṢAYA

"FIELD OF USAGE"

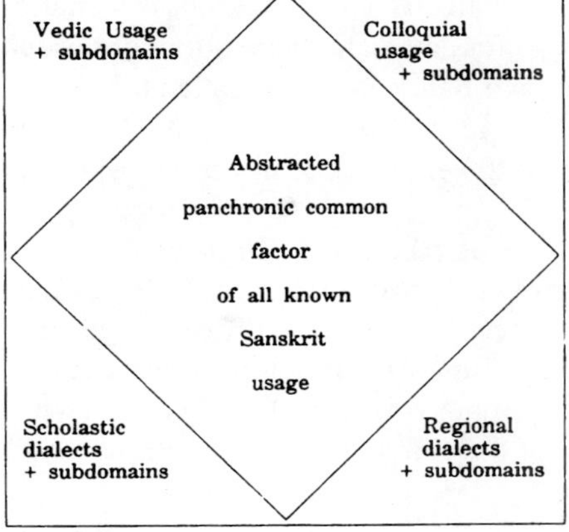

We may characterize this conception in the following way. The main assumption here appears to be that a grammar deals with all the known facts about a language. Here the conception of the "same language" is basically a sociocultural conception of identity. A person today is unlikely to say that Chaucer and Walt Whitman wrote in the "same language". There is a much greater awareness and acceptance of historical change among modern speakers of English. This evidently was not true for ancient India.

At this point however, we must clearly distinguish at least two separate strands of thoughts in the works of Kātyāyana and Patañjali, which probably did not exist in Pāṇini's conception of *prayoga-viṣaya* "field of usage". While describing instances of dialectal variation, Patañjali accepts the notion that certain expressions are found to be restricted in their usage to particular domains (*te te śabdās tatra tatra niyata-viṣayā dṛśyante, Mahābhāṣya* (K), Vol. I, p. 9). But the same grammarian supports a philosophical doctrine of the eternality of the Sanskrit language and argues on the basis of this doctrine that there can be no restriction whatsoever on the speakers of Sanskrit, and that Pāṇini's references to various regions and teachers, therefore, must be interpreted only as expressions of respect.[80] Clearly there is a difference of opinion between Patañjali, the upholder of the religious doctrine of eternality of Sanskrit, and Patañjali, the keen observer of regional variation - the linguist. However, these two Patañjalis occupy the same physiological space. Like a person with two personalities, sometimes one dominates the other, but sometimes the latter dominates the former. This is why we often find seemingly contradictory statements in the *Mahābhāṣya*; they are reflections of the different personalities of the same person. The field of usage of Sanskrit for Patañjali, the linguist, is as colorful as it is for Pāṇini - it contains dialectal and other kinds of variation. However, the same field of usage for Patañjali, the religious philosopher - promoter of the notion of eternal Sanskrit -, is a flatland which is flatter than the flatland of Pāṇini. Thus, while reading the *Mahābhāṣya,* it becomes incumbent upon us to keep track of these two personalities of Patañjali.

10. The main concern of these post-Pāṇinian philosopher- grammarians is with the notion of *sādhutva* "correctness". Kātyāyana says that the goal of Pāṇini's grammar is to teach correct usage of Sanskrit (*sādhv-anuśāsana*).[81] This grammatical notion of correctness is not a secular notion for these grammarians. It is directly linked with the notion of the meritoriousness of the correct usage. Kātyāyana says:[82]

> While the relationship between words and meanings is established by the usage in the world (of a certain expression) to denote a certain meaning, the science of grammar makes a regulation concerning the religious merit (produced by the use of words), as is commonly done in worldly conventions and Vedic rituals.

In terms of this merit-producing capacity of the correct Sanskrit usage, Kātyāyana explicitly likens it to the similar capacity of the Vedic scriptural words.[83] As merit-producing words, all dialectal usages are equally acceptable, as long as they are correct usages. Thus, there is no difference between them as far as the question of correctness and meritoriousness is concerned. Since Kātyāyana and Patañjali place supreme value on these two concepts, it is inevitable that the value of other distinctions in their eyes is diminished considerably. It is for this reason that the same Patañjali who accepts the fact of regional dialectal variation in one context argues in another context against the dialectal value of Pāṇini's references to regions and teachers. It is almost like saying that there are dialectal usages in Sanskrit, and yet it is not the business of grammar to deal with such distinctions which are inconsequential for religious merit. The business of grammar is to say which usages are correct and therefore meritorious. Thus, we can say with confidence that while the actual field of usage was most probably as variegated for Patañjali as it was for Pāṇini, the same field of usage viewed through the monocle of Patañjali the philosopher appeared flatter than ever before. Thus the field of usage for Patañjali is not actually very flat. It has been deliberately flattened by his other personality.

11. Granting that the linguistic panchronic flatland of Kātyāyana and Patañjali, in their perception as philosophers, is flatter than that for Pāṇini, one finds further interesting dimensions to this flatland. While it is panchronic in terms of being inclusive of usages of older and newer states of Sanskrit, we find that it rests primarily on a synchronic factor, i.e. *the contemporary standard usage of the language and the contemporary knowledge of the past linguistic usage.* While Kātyāyana believes that the language and its meaning are established by the usage of the world (*loka*),[84] the standard of spoken Sanskrit has been defined by Patañjali in terms of the usage of a very small community of *śiṣṭa*s "élites".[85] Patañjali's detailed discussion of this notion is as follows:[86]

> Q: Who are the *śiṣṭa*s?
> A: They are the grammarians.

Q: How is it?

A: Correct usage of language presupposes the science of grammar and the grammarians know the science of grammar.

Q: But if the correct usage of language presupposes the science of grammar, and if the science of grammar presupposes the correct usage of language, then this definition becomes circular. Circular definitions are not valid.

A: Then we will define *śiṣṭas* by their way of life and place of residence. That particular way of life is found only in the region of Āryāvarta.

Q: Which province is Āryāvarta? It lies to the east of the Ādarśa region, to the west of the Kālaka forest, to the south of the Himālayas and to the north of the Vindhya mountains. Those selfless Brāhmaṇas who live in this Āryāvarta, the land of the Āryas, who just store a basketful of grains, and have attained the highest wisdom in some branch of learning for its own sake, they are the *śiṣṭas* 'the normative speakers of Sanskrit'.

Q: If these *śiṣṭas* are the decisive standard for (the correctness of) words, what then is the function of the *Aṣṭādhyāyī*?

A: The *Aṣṭādhyāyī* aims at helping one recognize the *śiṣṭas*.

Q: How can the *śiṣṭas* be recognized by means of the *Aṣṭādhyāyī*?

A: One who studies the *Aṣṭādhyāyī* observes another person who is not studying it, but (nevertheless) is using words taught in it. He (i.e. the observer) then reflects: It must be either his born nature or divine grace that he does not study the *Aṣṭādhyāyī* and yet uses the correct words taught in it. He must also know other (correct) forms (which are not directly taught by the *Aṣṭādhyāyī*). Thus the *Aṣṭādhyāyī* aims at helping one recognize the *śiṣṭas*.

This is Patañjali's conception of how the grammarians derive their ideas about standard linguistic usage.

12. Kātyāyana and Patañjali consciously, but probably not deliberately, connected their notion of correct usage of Sanskrit with that of *dharma* "religious merit", and a similar connection actually holds between what the grammarians considered to be the standard for Sanskrit usage and what the ancient religious-legal texts in India considered to be the standard for the right kind of behavior. Discussions about how one should find out what to do when there is a doubt about a ritual activity or behavior are found in early Vedic texts. There is an interesting mix of the notion

of ancient traditions and contemporary sources for the knowledge of these ancient traditions. The *Ṛgveda* (8.30.3) says: "Do not take us far away from the path prescribed by Manu which has come down to us from our forefathers." But then how do we know what that ancient path prescribed by Manu was? The *Śatapatha-Brāhmaṇa* (8.6.3.18) says: *ye vidvāṃsas te manavaḥ*, "Manus are those who are learned." In the *Taittirīya-Upaniṣad* (1.11.1-4), the teacher after teaching the Veda instructs the pupil: "Do not neglect the learning and teaching of the Veda. ... If there should be any doubt in thy mind with regard to any sacred act or with regard to conduct, then in that case conduct thyself as Brāhmins who possess good judgement to conduct themselves, whether they be appointed or not, as long as they are not too severe and are devoted to sacred duties." It is understood that the Vedas are the source for the knowledge of sacred duties, but the Vedas do not tell us about everything that we want to know. In that case we should go to the contemporary repositories of that Vedic knowledge. These selfless learned Brāhmaṇas are assumed to know more than what appears in the known Vedic texts because their traditions are based on a larger corpus of Vedic texts which is not fully available to us. Such is the logic behind this practice.

These notions get solidified in the Dharmaśāstras. The *Āpastambīyadharmasūtra* defines *dharma* "virtuous conduct" by making a reference to the practice of the Āryas. It says (1.7.20.7-8): "That is *dharma* whose practice is praised by the Āryas, and what they blame is *adharma*. One should regulate the course of one's action according to the conduct which in all countries is unanimously approved by the Āryas, who are properly obedient, aged, of subdued senses, neither given to avarice, nor hypocrites." In his translation, Georg Bühler (1898: 46) renders the term *ārya* by "men of three twice-born castes." However, a comparison with other Dharmaśāstras indicates that it most likely has a regional reference to the upper-caste inhabitants of the region of Āryāvarta. The *Baudhāyanadharmaśāstra* (1.1.1.4-5) says: "The practice of the *śiṣṭas* is the third source for the sacred law. *Śiṣṭas* indeed are those who are free from envy, free from pride, contented with a store of grain sufficient for ten days, free from covetousness, and free from hypocrisy, arrogance, greed, perplexity and anger. Those are called *śiṣṭas* who in accordance with the sacred law have studied the Veda together with its appendages and know how to draw inferences from that and are able to adduce proofs perceptible by the senses from the revealed texts." But apart from this general description, this text also brings in the factor of regionality (1.1.2.9): "The country of the Āryas (Āryāvarta) lies to the east of the region where the river Sarasvatī disappears (*adarśana*), to the west of the Kālaka forest, to the north of the Pāriyātra (= Vindhya) mountains, and to the south of the Himālayas. The rule of conduct which prevails there is authoritative." There are many other Dharmaśāstras which have similar passages.[87] These passages are almost totally identical with the definition of the word *śiṣṭa* given by Patañjali. They all refer to the same community. The standards for linguistic usage and proper sacred and secular conduct are derived from the same community of *śiṣṭa*s in the land of Āryāvarta.

In addition to bringing up the Dharmaśāstra notion of *śiṣṭa*, Kumārila in his *Tantravārttika* also brings up an argument which reminds us of Patañjali's words. Kumārila says:[88]

> It is not always necessary that the good men, in all that they do, should always recall the scriptural authority for their actions; the fact is that from times immemorial we have always found the practice of good men to be in keeping with the scriptures. ... People come to be recognized as 'good' by always acting in accordance with the direct teachings of the Veda; and when they have thus acquired the title of 'good', even if they happen to do something else, in accordance with a fixed tradition (but without express support of the Veda), such actions are believed to have the character of *dharma*.

This is similar to Patañjali's *śiṣṭa* who is recognized as being a *śiṣṭa* precisely because his usage exhibits his conformity to the rules of Pāṇini, but that once he is recognized as a *śiṣṭa*, his other linguistic usage, for which there may not be express sanction in Pāṇini, is also accepted as standard Sanskrit usage. Like Kumārila's notion that the conduct of those who are already accepted as *śiṣṭa*s may not always have express support in the Vedas, and yet such conduct can be based on immemorial traditions, Patañjali's *śiṣṭa*s also use expressions for which there may not always be express support in the *Aṣṭādhyāyī*. Yet these usages are not considered to be their new innovations. On the contrary, these are looked upon as being ancient usages, which just escaped the attention of the earlier Sanskrit grammarians.

13. In terms of theological theory, Patañjali believes that Sanskrit is an eternal language and that it exists independently of its particular manifestations in history and geography. However, a grammatical description of this eternal language, like that of the eternal *dharma*, can be based on

only what we know about it, and hence it is important to know the sources of our knowledge. Considering the fact that the Vedic traditions were preserved mainly by oral transmission in India, the knowledge of these Vedic traditions for the current generation had a necessary synchronic aspect. Thus, it is significant that Patañjali's linguistic élits were not the common folks speaking this language out on the street. They were the small community of selfless and learned Brāhmaṇas of Āryāvarta "who have attained the highest wisdom in some branch of learning." This is the real distinction between the notions of *loka* "world [of speakers]" and *śiṣṭa* "élite, standard speakers". In this light, we can understand Kātyāyana's statement in a better way:[89] "While the relationship between words and meanings is established on the basis of the world (and not on the basis of what a grammarian does), the science of grammar simply makes a regulation concerning merit, i.e. only correct words will produce religious merit." Thus, the usage of language as such is uncontrolled by the science of grammar and the world at large goes on speaking the language with its own propensities. However, on the basis of the usage of the *śiṣṭas*, Sanskrit grammarians were able to assert that only those usages which are approved by the *śiṣṭas* generate merit, or social prestige as we might say today.

Sanskrit grammarians based their notion of the "field of usage" on this source of information and authority, i.e. the community of *śiṣṭas*. This source has both synchronic and panchronic dimensions at the same time. They, the *śiṣṭas*, are the repositories of traditional Vedic texts, and they are also speakers of the contemporary standard Sanskrit. But beyond these distinct diachronic and synchronic dimensions, they must also have an ability to effectively link these diachronic and synchronic states of Sanskrit in the course of ritual. This necessity is created by what is known as *ūha*, whereby a given *mantra* in a Vedic text must be ritually and linguistically recontextualized for another ritual by changing the cases, genders, numbers, persons etc.[90] This is the active link known to grammarians which joins the diachronic and synchronic facts of Sanskrit in a common purposeful utilization.[91] This makes these different states of Sanskrit something like different registers for a given *śiṣṭa*, rather than being two totally distinct states of a language being viewed by a historical linguist.

14. I have already spoken about the two personalities of Patañjali, i.e. Patañjali, the philosopher and theologian, and Patañjali the keen grammarian and observer of linguistic facts. Most of the purposes for studying

the science of grammar mentioned by Patañjali are religious and the most important of these purposes is that of *veda-rakṣā* "preservation of the Vedic traditions" from further deterioration.[92] In connection with this preservation of the Vedas, we may also note that the restriction that only the correct Sanskrit usage produces merit applied just to the context of sacrificial performances and not elsewhere.[93] Thus by Patañjali's own admission, the usage of Sanskrit was very closely connected with the notions of sacrificial performances and preservation of the Vedas. While placing the highest value on the notion of eternal Sanskrit and on Pāṇini's grammar as a mechanism to describe it, he at the same time leaves open the possibility of the contemporary usage of Sanskrit being somewhat different from that described by Pāṇini. Patañjali narrates the story of a grammarian who is offended by a chariot-driver (*sūta*), because the chariot-driver claimed to know the desired usage (*iṣṭi*). The obstinate grammarian insisted only on what could be derived by his rules (*prāpti*).[94] Patañjali advises the grammarian to accept the newly discovered desired usage and modify his rules. However, Patañjali would not go further and call this a "new" usage. For him, it could only be an ancient usage which was "newly discovered". For Kātyāyana and Patañjali, all such newly discovered Sanskrit usages of the *śiṣṭas* must be incorporated into the grammar. But there are no new usages. All such usages are probably ancient usages which were current in some other region, and they were simply not known to earlier grammarians.[95] Thus, these grammarians tried to arrive at a compromise of these two totally different sets of expectations.

15. From the theoretical point of view of this eternal Sanskrit, no new facts of language can come to light, because there can be no new facts. Only previously unknown facts can become newly known. Thus, the theory of eternality of Sanskrit separates the existence of language from its attestations in history. The grammarian, while committed to the notion of eternal Sanskrit, still aims at gethering the most up-to-date information about this language from the contemporary linguistic élites, who are at the same time repositories of traditional learning. Thus, in terms of its informational base, the grammar was supposed to cover the most up-to-date information about this language. While the eternal language itself was beyond the notion of change, the information available about this eternal language, however, could change with each succeeding generation.

There is a statement in Bhartṛhari's *Dīpikā* which brings in an interesting theological angle to the discussion of language, its eternality and change. Bhartṛhari says:[96] *niyata-kālā hi smṛtayo bhavanti*, "Recorded memories of sages (such as law-books or grammatical descriptions) are restricted to certain spans of time." With this statement, Bhartṛhari brings in a Dharmaśāstra notion into grammar, since both the law-books as well as grammatical descriptions are considered to be *smṛti* "revered memories of ancient sages". While, in theory all *dharma* texts are eternally valid, certain *dharma* rules are applicable only in certain *yuga*s "spans of time". By using this notion, the law-givers of ancient India argued, for instance, that customs such as the sacrifice of cows and ritual drinking of wine were no longer applicable in the current age. These customs were acceptable in earlier ages. Thus, by redistributing the scope of application for different Dharmaśāstra texts, the law-givers tried to accommodate historical changes, without at the same time abrogating the eternal validity of any text. It is not clear whether such an argument would have been acceptable to Patañjali. However, he is willing to accept that there are expressions which occur in Vedic domain which no one used in his contemporary spoken Sanskrit. The important point is that he would be unwilling to accept that the Vedic domain is no longer current. The Vedic texts, since they were preserved by the contemporary reciters and used by the priests in rituals were equally current for Patañjali.

16. Given the notion of eternal Sanskrit, the ideal method of grammatical description was to take a common factor of all known Sanskrit usage, and treat all other non-common facts as belonging to the respective domains and subdomains. Louis Renou says:[97]

> The grammar of Pāṇini does not concern the bhāṣā alone, but quite a common language, absorbing *chandas* and *bhāṣā* ... which absorbs in a single description the facts of *chandas* and elements of spoken language. The *chandas* therefore do not represent in any way a state of language distinct from the normal; it is in the interior of a common language, a fringe of archaisms or 'diversities' which for some reason or other mark the margin of a system.

Renou's description is quite accurate, but he does not deal with the reason for this system of description being what it is. It is clear that Pāṇini and his followers, like their other co-religionist colleagues, believed that the Vedic texts and the Sanskrit language were eternal entities. For the actual description of the language, there was a model in the ritual texts. One finds a similar model, for instance, in the *Aśvalāyana-Gṛhyasūtra* (1.7.1-2):

> The practices of various regions and towns vary widely. Here we will describe what is commonly shared by them.

These texts on *dharma* also describe uncommon practices which belong to particular localities, but they are described as deviations or exceptions. Just as each projection that is used in geography to draw the map of the spherical earth on to a flat plane involves its own distinct distortions, the same way each descriptive model accepted by linguists and culture-historians tends to distort the original facts in some peculiar ways. While each projection facilitates a particular understanding of the given data, it at the same time suppresses other perceptions of the same data. As such, each model presents its own ideology with which to interpret the given data.

17. Let us briefly look at the model of description adopted by Indian grammarians and law-givers and compare it with some other dominant models in linguistics. In modern linguistics, one clearly makes a distinction between historical linguistics and descriptive linguistics. In a strict sense, descriptive grammars deal with the synchronic states of languages at particular points in time. Each state is then studied and described independently. When we have many descriptive grammars of many successive states of a language, then by comparing and contrasting these successive states one can write a historical grammar of that language indicating losses, developments and retentions. Thus a clear sense of the temporal sequence of changes is constantly maintained in modern linguistics. This can be seen from the figure below:

DIAGRAM B

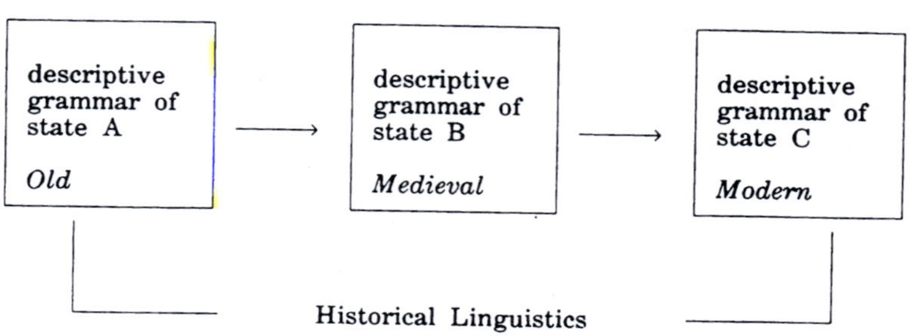

Another important distinction that has been brought out in modern linguistics is that between studies of language families which attempt to trace features of languages to their commonly shared ancestor, and studies of diffusion of features across languages belonging to different language families. Thus, the features of a given language may be a result of both of these processes working together, along with other processes such as dialect mergers etc. Models in modern linguistics are designed to bring out these various dimensions of languages under consideration.

In contrast with these modern models, the model adopted by Sanskrit grammarians highlights different features of the language data. It combines what we would consider historical states with synchronic states of the language and compresses all this data into one body before it begins to sift it out again. In trying to sift out this data again, it does not worry about the distinction of historical versus synchronic. The distinction it is concerned with is that of commonly shared features versus features restricted to particular domains. The model does not worry about the historical sources of these various features. Given this primary distinction, it then formulates its basic rules to describe the commonly shared features, and then tries to account for the features restricted to particular domains by formulating deviation-rules. If one wants to get a complete picture of the language of a particular domain, then one can simply look at the rules which apply to the commonly shared features and then add to them the rules which are particularly restricted to that domain. This totality will give us an idea of how Pāṇini conceived the total linguistic usage of that domain. For instance, let us consider the following rules:[98]

P.1.4.80 (*te prāg dhātoḥ*): "Items defined as *gati* (inclusive of the commonly known *upasargas*) occur before the verb-root."

P.1.4.81 (*chandasi pare 'pi*): "In the domain of *chandas*, these items can occur even after the verb-root."

P.1.4.82 (*vyavahitāś ca*): "(In the domain of *chandas)*, these items can occur even separated from the verb-root by other words coming in between."

Here, the first rule is the general rule applicable to the abstracted common factor, while the two later rules apply to the specific domain of *chandas* "Vedic language". To get a complete idea of what happens in the domain of *chandas*, we must take all the three rules together to build a Pāṇinian conception of the domain of *chandas*. This is illustrated in the following diagram:

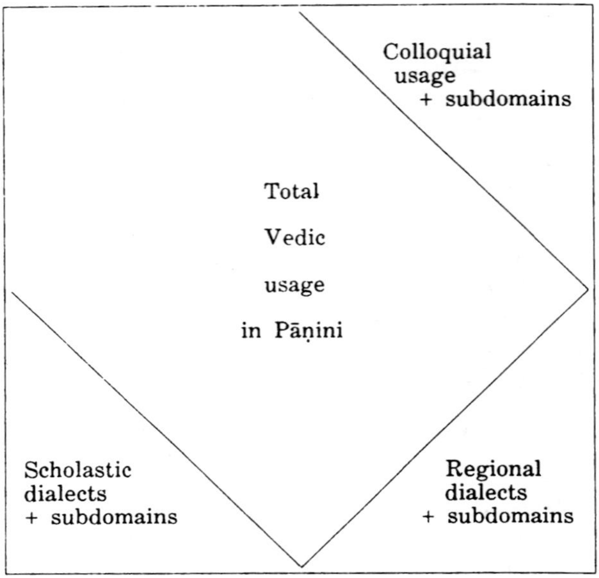
Colloquial
usage
+ subdomains
Total
Vedic
usage
in Pāṇini
Scholastic
dialects
+ subdomains
Regional
dialects
+ subdomains

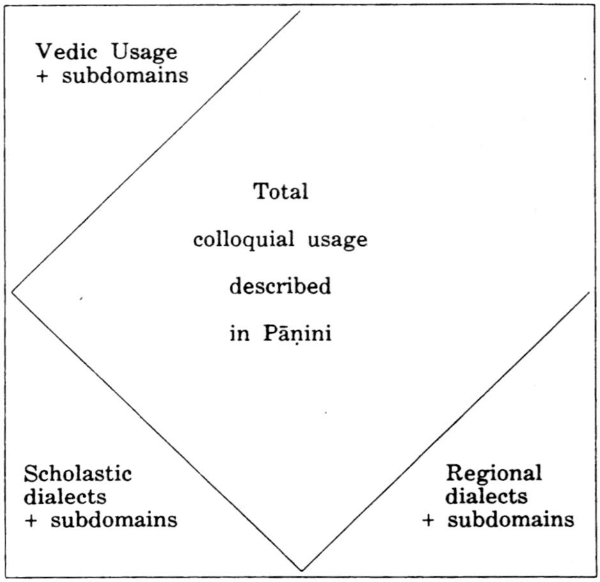
Vedic Usage
+ subdomains
Total
colloquial usage
described
in Pāṇini
Scholastic
dialects
+ subdomains
Regional
dialects
+ subdomains

18. Pāṇini makes no claims that his grammar represents a description of human mind. The overt claim is simply that his grammar accounts for all the usages known to him. However, one can certainly see that this model has useful dimensions. I will briefly deal with two such aspects which seem to be significant to me. The first aspect is that of the use of this grammar for teaching traditional Pandits in India. The traditional Sanskrit Pandits at the time of Pāṇini were interested in acquiring mastery over both the Vedic language and the contemporary Sanskrit. The grammar was a tool for this purpose.[99] For Pāṇini's grammar as a tool for teaching and learning, the principle of economy was very important. One way this economy has been achieved by Pāṇini is by making a distinction between commonly shared features and features restricted to particular domains.[100] Thus, if one were to have full descriptions of each of these domains, and if a student were to study all these full descriptions, then there would be a tremendous waste of effort. He would be repeating a great deal of the same rules in each domain. This problem has been avoided by Pāṇini by choosing the particular model. One sees the same advantage in the use of this model in the Dharmaśāstras.

The second dimension of Pāṇini's model is that it may possibly be a good representation of the mind of a *śiṣṭa* such as Pāṇini himself. As we have seen, these learned *śiṣṭas* stored all these different states of Sanskrit ranging from Vedic to contemporary colloquial in their mind and actively linked them in their use in ritual. Thus, for them, these were not distinct languages or states of a different language to be looked at for purely academic purposes. They were, to use a modern term, different registers of the same person, and he needed to have the ability to switch from one to the other freely. In his mind he had a combined ability and storage for all these different domains. Pāṇini's model may be said to provide an economic way of dealing with such a psycholinguistic question, though I must categorically state that the tradition has made no such claim on his behalf. The advantage in using Pāṇini's model for such purpose is that it opens up for a modern linguist a different way of looking at his subject, and a way out of the difficulties of purely diachronic and synchronic grammar.

One may make the following observations. The linguistic abilities of an eighty year old person living in New York would represent a piling up of his acquisition for all these years in addition to the horizontal experiences of acquiring many social dialects. These then become different registers in his linguistic repertoire and he can freely move from one to the other in different contexts. Thus the linguistic abilities of a person represent all this cumulative experience. If one views aids such as access to writing and reading, and to memorization as in ancient India, then one may say that these aids extend the human ability of access to information and to increased accumulation of information in the mind. The *śiṣṭas* in ancient India represented this kind of cumulative experience and ability to deal with Vedic and contemporary Sanskrit as different registers to be used for different purposes. Thus, instead of looking at Pāṇini's grammar and its model as being a purely theoretical device for compressing historical and synchronic states of Sanskrit into one database, one may look at it as a possible representation of the abilities of *śiṣṭas* in ancient India to use different speech-registers available to them. This is of course a non-theological interpretation of Pāṇini's model - a reinterpretation, rather than a claim on behalf of Pāṇini.

19. There is also another valuable dimension to the model of description seen in the works of Patañjali and later grammarians such as Bhartṛhari. In the Pāṇinian tradition, one comes across a notion that a grammar must be continually fine-tuned in light of the new information provided by each new generation of *śiṣṭas*.[101] Each new generation of these linguistic élites may provide previously unknown facts about this eternal language. Thus the grammar of this eternal language is in theory, quite paradoxically, not eternal. It has to be a continually changing entity. Perhaps some of this notion may go back to Pāṇini himself. Pāṇini clearly built upon grammars of his predecessors and modified them where he thought it was appropriate. But there probably was no difference of theological opinion between his predecessors and himself concerning the notion of eternal Sanskrit. Secondly, one may look at his use of "open-ended" devices such as the use of *ākṛti-gaṇas*, lists of words which are open-ended.[102] The commentators say that one can add to these open-ended lists new items by checking the usage of the *śiṣṭas*.[103] It makes this grammatical model quite different from anything known to the West. It is a living organism which, in theory as well as in practice to some extent, continues to grow with the language and ever remains aware of and inclusive of newly discovered facts about this eternal language. Traditional grammarians achieved this open-endedness either through the explicit means of modifying Pāṇini's rules, or through the implicit means of reinterpreting his rules, and adding to his grammar newer maximes of interpretation.[104] These maxims may be historically un-Pāṇinian and may make Pāṇini's system less scientific by blocking its potential for falsifiability,[105] but these maxims kept the system open-ended and capable of being inclusive of later linguistic developments.

20. Finally, I would like to briefly deal with two theoretical consequences of this notion of eternal Sanskrit. Both of these concern the relationship of Sanskrit with Prakrit languages. For Sanskrit grammarians, Sanskrit was the only eternal language, while Prakrits were clearly not eternal. They labeled these Prakrits by the derogatory term *apabhraṃśa* "degenerate languages". Obviously, Sanskrit being conceived of as an eternal language could not have any degeneration of its own, but other languages did.

Bhartṛhari's *Vākyapadīya* is a great compendium of Sanskrit philosophy of language. He discusses many views on a given subject, sometimes not clearly indicating his own preferences. According to what seems to be the dominant view in his work, an *apabhraṃśa* word lacks proper grammatical processing.[106] According to this view, the degenerate forms cannot convey meaning directly to the listener the way proper Sanskrit words can. The eternal relationship between words and meanings is true only for the Sanskrit language which is eternal. The degenerate forms spoken by a person are claimed to remind the listener the proper Sanskrit forms which then convey the particular meanings (*Vākyapadīya* I. 150, 151 and 153). From the same hieratical perspective, Bhartṛhari charges that the divine Sanskrit language has been variously mutilated by deficient people and that there can be no legitimate status for *apabhraṃśa* (*Vākyapadīya* I. 155). In this connection, one may say that the theology of eternal Sanskrit prevented Sanskrit grammarians from conducting an objective study of bilingualism and bilingual communication.

The second consequence of the notion of eternal Sanskrit was that it forced Prakrit grammars to adopt a particular model for describing Prakrits. This consequence is directly related to the first consequence described above. Prakrits were given no independent standing by the Brahmanical writers and they could be studied only in relation to the eternal Sanskrit. The only relation that held between the eternal Sanskrit and Prakrits, according to Indian grammarians, was that of successive degeneration of Sanskrit at the hands of incapable speakers. That was felt to be the origin of and the cause of the development of Prakrits. Thus, the most obvious model for describing Prakrits was that of successive degeneration. Prakrit grammars that are available to us show this structure uniformly. They first offer a set of rules to "convert" Sanskrit into one of the dominant Prakrits, usually the Mahārāṣṭrī Prakrit. Then follow other sets of rules to convert this Prakrit successively into other Prakrits. Thus Prakrit grammars have the descriptive model of successive degeneration of Sanskrit, and it seems most likely that this is the result of the doctrine of eternal Sanskrit.

The descriptive terminology used in this connection shows an assumption of history for Prakrits, with no such corresponding history for Sanskrit. The terms are: *tat-sama* "Prakrit words which are identical with the corresponding Sanskrit words", *tad-bhava* "Prakrit words which are not identical with the corresponding Sanskrit words, but are born from them through sound-changes etc.", and *deśya* "regional or local words which cannot be traced to Sanskrit". Obviously, the terminology assumes a history for Prakrits, but not for Sanskrit. Useful as these distinctions are, they sometimes project a pseudo-history. For instance, in terms of the modern concept of linguistic history, the Sanskrit word *gṛha* "house" becomes *geha* in Prakrit, but this Prakrit word was borrowed back into Sanskrit. Thus, Sanskrit now has both *gṛha* and *geha,* while Prakrits have *geha* (besides other derivatives such as *ghara*). Interestingly, in terms of the available terminology, the word *geha* now becomes a *tat-sama* word, because it is identical with an attested Sanskrit word. One no longer needs to consider it as a *tad-bhava* word and link it with the Sanskrit word *gṛha*. Thus, this terminology, by denying a history for Sanskrit, creates a pseudo-history for Prakrits. However, if one looks at this terminology as a language-learning device, then it still makes good sense to classify *geha* as a *tat-sama* word. If one has learned it while leaning Sanskrit, then one need not learn it again while studying Prakrits. However, the underpinnings of the terminology are not purely the practical necessity of teaching languages. It is the theology of Eternal Sanskrit.

21. In conclusion, we may point out that the notion of the Divine Eternal Sanskrit was not the creation of Sanskrit grammarians. This notion in its various forms goes back to ancient Vedic texts.[107] However, it was culturally such a dominant notion that Sanskrit grammarians had to accept it, promote it, and work within its parameters. As we have shown in this paper, these grammarians performed their task with enormous ability, intelligence and thoroughness. The grammars clearly served the purpose that they were designed to serve - to maintain our understanding of the Sanskrit language. This notion of eternal Sanskrit was, for Sanskrit grammarians, not just a background idea, but it was a "paradigm" for their sciences. The tradition of Sanskrit grammarians never saw a "paradigm-change".[108] That was brought about by the Western science of linguistics.

V

SANSKRIT GRAMMARIANS: DIFFERING PERSPECTIVES IN CULTURAL GEOGRAPHY

1. For the past several years, I have been interested in investigating the various factors - the usually unstated factors - which possibly and probably underlie works of Sanskrit grammarians. It is these factors which may perhaps explain to us why the grammarians formulated their grammars in the particular way in which we have them. Without an understanding of these factors, we can only scratch the surface of these grammatical texts because we will not have even a hypothetical access to the intentionality of their authors. These factors are varied in themselves because essentially these factors, in principle, are the totality of the cultural, geographical, political, religious and other parameters within which these grammarians lived and which consciously or unconsciously helped to build their general intellectual framework. Their grammars are the natural results of this larger intellectual and cultural framework and therefore it is crucial to have an understanding of this larger cultural framework. This is important not only from the general interests of Indian history, but also for a better understanding of several grammatical doctrines such as that of *śiṣṭa-prayoga* "standard usage". In my "Historical Change and the Theology of Eternal Sanskrit" (included in this volume), I have discussed in detail several cultural and theological factors which form the basis of the intellectual framework of Sanskrit grammarians. In this chapter, I shall discuss some of the geographical and geopolitical factors which underlie the intellectual framework of these grammarians.

2. While the tradition tells us that Pāṇini hailed from the town of Śalātura near modern Peshawar, I have argued in my recent work (Deshpande, 1982a; Deshpande, 1983b; and Deshpande, 1988) that there is syntactic and phonological evidence in the *Aṣṭādhyāyī* to show that Pāṇini was

principally a "frontier grammarian". Sometime ago I came across a long abstract of a paper by Shiva G. Bajpai given at the fourth World Sanskrit Conference held at Weimar in 1979. This paper is titled "Greek *Praisoi* and Sanskrit *Prācya*: Problems of Identification and its Historical Significance." I have not been able to obtain the full text of this paper, but the detailed abstract of the paper is sufficient to give the reader a good idea of the principal arguments. This paper prompted me to think further on the geographical and geopolitical dimensions involved in the frameworks adopted by Sanskrit grammarians. Let me first give a brief resume of Bajpai's abstract, and then I will proceed with my own ideas.

3. According to Bajpai (1979: 80), "the cumulative Classical evidence shows that the Praisoi occupied the entire Ganga plain. That their frontier might have extended further northwest is not altogether improbable." He further states (p. 80): "the Sanskrit versions of Prācya derived from the Brāhmaṇas, Dharmasūtras, and Purāṇas, which have been so far proposed by the modern scholars for the identification of the Praisoi, are definitely in conflict with the Classical view because none extends westward far enough into upper Ganga plain, being limited to Kālakavana near modern Allahabad. ... These versions of Prācya are based on the conception of the fivefold division of India, which was unknown to the Classical (Greek) authors." Then Bajpai brings in evidence from Pāṇini's grammar to show the existence of another Sanskrit version of Prācya which is in accordance with the Classical (Greek) evidence. Bajpai takes the Pāṇinian divisions Udīcya and Prācya and identifies the traditionally quoted dividing river Śarāvatī with Sarasvatī.[109] According to him (p. 81), this Pāṇinian view then "concurs with the Classical (Greek) notices of the Praisoi and accords fully with the northwestern limits of the Nanda empire." Bajpai concludes by saying (p. 81) that his analysis "provides the northwestern perspective of the geopolitical and cultural entity of Prācya which is characteristically different from that centered on the middle region (*madhyadeśa*) as found in the Brahmanical and Buddhist sources. ... It cannot be claimed that the classical authors derived knowledge directly from the *Aṣṭādhyāyī*. But their informants from Punjab could, or at least hold a view consistent with that of Pāṇini, who was himself a northwesterner and composed his treatise in that region."

4. Having thus summarized Bajpai's arguments, I would like to point out that my own recent researches (Deshpande, 1982a; 1983b; and 1988) based on syntactic and phonological evidence show that Pāṇini was most certainly maximally familiar with the peculiarities of the language of the

northwest. To add to Bajpai's analysis, it may also be pointed out that while Pāṇini uses the terms Udīcya and Prācya, and probably viewed a river in Punjab as the dividing line between these regions (Śarāvatī = Satlaj),[110] it is important to note that he does not use the term *madhyadeśa* or *madhya* to refer to any geographical area. Thus, it is clear that from his northwestern perspective there is the division between the northern and the eastern regions, but that there is no region considered to be the *madhya* "center" or "central region". In contrast with this twofold division in Pāṇini, one finds a threefold division in the works of Yāska and Patañjali, who use the term *madhya* in addition to the term *prācya* and make a reference to the usage of the Āryas[111] - a term which in the context of the description of regional dialects clearly seems to hint at the region of Āryāvarta. This region is explicitly defined by Patañjali as the area between Punjab and Prayag, limited by the Himalaya in the north and the Vindhya in the south.[112] Thus there is a divergence between the perspective of Pāṇini on the one hand and the perspective of Yāska and Patañjali on the other. While the first perspective is the northwestern perspective, the second one is the northcentral or the northeastern perspective. In the following paragraphs, I shall explore the cultural and the grammatical significance of this division of opinion.

5. I would like to slightly differ from the analysis given by Bajpai. We have to be careful in calling Pāṇini's perspective a northwestern perspective. While in terms of his emphasis and acquaintance, Pāṇini's perspective is a northwestern perspective, it is, however, clear that he does not view the northwest as the center of his cultural universe. Pāṇini's use of the term Udīcya for his own region shows that he acknowledges that he is in the northern or the northwestern corner of a cultural universe which covers the Indian mainland. The geographical non-centrality of his own region in terms of his terminology is very significant in that his region was admittedly not at the center of the Brahmanical cultural universe. A true northwestern perspective would have placed the northwestern region at the center of its cultural geography. Such for instance is the case of the Vedic expressions *pañca janāḥ* "five tribes" or *sapta sindhavaḥ* "(the region of) the seven rivers". Such terms do not define their own identity by referring to some other notion of geographical or cultural "center". These terms are insular and hence internally defined. They show no awareness of or participation in a larger geographical or cultural universe, and hence are far more ethnocentric in their reference. They represent a notion of people who viewed themselves to be in the center of their universe - a conception commonly found among tribal peoples. One may

also compare the ritual notion of the Vedic Aryans which makes the Vedi or the sacrificial altar the farthest end of the universe and the sacrifice its center - *iyaṃ vediḥ paro antaḥ pṛthivyā ayaṃ yajño bhuvanasya nābhiḥ*, *Ṛgveda*, 1.164.35ab. Such a statement may be interpreted to mean that the migrating Vedic tribes had no fixed geographical center in any region, but that the center of their ritual and cultural universe moved along with them. Wherever they went and performed their rituals, they were always at the center of their universe.

6. Pāṇini who uses the terms Udīcya and Prācya thus cannot be said to have believed that he was at the center of the Sanskrit speaking universe. While he does not use a term such as *madhyadeśa* or *madhya* to indicate any such geographical or cultural "center", his terminology shows his clear awareness of the extensive use of Sanskrit in the Indian mainland and his reluctance to consider any of the regional varieties as being particularly central or more authoritative. In principle, his grammatical description has no regional bias or focus. It is not aimed at describing the linguistic norms of any particular region which he considered to be the center of the Sanskrit-speaking universe. His general rules apply to the abstracted common factor of all known linguistic data - diachronic as well as synchronic. Thus, Renou rightly says (1941: 248-9):

> The grammar of Pāṇini does not concern the *bhāṣā* alone, but quite a common language, absorbing *chandas* and *bhāṣā*... which absorbs in a single description the facts of *chandas* and elements of spoken language. The *chandas* therefore do not represent in any way a state of language distinct from the normal; it is in the interior of a common language, a fringe of archaisms or 'diversities' which for one reason or other mark the margin of a system.

We may extend Renou's description to geographical dialects in Pāṇini. Theoretically speaking, Pāṇini's term *bhāṣā* represents the abstracted common factor of all known regional and scholastic dialects, excepting the language of the Vedic texts or *chandas*. The peculiarities of these various dialects are described as exceptions to the abstracted norm called *bhāṣā*. Thus, in principle, his grammar does not intend to present the northwestern dialect as being the central dialect, though as a matter of fact, his being a northwesterner naturally makes his abstracted common factor somewhat more akin to the northwestern usage. But clearly he does not intend to project the northwestern usage as the more superior usage, as for instance is done by the author of the *Kauṣītaki-Brāhmaṇa* (7.6): "The best form of speech is spoken in the north (west), and hence people go to the north (west) to learn (that form of) speech" (*udīcyāṃ ha vai diśi prajñātatarā vāg udyate / udañca eva u yanti vācaṃ śikṣitum /*). Unlike the preference so clearly expressed by the *Kauṣītaki-Brāhmaṇa*, Pāṇini followed a more neutral method of abstracting the common factor of all domains of usage and then describing the non-common factors as being exceptions to this abstracted common factor. This method is also seen in works such as the *Āśvalāyana-Gṛhya-Sūtra* 1.7.1-2 which says that the religious traditions of various regions, villages and families are widely divergent and that it will describe only what is commonly shared by all of them (*yat tu samānaṃ tad vakṣyāmaḥ*). But we must at the same time note that while most *Dharmasūtras* make the region of Āryāvarta the most superior Aryan region - its practices to be emulated by other regions -, Pāṇini seems to have observed strict neutrality in this respect.

7. One may advance a conjecture to explain this neutrality. It may be remembered that the politically dominant empire of the Nandas was in the Prācya region. Whether Pāṇini lived in the eastern province of Darius's Iranian empire or not may never be fully decided, but certainly the region which he belonged to was at that time not a politically dominant region and could not expect to impose its linguistic or cultural norms on the bulk of the Sanskrit-speaking region which was in the east. Pāṇini's region was on the margins of bigger political entities, but was not itself the focal point of any such influential empire. The traditional stories inform us that Pāṇini had to go Pāṭaliputra, the capital of the Nandas, to gain recognition.[113] Thus, Pāṇini perhaps chose not to recognize openly the political superiority of the Prācyas, nor could he proclaim the Udīcyas to be superior, since they were politically the dominated region, rather than being the dominant one. Thus, he chose a more neutral framework which described regional variation without bringing in the notion of the superiority of one region over others.

8. We may contrast this situation seen in Pāṇini's *Aṣṭādhyāyī* with the situation as it can be inferred from Yāska's *Nirukta* and Patañjali's *Mahābhāṣya*. On the basis of lingüistic evidence, I have argued elsewhere that Yāska most likely came from the Prācya region.[114] Yāska and Patañjali have the notion of Ārya as a regional term referring to the region of Āryāvarta. They also use the term *madhya* along with the term *prācya*. This generally seems to point to a more northcentral or a northeastern perspective. Patañjali's *Mahābhāṣya* provides a much more detailed picture of this eastern cultural perspective. Patañjali is traditionally

associated with Pāṭaliputra and the Brāhmaṇa king Puṣyamitra Śuṅga who came to the throne after assassinating the last Maurya king. While Patañjali's *Mahābhāṣya* is ostensibly a commentary on Pāṇini's *Aṣṭādhyāyī* which originated in the northwestern region of India, Patañjali regards the *Aṣṭādhyāyī* as a means of recognizing speakers of the standard usage of Sanskrit from the region of Āryāvarta. His discussion of the standard usage of Sanskrit is fascinating and may be quoted at length:[115] "Who are the *śiṣṭa*s 'linguistic elites'? (They are) the grammarians. How is it? Correct usage of language presupposes the science of grammar and the grammarians know the science of grammar. But, if the correct usage of language presupposes the science of grammar and if grammar presupposes the correct use of language, then this definition becomes circular. Circular arguments do not stand valid. Then, we define *śiṣṭa*s by their way of life and place of residence. That particular way of life is found only in the region of Āryāvarta. What province is Āryāvarta? It lies to the east of the Ādarśa region, to the west of the Kālaka forest, to the south of the Himālayas, and to the north of the Vindhya mountains. Those Brāhmaṇas who live in this Āryāvarta, the land of the Aryans, who just store a basketful of grain, who are selfless and have attained the highest wisdom in some branch of learning for its own sake, they are the *śiṣṭas*. If these *śiṣṭas* are the decisive standard for correctness of words, then what is the function of the *Aṣṭādhyāyī*? The *Aṣṭādhyāyī* aims at helping one recognize the *śiṣṭas*."

It is important to note that the region regarded by Patañjali to be the Aryan region par excellence does not include Pāṇini's birthplace, because one may safely conclude that, like most of the Dharmaśāstras,[116] the northwestern regions were impure regions for Patañjali. According to his description, the northwestern region is occupied by the non-Aryan Yavanas, Ionian Greeks and Śakas (Deshpande, 1979a: 117.) Patañjali's claims about linguistic superiority of Āryāvarta are in line with similar cultural claims in the Dharmaśāstras. For instance, Manu says:[117] "From a Brāhmaṇa, born in this country of Āryāvarta, let all men on earth learn their ways of behavior." Patañjali's claim is similar in the context of standard Sanskrit. One can certainly make an educated guess that Patañjali's linguistic claims are in part a reflection of the Brahmanical political power of the Śuṅgas, whose empire almost coincides with the boundaries of the region of Āryāvarta.[118]

9. On this last point, there is some contrast in the notion of Āryāvarta as seen in Patañjali and in some of the Dharmaśāstras. This difference is

quite subtle, and yet may reflect some difference in perspective. For instance, Manu (*Manusmṛti*, 2.21-22) says: "The region which lies between the two divine rivers Sarasvatī and Dṛṣdadvatī, that which has been created by gods, they call Brahmāvarta. The Kurukṣetra, the Matsyas, as also the Pañcālas and the Śūrasenas - this is the region of the Brahmarṣis, immediately after Brahmāvarta. That which lies between the Himalayas and the Vindhyas, and which is also to the east of Vinaśana and to the west of Prayāga, that region is called Madhyadeśa. The tract between those two mountains which extends as far as the eastern and the western oceans, the wise call Āryāvarta." Here there are four concentric regions and the innermost regions are the purest and holiest compared to the outermost regions. Thus, Manu's Āryāvarta is much larger and wider than that of Patañjali. Patañjali's Āryāvarta corresponds rather to Manu's Madhyadeśa. However, inside that Madhyadeśa, for Manu the center of purity and importance is more to the west, nearer to the lands of the Kurus and Pañcālas, rather than toward the east in the direction of Magadha. Manu thus represents a different geocultural perspective as compared to Patañjali. It may be conjectured that Manu's geocultural perspective is the Kuru-Pañcāla perspective - which as seen in the Mahābhārata was opposed to the powers in Magadha. In Patañjali, while the same general region is holy, the center of gravity may have shifted more to the east - closer to Pāṭaliputra, the capital of the Śuṅgas.

10. In support of looking for the political underpinnings of the descriptive framework of Sanskrit grammarians, I would like to refer to a recent discussion by K.R. Norman. Both the Jainas and Buddhists (of the Theravāda school) claim that Māgadhī (or Ardhamāgadhī) which was the language of the "original" scriptures, is the original language of all beings. Jainas say that when Mahāvīra spoke in Ardhamāgadhī, it was automatically converted to the language of the listeners.[119] While one may look at these as pure religious doctrines, they in fact contain a reflection of the political domination of the Magadha region during the period of the Mauryan empire (Norman, 1980: 67).

I fully agree with the political motivation which Norman finds in these Buddhist and Jaina assertions. Thus it is clear that the Jaina and the Buddhist claims of superiority for their scriptural Māgadhī represent the Māgadhan geopolitical perspective. The difference between Patañjali's perspective and the Jaina and the Buddhist perspectives lies probably in their being associated with different political regimes from the same region. Patañjali shares in the glory of the revivalist Brahmanical Śuṅgas, while the Jainas and the Buddhists reflect the domination of the preceding Mauryan empire.

11. On the other hand, all the Prakrit grammars available to us show a more western or perhaps south-western perspective. They generally make Mahārāṣṭrī the principal Prakrit and then write rules to derive other Prakrits from it, Māgadhī coming as the third or fourth Prakrit. This is also in line with the situation in Sanskrit dramas. In Sanskrit dramas, upper-class females and middle-class males speak Śaurasenī in conversation and Mahārāṣṭrī in poetry, but Māgadhī is reserved for fools, thieves etc. It is clear that both Sanskrit dramas and Prakrit grammars share in this tendency of placing Māgadhī at the lower end of prestige. This is also seen in Rājaśekhara's *Kāvyamīmāṃsā* (p. 50) where he says that a good poet should have servants fluent in Apabhraṃśa, and maidservants fluent in languages like Māgadhī. His wives should be fluent in Sanskrit and Prakrit. It is important to note that Prakrit for Rājaśekhara refers not to Māgadhī, but to Mahārāṣṭrī. It would seem most likely that such a westerly or south-central geopolitical perspective would develop during the shift of political power away from the Magadhan region during the period of Sātavāhana ascendancy. Thus the above discussion shows that shifting geopolitical and geocultural perspectives underlie the works of Sanskrit grammarians, Prakrit grammarians, Sanskrit dramas etc. and an understanding of these shifting perspectives may afford us a better sociolinguistic appreciation of the complex history of India.

VI

RĀJAŚEKHARA ON ETHNIC AND LINGUISTIC GEOGRAPHY OF INDIA

1. Rājaśekhara's *Kāvyamīmāṃsā*, written around 900 A.D., besides being an important text on Sanskrit poetics, contains a great deal of information on other topics which a good poet was supposed to be familiar with. This work contains information on ethnic and linguistic geography of India which has proved to be useful to students of India's cultural history. In this paper, I shall discuss some of the passages in this text which deal with ethnic and linguistic geography, and I shall briefly compare and contrast Rājaśekhara's conceptions with modern conceptions about India's linguistic and ethnic history.

2. While modern historians of India have made use of all the available sources of information in constructing India's past, linguists in the last two hundred years have advocated various theories about migrations of Aryans and non-Aryans into and within India. Theories about "inner" and "outer" Indo-Aryans, early and late migrations, greater or lesser contact with various ethnic groups, Emeneau's "India as a Linguistic Area" and Southworth's "linguistic archeology" are some of the examples of the contributions of modern linguists to the reconstruction of Indian linguistic and ethnic history. While most of this work has been exciting, a time has come to compare and contrast these theories with what the occupants of the Indian subcontinent themselves thought about their own linguistic and ethnic composition. A few years ago, I attempted to reconstruct a history of socio-linguistic attitudes in India (Deshpande, 1979a). This work is an investigation into what Indians themselves thought, and think, about their own socio-linguistic identity and that of others. In the course of this investigation, I made substantial use of the material provided by Rājaśekhara in his *Kāvyamīmāṃsā*. The present paper takes a closer look

at some of Rājaśekhara's conceptions and compares and contrasts them with conceptions in modern Indian linguistics and anthropology.

3. For whatever reasons, ancient India was not interested in maintaining a strict record of its "matter of fact" history (Deshpande, 1979b). What her literature presents to us are more often than not synchronic flashes of information. If on the basis of independent evidence, we could date, or at least sequentially order these flashes of information, we can construct a skeletal history. In what follows, I shall briefly present a series of such flashes of information within this series. Schwartzberg's 1978 work, *A Historical Atlas of South Asia*, also adopts a similar approach and maintains that a comparison of various sequential flashes yields a valuable amount of information about migration of peoples, changing political and cultural boundaries etc.[120]

4. The *Ṛgveda*, composed primarily in the northwestern corner of the Indian subcontinent around 1500-1000 B.C., refers to non-Āryans not only as *dāsa-varṇa*, "the Dāsa race", but the armies of the Dāsas, claimed to have been destroyed by Indra, are called *kṛṣṇa-yonīḥ* "of dark origin" (*Ṛgveda* 2.20.7). See Map 1. The Vedic Aryans seem to have perceived the non-Aryans, even in Punjab, as being of darker complexion. As Aryans moved into the interior of India, see Map 2 for Southworth's reconstruction, there was a gradual process of naturalization or indigenization of Aryans and Aryanization of non-Aryans (Southworth, 1974; Deshpande, 1979a and 1979b). This process was by no means smooth and uniform. It involved many violent social, religious, political and other conflicts, impositions and adjustments, and resulted in various groups holding different opinions on questions of identity, Aryanhood, Barbarianness etc. By the time the Buddhist and the Jaina canonical texts and the Hindu Dharmaśāstras were formulated, there were several competing conceptions of Aryanhood and Aryan lands. As shown in Map 3, the Brahmanical conception of Āryāvarta was different from the Jaina conception of Aryan lands. I have discussed these two conceptions in detail elsewhere (Deshpande, 1979a: 43-54). While the Brahmanical Āryāvarta was a region to the north of the Vindhyas, to the south of the Himalayas, to the east of Punjab and to the west of Allahabad; the Jainas considered the whole of north India, from the Indus river in the west to Bengal in the east to be the Aryan region. Suffice it to say that the Jaina conception of Aryan lands includes those regions which were considered by the Brāhmaṇas of the Midland to have been inhabitated by "impure and

mixed" populations. There was tension between indigenized Aryans and Aryanized indigenous populations in different parts of India. The Brahmanical conception of Aryan region was not a monolithic conception either. Map 4 shows a significant stratified conception occurring in Manu's law-book. Manu says (*Manusmṛti* 2.21-22):

> The region which lies between the two divine rivers Sarasvatī and Dṛṣadvatī, that which has been created by gods, they (the sages) call Brahmāvarta. The Kurukṣetra, the Matsyas, as also the Pañcālas and the Śūrasenas - this is the region of the Brahmarṣis, ranked immediately after Brahmāvarta. That which lies between the Himalayas and the Vindhyas, and which is also the east of Vinaśana and to the west of Prayāga, that country is called the Madhyadeśa ("Midland"). The tract between those two mountains which extends as far as the eastern and the western oceans, the wise call Āryāvarta.

The conception of Madhyadeśa in Manu corresponds to the notion of Āryāvarta mentioned earlier, while Manu's Āryāvarta is identical with India north of the Vindhyas. Manu's conception gives us concentric circles of ranking showing that it is a hierarchical conception. The Lawbook of Sumantu makes this very clear (Gharpure, 1946: 13):

> Brahmāvarta is the best region; the region of the Brahmarṣis is next to it; the Madhyadeśa is lower than that; and the Āryāvarta is inferior still.

Outside of this region is the region of Mlecchas, non-Aryans or foreigners. In fact, the farther one goes from the Brahmāvarta, the mixture with Mlecchas increases, and it is this increasing loss of purity which makes these regions increasingly non-Aryan. The Lawbook of Viṣṇu states (Gharpure, 1946: 14):

> The country where the adjustment of the four Varṇas does not exist, such region should be known as the Mlecchadeśa; and the other has been stated as Āryāvarta.

A possible implication of this statement is that a Mleccha region could be turned into an Aryan region if the Aryan social system could be established in that region. This explains the increasing scope of Āryāvarta, and yet a distinction between more Aryan and less Aryan seems to have remained, and this has been reflected in the hierarchical concentric circles in Manu's conception.

5. While the center of gravity in Manu's conception of Aryan lands lies more to the west, the statements in the *Brāhmaṇa* literature affirm the linguistic superiority of the northwestern region (Deshpande, 1977-78: 121ff). In later times, this center of gravity shifts further to the east. The center of gravity of the Śuṅga empire, which led the renaissance of Hinduism after the Mauryan rule, lies in the region of Magadha (Schwartzberg, 1978: 20, 145; Deshpande, 1979a: 107, fn. 24). The older Brahmāvarta is, by this time, dominated by the Indo-Greeks who are considered to be Mlecchas by the Brahmanical tradition.[121] The great Sanskrit grammarian Patañjali lived during this period, and Map 5 shows the dimensions of the Brahmanical Śuṅga empire and the region in which Patañjali lived during the second century B.C. Patañjali's Āryāvarta is identical with Manu's Madhyadeśa. It lies to the east of Punjab and to the west of Allahabad (D.R. Bhandarkar, 1931: 110; and Deshpande, 1978: 100-103). Patañjali does not espouse the conception of Āryāvarta as the whole of north India. The western boundary of Patañjali's Āryāvarta is practically the western boundary of the Brahmanical Śuṅga empire. Beyond this are the Indo-Greeks, the Yavanas. Patañjali has not extended the eastern boundary of his Āryāvarta beyond Allahabad. It seems that Brahmanical influence in the regions to the east of Allahabad was much weaker (D.R. Bhandarkar, 1931: 107ff). Patañjali says that a Brāhmaṇa is *gaura* "fair" and that no person with the color of black lentils can be recognized as a Brāhmaṇa.[122] It may be noted that he is not referring to Aryans as such being fair, but to Brāhmaṇas alone. Brāhmaṇas in the late classical period considered themselves to be the only survivors of the old Vedic society and believed that there were no true Kṣatriyas in the world any longer.[123] There are indications in Kātyāyana's Vārttikas on Pāṇini's grammar that the relations between Brāhmaṇas and Kṣatriyas were deteriorating (Deshpande, 1979a: 110, fn. 48). By the time of Patañjali, only the learned Brāhmaṇas of Āryāvarta were viewed as being the speakers of the ideal form of Sanskrit, and others were simply viewed as being non-standard. This is an indication of a widening gap between the Brāhmaṇas and the rest, and this eventually leads the Brāhmaṇas to consider all the non-Brāhmaṇas to be Śūdras. This is evident particularly in Bengal and parts of south India.[124]

6. Having glanced at these older conceptions, let us now turn to Rājaśekhara's work. Map 6 shows the broad divisions of India into Uttarāpatha, Paścāddeśa, Madhyadeśa, Pūrvadeśa and Dakṣiṇāpatha.[125] If we look at the detailed lists of "countries" or peoples in these different

divisions as provided by Rājaśekhara, some important facts are highlighted. The list of peoples in the Uttarāpatha shows the maximum concentration of "foreign" peoples such as Śakas, Hūnas, Kulūtas, Kīras etc. In fact it is hard to find even one name in this list which can be identified with the older Aryan tribes known from the Vedic and epic literatures. Therefore it is no wonder that the Dharmaśāstras viewed this region to be an "impure" region inhabited by mixed populations. The descendants of the Vedic Aryans were evidently pushed further east by these post-Aryan invaders. Languages, peoples and cultures in Sindh, Punjab, Rajasthan, Kashmir and most other parts of India have been affected by these post-Aryan invasions and settlements.

7. Previously I have referred to certain attitudes concerning complexion in India. Vedic Aryans in Punjab refer to their non-Aryan enemies as being of dark complexion. Later on Patañjali says that Brāhmaṇas are fair while non-Brāhmaṇas are dark. Obviously, in the region where Patañjali lived, the fair Brāhmaṇas must have been greatly outnumbered by the darker non-Brāhmaṇas. While these are stray statements about complexions of certain groups, a detailed complexion-geography does not emerge until the *Kāvyamīmāṃsā* of Rājaśekhara. The *Nāṭyaśāstra* of Bharata does say that Śakas, Yavanas, Pahlavas and Bāhlīkas in the northern direction should be shown as having a fair complexion,[126] but this text does not offer a detailed complexion-geography.

8. Map 7 shows Rājaśekhara's conception of regional distribution of complexions. This is a significant picture, and it helps remove some of the commonly held beliefs based on a person's complexion. It is to be noted that some difference was felt between the fair complexions of the upper and lower northwestern regions, as well as between the darker shades found in the eastern and southern regions. It is to be particularly noted that despite the fact that a great deal of mixture took place in the northwestern regions, the complexions in Uttarāpatha somehow remained by and large fair. The word *gaura* which is used by Patañjali to describe the complexion of Brāhmaṇas in the eastern region is used by Rājaśekhara here to describe the complexion of a population which included Śakas, Yavanas, Hūṇas and other foreign elements. This agrees with the statement of the *Nāṭyaśāstra* mentioned earlier. It is clear from Patañjali's statement that only the minority community of Brāhmaṇas in the eastern region was fair in contrast with the larger non-Brāhmaṇa masses. On the other hand, the situation in the northwestern region seems

to have been quite different. Here the majority of the population was relatively fair in its complexion. This makes us aware of the fact that the fair complexion of a person in India is no compelling evidence of his historical Aryan origin. D.R. Bhandarkar also makes the same point in his fascinating discussion of the foreign elements in the Hindu population.[127]

9. According to Rājaśekhara, the complexion of people in the southern region was *kṛṣṇa* "dark", while the complexion in the eastern region is said to be *śyāma* "light dark". The Kirātas or Tibeto-Burmans in the upper northeastern regions are often described as having golden or yellow complexion (S.K. Chatterji, 1950: 165), and the lower northeastern region can be viewed as an area representing a mixture between the northeastern yellow Kiratas and the darker Dravidians and Muṇḍas.[128] This conception is very similar to Herbert Risley's ethnic classification of this region. See Map 12. Risley holds that the population of Bengal and parts of Bihar and Orissa is Mongolo-Dravidian. The term Mongoloid in Risley's classification refers to Tibeto-Burman stocks, while the term Dravidian includes Muṇḍas.

10. The Madhyadeśa, according to Rājaśekhara, was inhabited by peoples of all complexions. This is a region of considerable overlap between north and south, east and west. The idea that there is an overlap of various systems, primarily north and south, in this region gets added support from other descriptions in Rājaśekhara's work. Map 8 shows that the region of Avanti, which fairly corresponds to Rājaśekhara's notion of lower Madhyadeśa, has both styles of dress, the northern Pāñcāla-Madhyamā as well as the southern Dākṣiṇātyā (*KM*, p. 9). Map 9 shows that the same region of Avanti has an overlap in respect of styles of amorous expression. It has the northern Sātvatī style as well as the southern Kaiśikī (*KM*, p. 10). Rājaśekhara's discussion also suggets that there was an overlap of the northern and southern literary styles in this region. See Map 10.

11. It may be pointed out that the complexion-geography and other cultural regionalities presented by Rājaśekhara help us chart outlines of some major ethno-cultural grids in classical India. In terms of complexion, there appears to be a significant boundary dividing the north and the west from the south and the east. There are sub-isoglosses dividing the north from the west and the east from the south. The major boundary in

Rājaśekhara's complexion-geography dividing the north and the sest from the south and the east may be compared with the dialect division in Ashokan inscriptions (Southworth, 1974: 210). Rājaśekhara's picture must also be contrasted with what we know from the *Ṛgveda*. At the time of the Ṛgvedic compositions, the enemies of the Aryans in the northwestern regions were described as *kṛṣṇa* "dark", while in later times, the darker complexions are mainly confined to the east and to the south and extend upto central India. This is perhaps an indication of ethnic displacement of darker complexions from the northwestern parts of India. That there was a major displacement of non-Aryan elements is supported by various kinds of evidence. The boundary of the Aryan homeland gradually moved eastward from eastern Punjab at the time of the *Ṛgveda* to Allahabad in the days of Patañjali. The *Mahābhārata* records various efforts made by the Pāṇḍavas to burn and clear forests and exterminate Nāgas and other tribes.[129] As a result of these Aryan efforts the region of Uttarāpatha and parts of Madhyadeśa were cleared of non-Aryan tribes. Joseph Schwartzberg (1978: 283ff) shows that non-Aryan tribal peoples survived on the fringes of this cleared area. Thus this region, the homeland of the Aryans, shows a predominant fair complexion. However, the post-Vedic invasions of Uttarāpatha and western regions resulted in many overlays of non-Aryan elements. But it seems that these elements were also fairer in complexion. Hence, the northwestern region did become more and more impure and mixed from a Brahmanical religious point of view, despite remaining fair in complexion. Thus over a period of centuries, the association of complexion with Aryanness and religious purity seems to have vanished completely.[130]

12. Rājaśekhara's description of the overlap of northern and southern cultural patterns and complexions in the region of Avanti or lower Madhyadeśa may be compared with some of the recent conclusions supporting this overlap. A study of patterns of kinship in India also shows that the regions of Gujarat, Maharashtra and Orissa represent the region of overlap between the Indo-Aryan kinship system and the Dravidian kinship system. While cross-cousin marriage is not found in the north, and while it is the preferred form of marriage in the south, both types survive in the above mentioned frontier belt.[131] See Map 11. To this we may add recent ideas advanced by S.B. Joshi and Franklin Southworth that Marathi probably developed from a pidginized form of Prakrit spoken by a predominantly Dravidian population.[132] This conception at this stage is still a hypothesis and not a completely proven thesis.

However, the origin of Marathi definitely lies in the phenomenon of overlap of the northern and southern social and linguistic systems in the region of Maharashtra. Rājaśekhara's description places this overlap in a region which is immediately to the north of current Maharashtra. It is very likely that this region of overlap has shifted southwards since the time of Rājaśekhara. Since some of Rājaśekhara's notions are derived from the *Nāṭyaśāstra* of Bharata, this overlap may be pushed back to about the beginning of the Christian era, if not earlier.

13. We may briefly compare Rājaśekhara's complexion-geography of India with Herbert Risley's ethnological geography of India. See Map 12. Though Risley's conceptions and terminology are now largely outdated, they represent a stage in the evolution of concepts about Indian ethnography and as such will always remain a matter of historical interest. Risley worked side by side with Sir George Grierson to whom we owe the monumental *Linguistic Survey of India*. Sir Herbert Risley was entrusted with a no less significant and demanding task, i.e. preparation of the Census of India. Like most western scholars of his time, Risley was indeed convinced of the notion of Aryan migrations into India as postulated by Indo-Europeanists and of the existence of the separate Dravidian linguistic family advocated by Caldwell. Risley groups Dravidians and Mundas under the same category of Dravidians and calls the Tibeto-Burmans by the term Mongoloid. He takes into account the Scythian (*śaka*) rule in Maharashtra, Gujarat and Sindh and proposes that the population of this region is Scytho-Dravidian. In the northwestern part of the subcontinent, he places the Turko-Iranian population. Here, he takes into account the Muslim invasions, which took place after the time of Rājaśekhara. It is interesting to note that this area was heavily influenced by foreign elements even prior to Rājaśekhara's time, and the only thing that changed was the fact that previous invaders were not Islamic, but the new ones were.

14. Risley's classifications show significant ethnic overlaps. According to him, the Dravidians extend far to the north and east where they merge respectively with Aryans and Mongoloids. This implies that at one time, the Dravidians had occupied all these extensive northern regions, though now they are mainly confined to the south. This agrees fairly well with the conclusions of modern research into India's linguistic history,[133] and is further supported by Rājaśekhara's complexion-geography and by his geography of cultural patterns. Risley's Indo-Aryan area largely corre-

sponds to Rājaśekhara's Uttarāpatha. Risley found certain common anthropometric features in this region and hence he lumped the people of this region into a single category of Indo-Aryans. This is quite similar to what Rājaśekhara does with respect to this region. Despite the fact that a great deal of ethnic intermixture took place in this region, Rājaśekhara finds a pervasive *gaura* "fair" complexion here, and he is aware that there is no connection between traditional Aryanhood and fair complexion.[134] The boundaries in Rājaśekhara's complexion-geography have certain close parallels in Risley's conceptions.

15. There are many other conceptions about the Indian linguistic geography in Rājaśekhara's work. I have dealt with them in detail elsewhere (Deshpande, 1979a: 28-33). While commenting on Pāṇini's grammar, Kātyāyana uses the words *laukika* "worldly" and *vaidika* "Vedic", instead of using the words *loka* and *veda*.[135] Patañjali in his remarks on Kātyāyana's statement says that Kātyāyana is a southerner and southerners prefer to use *taddhita*-derivatives.[136] Patañjali, however, does not provide a complete geography of such grammatical features. According to Rājaśekhara (*KM*, p. 22), the people of Vidarbha prefer more nominal constructions, but avoid long compounds. The people of the Gauḍa country (= Bengal) prefer long compounds. Southerners prefer the use of *taddhita*-derivatives, while the northerners prefer *kṛt*-derivatives. Then he says that all good poets prefer using verbs. Since Rājaśekhara himself belonged to Madhyadeśa, this may perhaps refer to the preference in that part of India. Though we do not have full confirmation for these descriptions from other sources, some of the details do find echoes elsewhere.[137]

16. Rājaśekhara's work also tells us about particular regions showing preference for particular literary languages (*KM*, p. 51). He says that the Gauḍas are more interested in Sanskrit, while the Lāṭas are more interested in Prakrit. The poets of Rājasthan, upper Punjab and Bhādānaka (?) are more fluent in Apabhraṃśa. The poets of Avanti, Vindhya and Daśapura prefer Paiśācī. Finally he says that a poet who lives in the Madhyadeśa is fluent in all languages. See Map 13. It is not clear why the preference for Sanskrit should have been viewed as being limited to Gauḍas. The reference to the region of Paiśācī in the vicinity of the Vindhyas finds support in the story of Guṇāḍhya's *Bṛhatkathā* (*Kathāsaritsāgara*, pp. 15ff). The close link between the dialects of Rajasthan and Apabhraṃśa can also be supported on the basis of modern conceptions (Chatterji, 1960: 104, 118, 182, 194). The claim that the

Lāṭas (= Gujarat) show a marked preference for Prakrit may be viewed in the light of the strength of Jainism in this region, and its use of Prakrit.

17. Rājaśekhara also informs us that various kings had peculiar linguistic inclinations (*KM*, 50). According to him, the king Śiśunāga of Magadha made a rule that no one in his harem should utter any retroflex sounds. This is an interesting reference, and is perhaps related to lack of retroflexes in Tibeto-Burman languages. Assamese, for instance, has only alveolars in place of dentals as well as retroflexes, and this has been explained as the influence of the neighboring Tibeto-Burman languages on this Indo-Aryan language. The king Kuvinda of Śūrasena (= Mathurā region) is said to have banned harsh consonant-clusters in his harem. This could be a reference to a kind of Prakrit where simplification of Sanskrit consonant clusters was commonplace. The king Sātavāhana of Kuntala made his entire harem a Prakrit-speaking place. This reference is quite interesting. The story of the origin of the Kātantra grammar as narrated in the *Kathāsaritsāgara* states that the Śātavāhanas were more proficient in Prakrit than in Sanskrit (*Kathāsaritsāgara*, pp. 18ff). The rise of the Mahārāṣṭrī Prakrit as the most dominant literary Prakrit may be related to the rise of the Sātavāhana power, when the center of political gravity in India shifted to the south-central region. Rājaśekhara says that the king Sāhasāṅka of Ujjayinī enforced Sanskrit in his harem. This may be contrasted with Rājaśekhara's own statement that the poets in the region of Avanti, Vindhya etc. preferred the use of Paiśācī. It may be that the kings who established themselves in a particular region brought with themselves certain preferences which were contrary to the local preferences. Another fact must also be noted. Rājaśekhara's orientation is not terribly historical either. His work is more of a traditional encyclopedia, rather than a cultural history. The kings whose preferences are noted by Rājaśekhara are separated from each other by hundreds of years. This affects the mutual comparability of his own statements. His perspective of Indian cultural history is perfectly atemporal, and this is quite in keeping with the general trend of the classical Indian mind (Deshpande, 1979: 12-13, 17ff).

18. Rājaśekhara also gives us information about the regional modes of speech and recital. His comments are often based on stereotypical ideas prevalent in India. Such ideas are found in other works, such as the *Kuvalayamālā* of Uddyotanasūri.[138] Here are Rājaśekhara's opinions (*KM*, pp. 33-4):

Māgadhas and others to the east of Banaras speak Sanskrit very well, but they do not do well in Prakrit. (This agrees with Rājaśekhara's opinion that the Gauḍa poets prefer to use Sanskrit.)

A Gauḍa reciter is neither clear nor yet confused, neither harsh nor yet soft, and neither with a low pitch nor with a high pitch. His recitation is like that of a horse.

A Gauḍa speaks Prakrit so bad, that either he should give up Prakrit, or Prakrit should change its nature. (This may be compared with the low status given to Māgadhī in Sanskrit dramas. Rājaśekhara himself gives Māgadhī the status of a maid-servant (*KM*, p. 50)).

Whatever be the sentiment, style or qualities, all the Karṇāṭas proudly emphasize their retroflexes. All Dravidian poets recite prose, verse or a mixed text in a musical way.

The Lāṭas hate Sanskrit,[139] but recite beautiful Prakrit poetry with their tongues rambling with the pleasure of uttering soft sounds.

The poets of Surāṣṭra, Travaṇa etc. recite even Sanskrit by mixing it with bits of Apabhraṃśa, thus making it more beautiful.

By the grace of Sarasvatī, the Kashmirians are good poets, and yet their recitation sounds like *gaḍūcī-gaṇḍūṣa* ("noises of puffing a hukka"?) to the ear.

Poets of the northern region recite with a nasal twang, despite their great refinement. (There are indications in Pāṇini's *Aṣṭādhyāyī* of this preferred nasality in his region, Deshpande, 1979a: 114, fn. 110).

Possessed of good qualities, with voice corresponding to the style, with the perfect arrangement of words and properly divided by caesuras, the beautiful recitation of the poets of the Pañcāla region flows into the ears like honey.[140]

19. What is the value of Rājaśekhara's information? It cannot be denied that Rājaśekhara had no conception of "history" in the modern sense of the term. His conception of India is that of a timeless storehouse, and his treatment of the subject is like an encyclopedia. However, he was not unique in holding such a perception of history. Pāṇini, Patañjali, Manu and others show the same panchronic perception of Indian culture (Deshpande, 1979b, 1978). However, Rājaśekhara's perception of India

is significantly different from that of Patañjali or Manu. To a certain extent it is somewhat similar to Pāṇini's percption of the Sanskrit language. Pāṇini does not present a particular regional variety of Sanskrit as being standard Sanskrit. He looks at every available kind of Sanskrit and takes care of this totality by making a distinction between the commonly shared core and the specific usages of particular historical or regional domains (Deshpande, 1978: 71-84). In contrast with this universality of approach, Patañjali concentrates on the region of Āryāvarta and its learned Brāhmaṇas for his standard of Sanskrit, and the implication of this clearly seems to be that other regions should emulate the élite behavior of this region (Deshpande, 1978: 99ff). This is also true of Manu's Lawbook which explicitly says (*Manusmṛti* 2.20): "From a Brāhmaṇa born in this country (=Madhyadeśa), let all men on earth learn their ways of behavior."

The perception of cultural variation in Rājaśekhara's work is of an entirely different order. There has been a great deal of change since the time of Patañjali and Manu upto the time of Rājaśekhara. While for Patañjali and Manu the Āryāvarta alone was the holy land, and all the outer regions were inhabited by fallen, impure and mixed populations, this view is no longer held by the time of Rājaśekhara. Rājaśekhara appreciates Sanskrit of the Gauḍas, poetry of the Kashmirians, Apabhraṃśa of Punjab, Prakrit of the Lāṭas and the recitation of the poets of Saurāṣṭra. All of these regions are impure, fallen and mixed regions in the lists of the earlier Dharmaśāstras (Gharpure, 1946: 16ff). The best literary Prakrit, Mahārāṣṭrī, and the best poetic style, Vaidarbhī, developed in regions outside the old Āryāvarta. Thus in Rājaśekhara's work, and other works of the classical period, we find a very different awareness and perception of India. Here, every region of India has a share in the glory of the land and hence the cultural geography in Rājaśekhara is more even-handed and generous in comparison with the heavy-handed treatment of non-Āryāvarta regions, non-Brahmanical peoples and non-Sanskrit languages in the works of Patañjali and Manu (Deshpande, 1979a: 7-10). For this reason, Rājaśekhara's cultural geography becomes significant for its approach and for its content. Though Rājaśekhara lived in a pre-modern age, as we have seen, his conceptions compare fairly well with those of a modern anthropologist like Risley. Therefore, in any historical reconstruction of India's cultural, anthropological and linguistic history, Rājaśekhara's *Kāvyamīmāṃsā* remains a very useful tool.

MAP 1

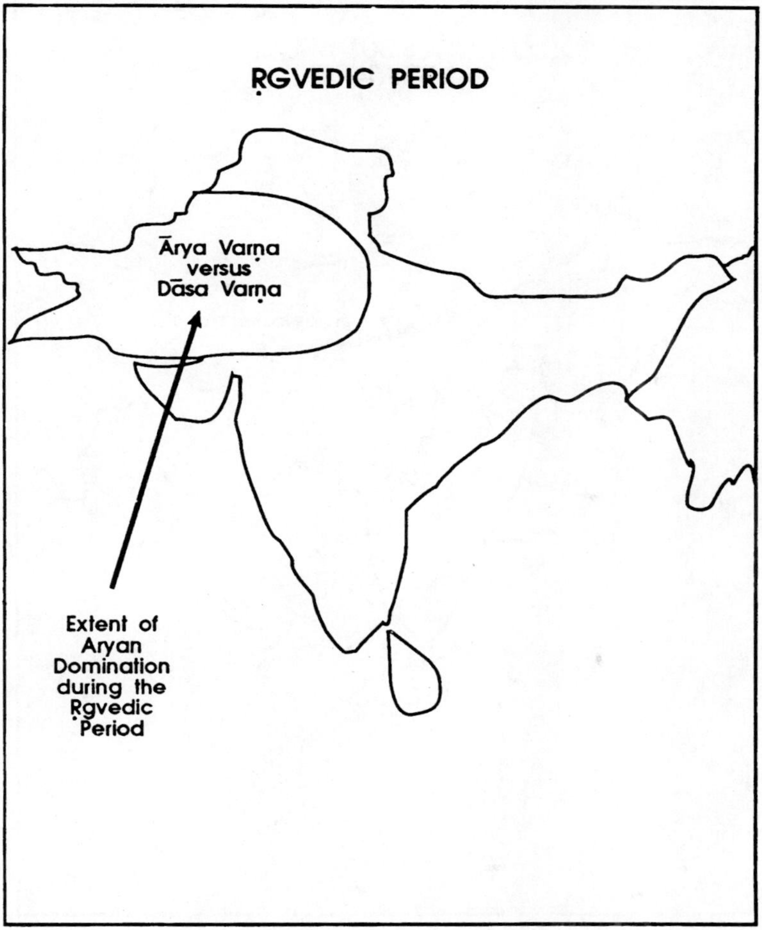
ṚGVEDIC PERIOD
Ārya Varṇa versus Dāsa Varṇa
Extent of Aryan Domination during the Ṛgvedic Period

MAP 2

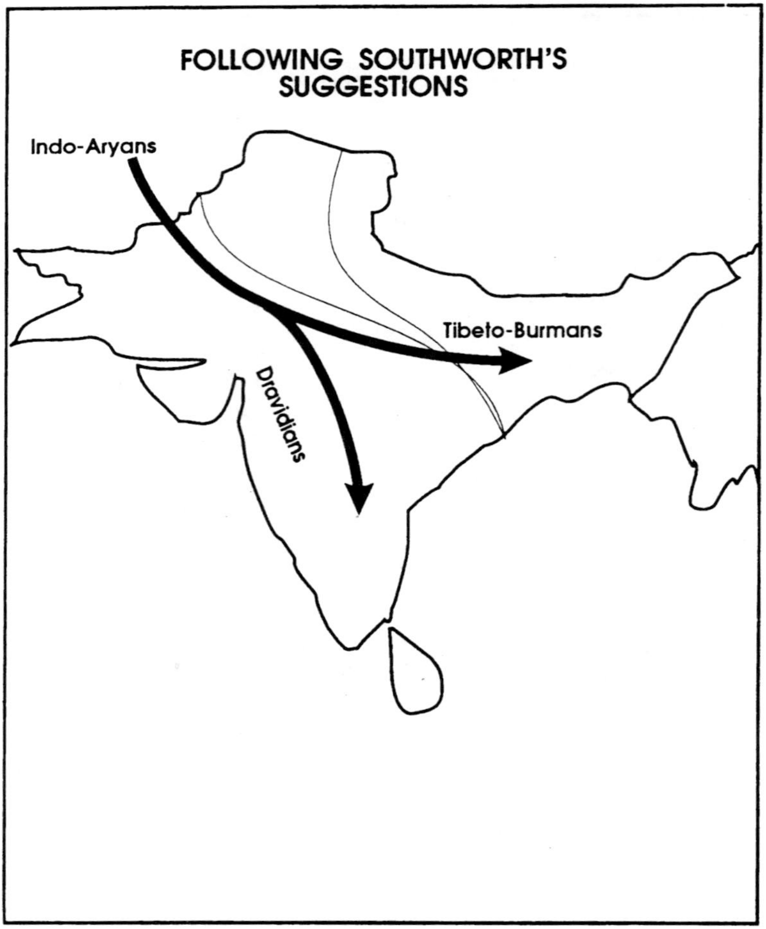
FOLLOWING SOUTHWORTH'S SUGGESTIONS
Indo-Aryans
Tibeto-Burmans
Dravidians

MAP 3

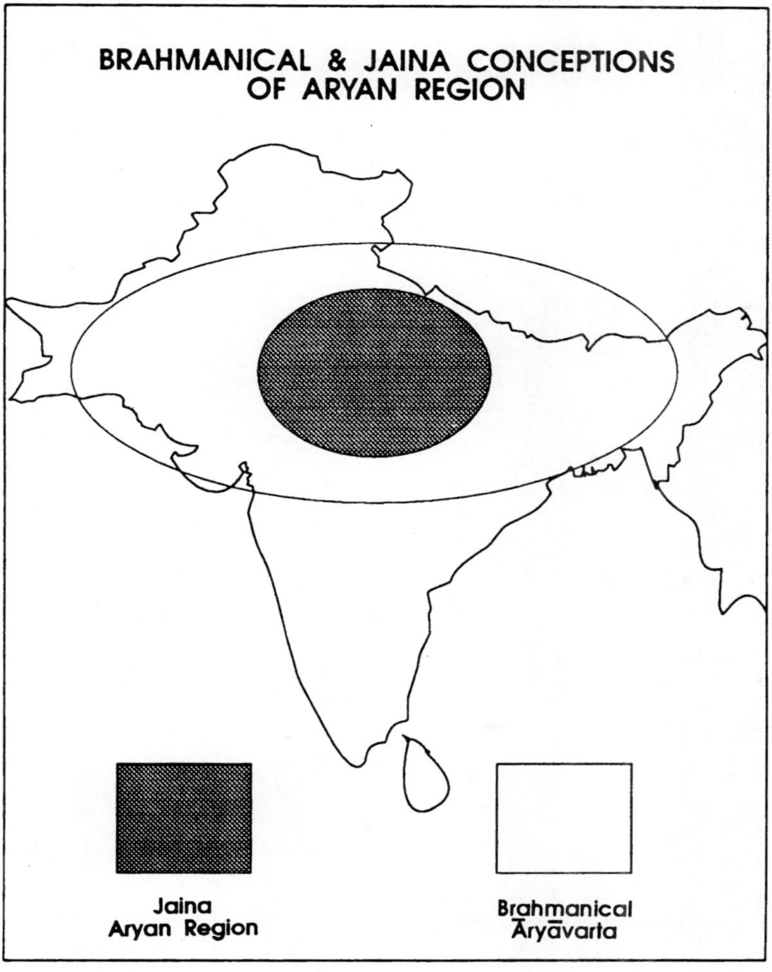
BRAHMANICAL & JAINA CONCEPTIONS
OF ARYAN REGION
Jaina
Aryan Region
Brahmanical
Āryāvarta

MAP 4

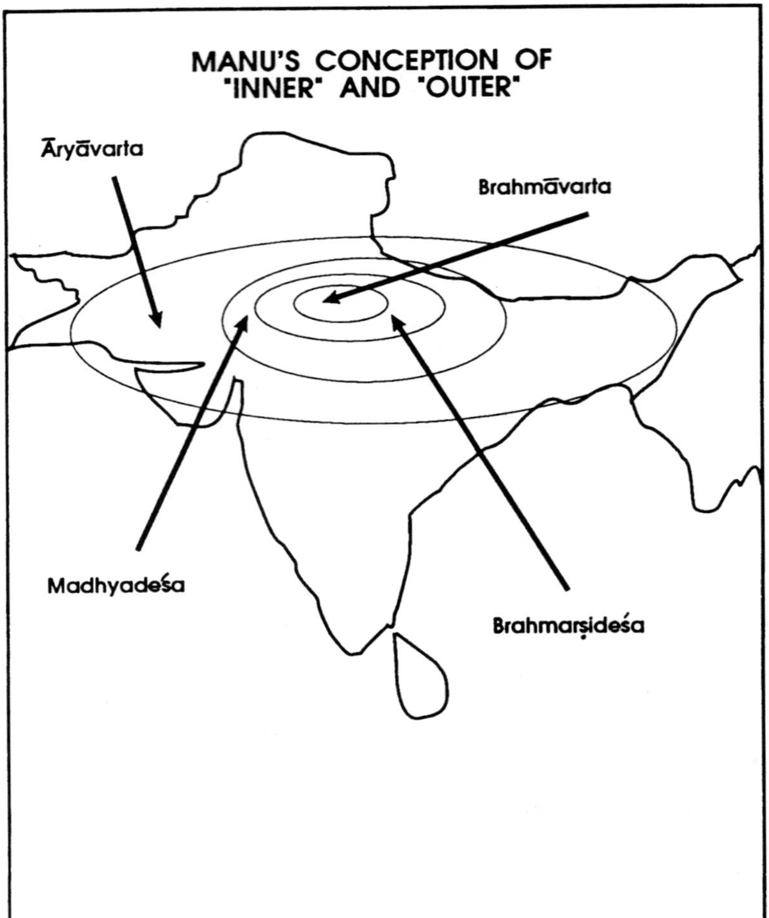
MANU'S CONCEPTION OF
"INNER" AND "OUTER"
Āryāvarta
Brahmāvarta
Madhyadeśa
Brahmarṣideśa

MAP 5

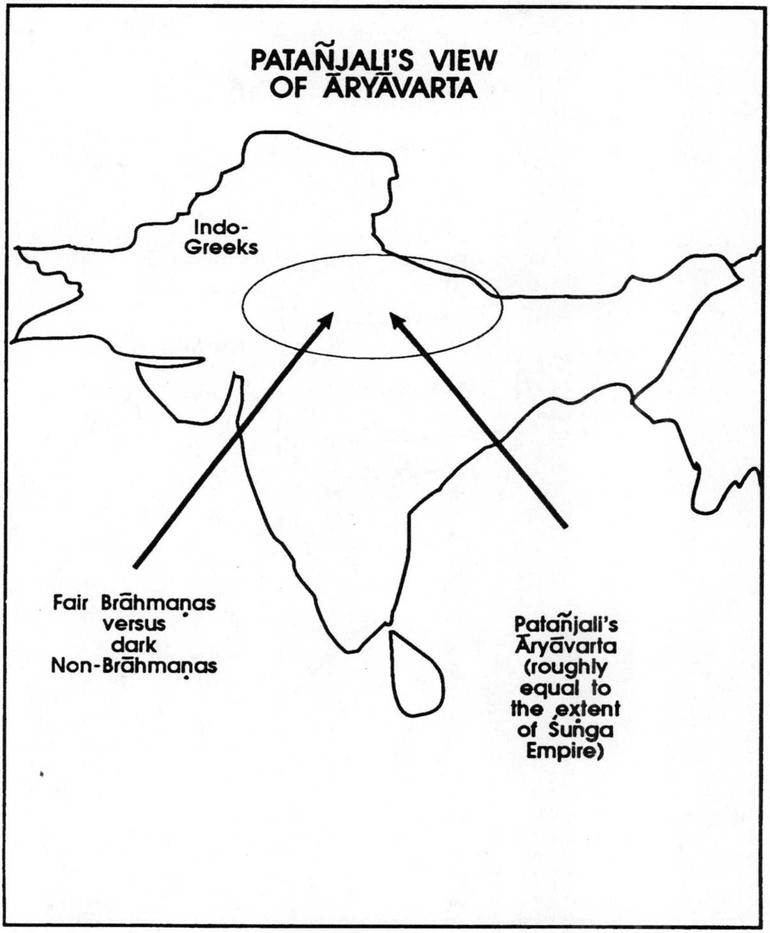
PATAÑJALI'S VIEW
OF ĀRYĀVARTA
Indo-
Greeks
Fair Brāhmaṇas
versus
dark
Non-Brāhmaṇas
Patañjali's
Āryāvarta
(roughly
equal to
the extent
of Śuṅga
Empire)

MAP 6

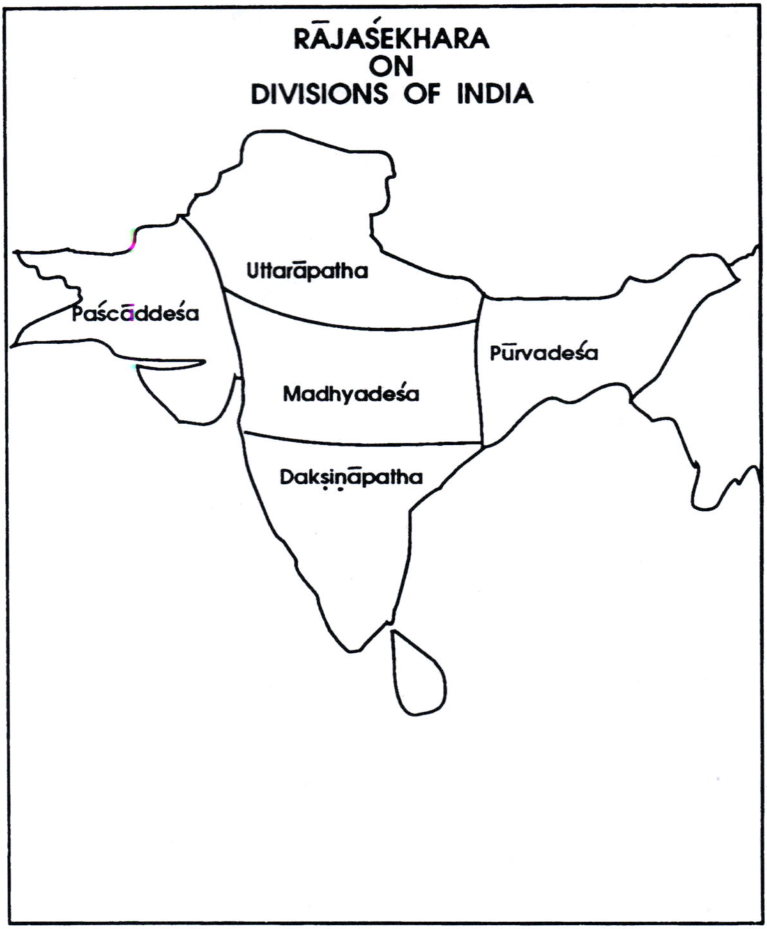
RĀJAŚEKHARA
ON
DIVISIONS OF INDIA
Uttarāpatha
Paścāddeśa
Pūrvadeśa
Madhyadeśa
Dakṣiṇāpatha

MAP 7

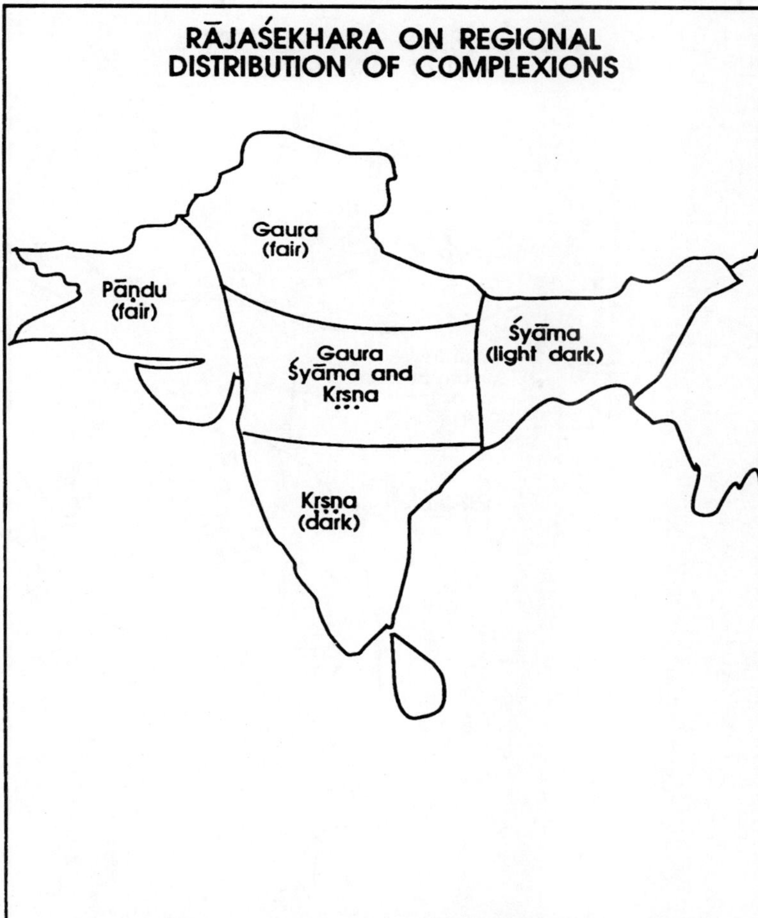
RĀJAŚEKHARA ON REGIONAL DISTRIBUTION OF COMPLEXIONS
Gaura (fair)
Pāṇdu (fair)
Gaura Śyāma and Kṛṣṇa
Śyāma (light dark)
Kṛṣṇa (dark)

MAP 8

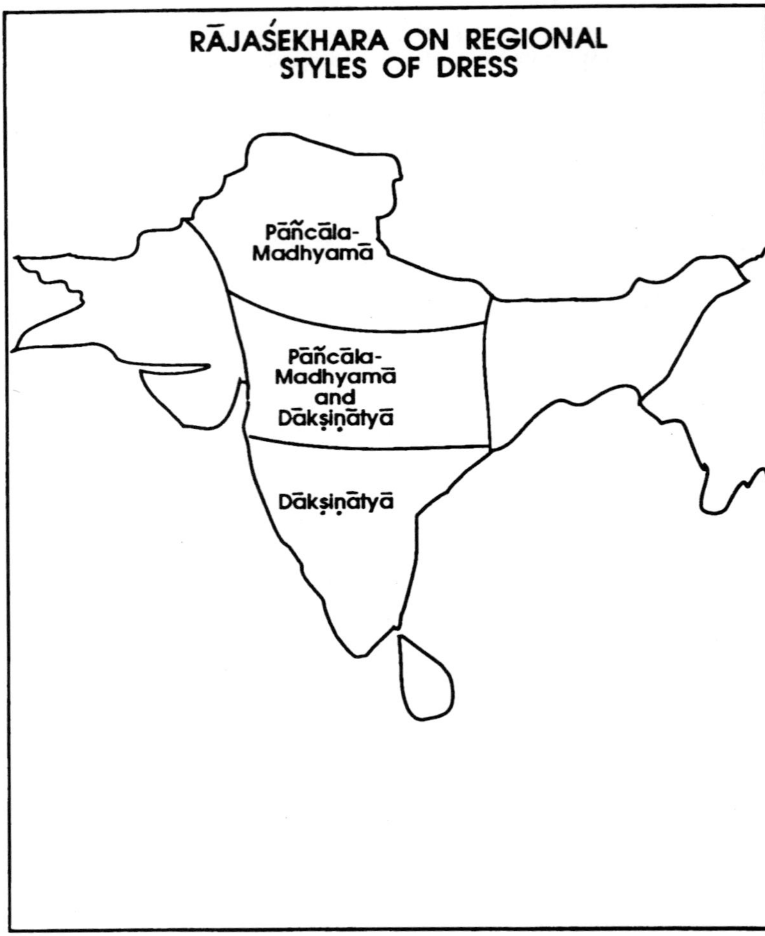
RĀJAŚEKHARA ON REGIONAL STYLES OF DRESS
Pāñcāla-Madhyamā
Pāñcāla-Madhyamā and Dākṣiṇātyā
Dākṣiṇātyā

MAP 9

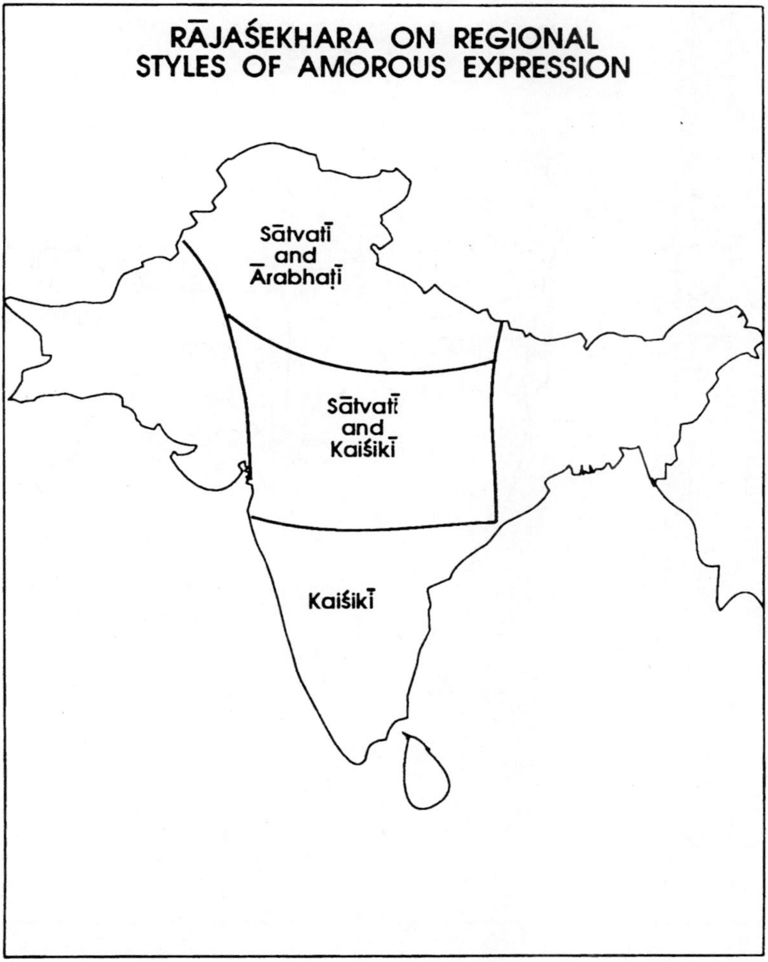
RĀJAŚEKHARA ON REGIONAL
STYLES OF AMOROUS EXPRESSION
Sātvatī
and
Ārabhaṭī
Sātvatī
and
Kaiśikī
Kaiśikī

MAP 10

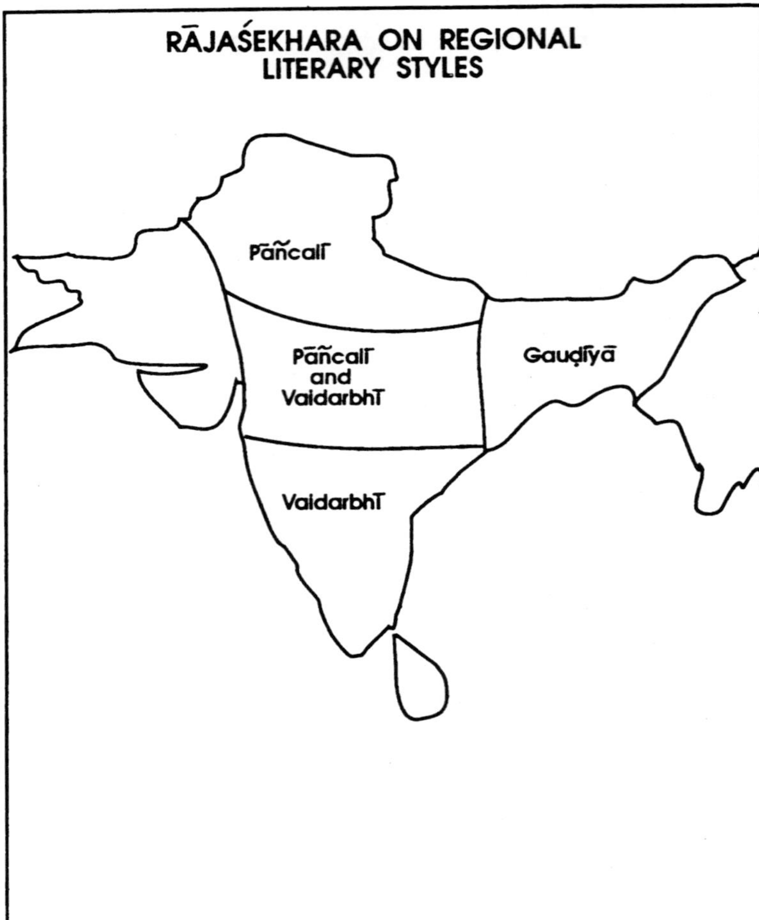

RĀJAŚEKHARA ON REGIONAL LITERARY STYLES

MAP 11

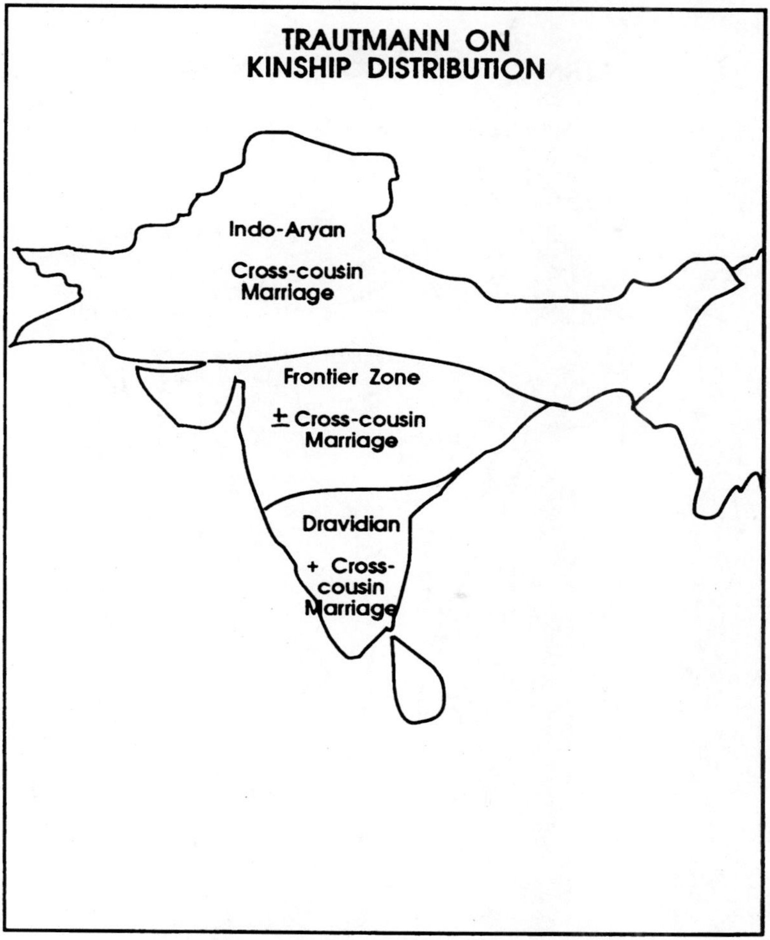
TRAUTMANN ON
KINSHIP DISTRIBUTION
Indo-Aryan
Cross-cousin
Marriage
Frontier Zone
± Cross-cousin
Marriage
Dravidian
+ Cross-
cousin
Marriage

MAP 12

HERBERT RISLEY ON ETHNIC DISTRIBUTION IN INDIA

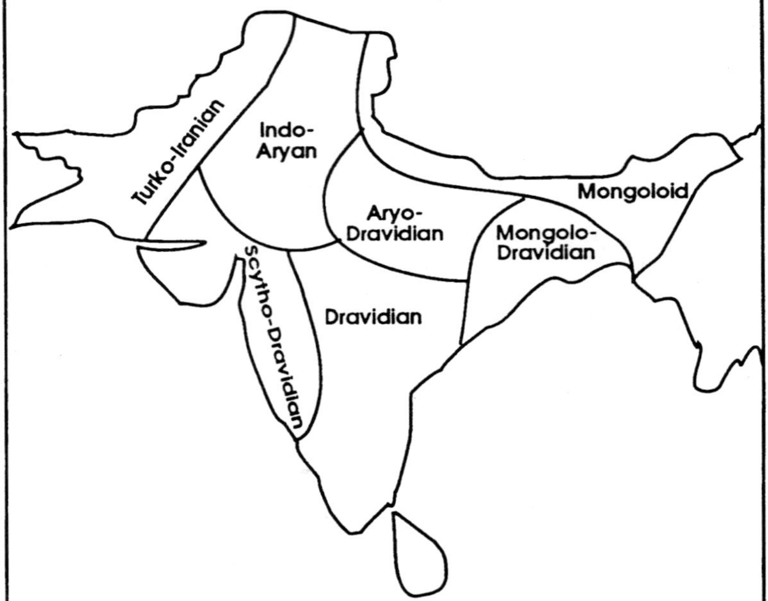

MAP 13

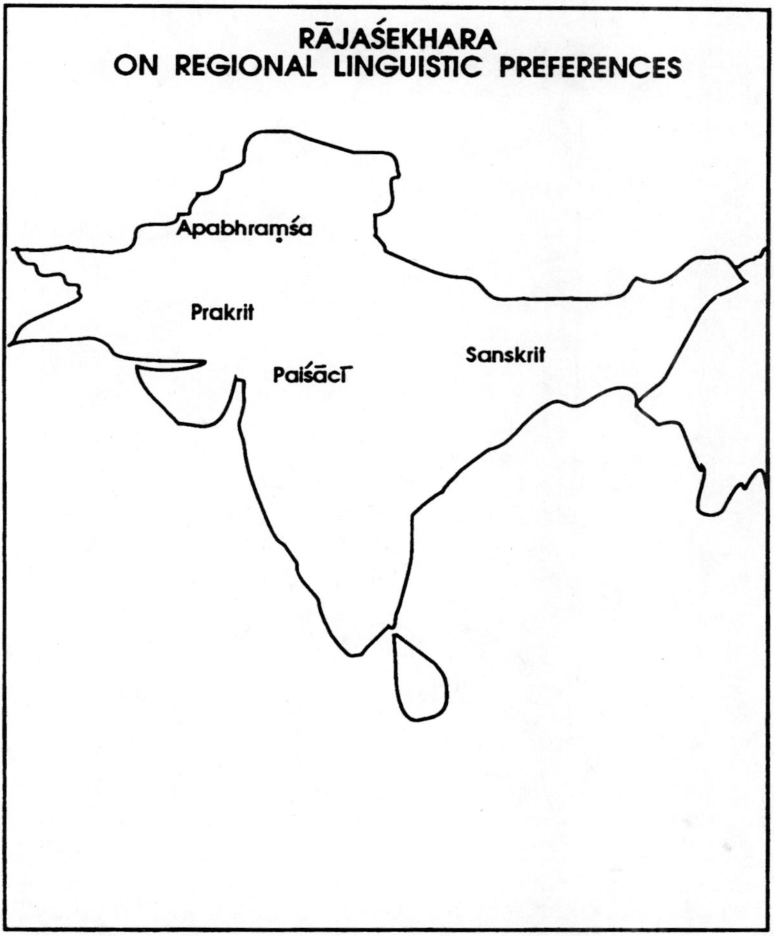
RĀJAŚEKHARA
ON REGIONAL LINGUISTIC PREFERENCES
Apabhraṃśa
Prakrit
Paiśācī
Sanskrit

VII

NATION AND REGION: A SOCIOLINGUISTIC PERSPECTIVE ON MAHARASHTRA

1. After India became independent in 1947, the Government of India adopted a policy in accordance with which the country was reorganized into linguistic states. While during the British rule, the provinces were simply administrative units and had no inherent factors uniting them from within, the policy of creating linguistic states officially accepted language as a principle uniting a region. For instance, the Bombay Presidency during the British rule extended from Sindh in the northwest to Karnataka in the south and was comprised of areas speaking Sindhi, Gujarati, Marathi and Kannada, not to speak of other minority languages in these regions. The Governer of Bombay administered this vast territory, and later the University of Bombay had all this region under its affiliation. The official language of administration being English, there was always a semblance of unity at the administrative level, but there was hardly any feeling of regional unity among the subjects of this vast Presidency. Before India achieved freedom, the region of Sindh was separated from the Bombay presidency in 1935. India achieved independence in 1947.

2. After independence, the Government of India initiated the policy of creating linguistic states, and yet, for several years, the Bombay state was still a bilingual state comprising the areas speaking Gujarati and Marathi. However, riots broke out in the fifties to have this region divided into two states, one speaking Marathi and the other speaking Gujarati. In Maharashtra, a Committee for United Maharashtra (*Saṃyukta-Mahārāṣṭra-Samiti*) was organized in which most of the non-Congress opposition parties joined hands, and this organization successfully led a popular campaign to have the separate state of Maharaṣhtra established for the Marathi-speaking people. In this popular campaign, the politicians and

the poets of Maharashtra invoked every conceivable argument to show the internal unity of the Marathi-speaking people.[141] This movement is important in that it shows how a people can unite for a certain cause, claim certain diachronic and synchronic factors as causes of this unity, and importantly, forget other diachronic and synchronic factors which in fact do divide them. However, the notion of the unity of a people is a subjective notion, and once developed it can be a very powerful instrument for political activity. The show of strength in these linguistic riots and demonstrations was so effective that the then Prime Minister Pandit Jawaharlal Nehru finally conceded to a partition of the bilingual state, and the modern state of Maharashtra was born out of this partition in 1960. Once this goal was accomplished, the parties which had come together to form the Committee for United Maharashtra could not stay united any longer, and their internal differences became once again the focus of their politics. However, these and later events in regional and national politics indicate the ability of the Marathi people to unite for a regional cause, and also indicate that in the absence of any such pervasive regional cause, internal differences of many sorts become dominant issues. In the present paper, I shall attempt to deal with the notions of "nation", "region", "unity" and "disunity" in relation to India in general and Maharashtra in particular. My approach is primarily historical and I shall concentrate mainly on socio-linguistic factors in the history of Maharashtra.

3. We shall begin with the notion of unity in ancient India. The fact that certain regions are geographically contiguous or that people in those regions speak languages which belong to what the academics consider to be a single language family is no reason for hoping to find unity among them. "Unity" does not exist apart from what is in the minds of those who feel that unity, and once they feel this unity, the felt unity in turn brings the people closer. According to modern historians of India, people belonging to different racial stocks and different language families arrived in India from different places at different times, and through their historical contacts, conflicts and compromises was built the unity and diversity of India as we know it today. There are traces of Negritos in India. The Austro-Asiatic peoples joined them later and still survive today in the form of Munda-Santal populations. Dravidians were the next to come, from the northwest (Kamil Zvelebil, 1972), and migrate into different parts of India. Then came the pre-Vedic and Vedic Aryans in various waves (Deshpande, 1977-8, and Deshpande and Hook, 1979) and migrated first from the west to the east and then to the south. The

difference between the "original Aryans" and modern Indo-Aryans is perhaps as wide as that between the Aśokan scripts and the modern Devanāgarī script (Oldenberg, 1896: 39-40). Gradually a fusion of these various peoples took place in India. The Aryans were Indianized, or rather indigenized, and the non-Aryans were Aryanized (Deshpande, 1979a; Deshpande and Hook, 1979; Nilakanta Sastri, 1967). These processes were not always either simple or peaceful, but were complex and often resulted in severe tensions which are reflected in claims and counter-claims to Aryanhood, prestige, authenticity and purity (Deshpande, 1979a).

4. While these complex processes were going on in India, and still go on today, they resulted in various kinds of cultural and linguistic patterns. By coming into contact with peoples of different racial, cultural and linguistic origins, each of the different groups borrowed something of others and transmitted something of their own to them. India was and is a "Melting Pot" in a much stronger sense than the United States to which this metaphor is customarily applied. This process of "melting" resulted in certain features emerging as pan-Indian, while many other features remained limited to smaller domains. These pan-Indian features, of whatever historical origin they may be, are shared by most of the Indian peoples, regions, cultures and languages. Thus cultures of different origins and languages of different families came to bear certain "Indian resemblances". In recent times, Professor M.B. Emeneau came to recognize what he called "India as a Linguistic Area" (Emeneau, 1956 and 1974). This notion has since then become a dominant notion in recent linguistic studies on India, and is intended to refer to the diffusion of linguistic features across language families and to the creation of an Indian linguistic norm shared by the majority of the languages of the region (Southworth and Apte, 1974, and Shapiro and Schiffman, 1981). Since then attempts have been made to view India as a cultural area on similar lines.

5. Were Indians themselves oblivious to this phenomenon? I think not. If we remove the mantle of mythology, the classical Indian literature shows an awareness of this notion of India as a cultural area. However, the classical authors were more concerned with the synchronic aspects of India as a cultural area, than with the historical origins of this phenomenon. For instance, the *Lawbook of Manu* takes for granted the existence of this racial and cultural synthesis and the remaining diversity and

explains to us its perception of the existing "system". It delves into mythology when it claims that the four-fold system of castes was created by God on the first day of creation and that all the peoples on earth then known to the Indians were somehow or other born out of legal and illegal mixtures of these original castes and through migrations to "impure" distant lands and "falling" from the original state of purity (Deshpande, 1979b, and V. Jha, 1970). Even the four castes are said to have originated from the same Cosmic Person, a symbol for ultimate reality (*Ṛgveda* 10.90.12). This also shows a conception of the ultimate unity of Indian peoples, with an acknowledgement of "subsidiary" functional diversification. According to the classical tradition recorded in the Dharmaśāstras, the cultural patterns expressed in these terms were eternal entities. From a modern academic point of view, this "history" is certainly unhistorical, and yet we must assume that it is a historically authentic and functional representation of how certain people felt about their cultural unity and diversity. As S.K. Chatterji points out (1962: 83): "A significant point in this reconstruction is that the great fact of different races of people having brought in diverse elements of Hindu culture ... has not been taken note of, either unwillingly, or deliberately and with a purpose." If indeed this reflects ignorance on the part of the classical Indian thinkers, this ignorance of "history" had a very positive and constructive synchronic aspect. This was not simple ignorance, but was an act of ignoring certain questions of historical origins to focus more positively on the synchronic social establishment. We cannot have a "Melting Pot" without this critical factor of "ignoring". Chatterji himself recognized this positive aspect (1962: 85): "Here was a deliberate sacrifice of history for a larger issue. And his larger issue was the reconstruction of a new historical standpoint, in which peoples of various races and colours and languages were looked upon as limbs of a single body, a body which came to be felt as an organic whole." If Chatterji is right, Manu was "using" history as a tool to bring about a new kind of Indian unity, and this may then be comparable to the use of reconstructed history in socialist countries of the world. However, I think that S.K. Chatterji is attributing to Manu a far wider theoretical and historical initiative than is warranted by the available evidence. It is not clear if Manu was "reconstructing" a new historical standpoint. I think Manu expressed an established historical standpoint which itself was a result of the historical process of cultural synthesis. There is no cynical distortion of facts, but an unconscious turning of convenient fictions into facts. I strongly feel that Manu expressesd the then existing Brahmanical ideology of India as a cultural area, and only in this limited sense anticipated M.B. Emeneau's concept of India as a linguistic area.

6. Given this early Brahmanical conception of India as a cultural area, we can discern important aspects of the early Brahmanical notions about what is pan-Indian and what is regional. The classical literature such as the works on Sanskrit grammar and the Dharmaśāstras by and large represents a dominant All-India point of view. It concentrates on those aspects of Indian culture which are not expected to vary from region to region. Ideally this upper class literature attempted to educate the élites all over India in the norms of the Āryāvarta.[142] It did recognize certain regional variations, but these variations were considered to be subsidiary and were not accorded the same status as the All-India elements. The Dharmaśāstra texts do refer to local customs such as the cross-cousin marriage in the south, but their main objective is to provide a pan-Indian system. The *Āśvalāyana-gṛhya-sūtra* (1.7.1-2) says that the religious practices of various parts of India and in various villages are somewhat different, but that it will only talk about what is shared in common by all the regions. There is also a recognition in these texts that the Vedas did not deal with regional Dharma, clan Dharma and caste Dharma, and that, for this reason, Manu and others had to specify some of these details (*Vāsiṣṭha-Dharma-Śāstra* 1.1.17). There is a feeling that the All-India elements existed somehow prior to the regional elements, and this affects the traditional Hindu conception of history. It starts with the notion of unity and then explains diversity as a historical development, and the diversity is viewed not only as a secondary factor, but it also stands lower in traditional religious valuation. This is the opposite of what a modern historian may think, and yet in substance it does refer to the same distinction between pan-Indian and regional traits. In dealing with characters in Sanskrit drama, Dhanañjaya's *Daśarūpaka* (II. 58, 61, 63-66) points out that the upper class characters in Sanskrit drama are more unified in their Sanskrit and Prakrit linguistic behavior and in their costumes etc., while lower class characters were supposed to be typically regional in their language and costumes. This normative statement is supported by the earlier literature on Sanskrit dramaturgy as well as by the Sanskrit dramas themselves. The upper class male characters in Sanskrit drama speak Sanskrit, while other characters speak various different Prakrits. The Śaurasenī and Mahārāṣṭrī Prakrits are used by upper class females and middle-class males, while Māgadhī and other Prakrits are used by lower class characters. The same upper class cultural

unity on the All-India level may be seen in the Brahmanical ritual patterns and in the identical way inscriptions from all over India describe numerous kings. The high-flown descriptions of kings in inscriptions all over India show the commonly shared Sanskritic notions about royalty. Thus, in general terms, the higher we go on the social scale, the more All-India cultural features come to the fore, while the lower we go on the social scale, the more things differ by region. This is true not only of ancient and medieval India, but also of modern India. The inventory of All India features is by no means static; gradually Persianization and Anglicization have greatly influenced the earlier Sanskritic All India features.[143]

CULTURAL UNITY AND DIVERSITY

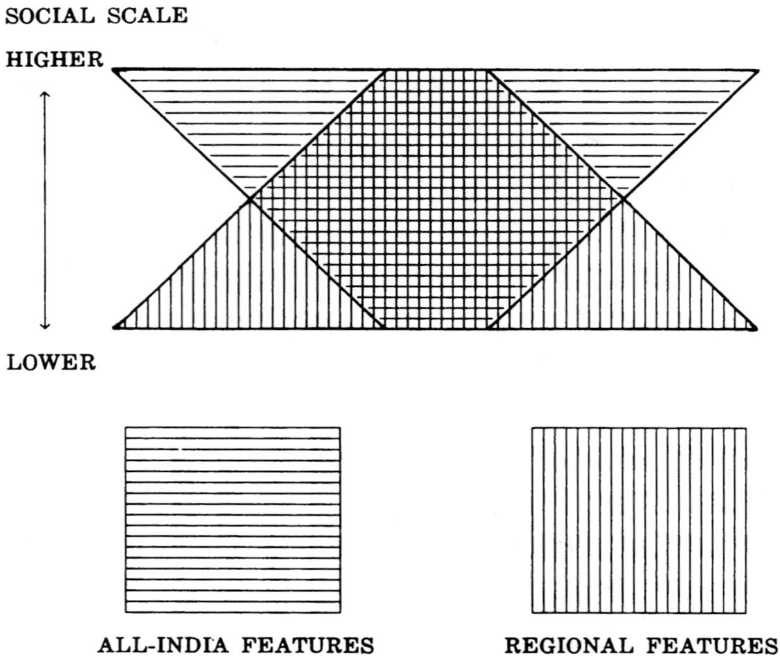

7. Having discussed these important general concepts, we shall now turn to the history of Maharashtra. What happens on the All-India level also happens in the region of Maharashtra on a somewhat smaller scale. Just as India has been described as a melting pot, similarly every region of India is a melting pot in its own way. Maharashtra is no exception. The history of the racial, cultural and linguistic evolution of Maharashtra shows numerous influences from time to time, and there is no reason to believe that the Maharashtrian peoples historically represent a single ethnic stock. Maharashtra is situated on the border between the northern Indo-Aryan region and the southern Dravidian region, and historically represents a region of overlap of these two, and perhaps other, systems. Irawati Karvé (1953: 11ff) shows how the kinship system in Maharashtra represents a mixture of Aryan and Dravidian systems, and this aspect has been recently reinvestigated by Trautmann (1979). In calling mother's brother's daughter *māme bahīṇ* "sister via maternal uncle", the Marathi language retains its Indo-Aryan heritage, but since many Maharashtrian communities allow the marriage of a person to his mother's brother's daughter, the Marathi kinship pattern reflects the dominant Dravidian practice. Karvé (1953: 8ff) shows that northern communities which migrated to Maharashtra, and which originally did not accept this marriage pattern, came to accept it in the course of time. Communities which have been in this region longer show a greater influence of this practice, while the communities which have been in this region for less time, show less influence. Similarly, within Maharashtra, this practice is less common in the northern regions than in the southern regions. In the southern regions of Maharashtra, several communities also allow marriage with father's sister's daughter. This shows much more Dravidian influence from the neighboring Dravidian-speaking regions (Karvé, 1953: 17ff). Karvé (1968) also attempts to show that the Deśastha Ṛgvedī Brāhmaṇas share with certain non-Brāhmaṇa castes, i.e. certain Marāṭhā and Kumbhār groups, certain blood-group characteristics. The historical implications of this study are unclear, and we may simply say that there is a great deal of similarity of various features across the caste-boundaries.[144] S.B. Joshi (1951, 1952) argues that Maharashtra originally was a Kannada-speaking region, and that Marathi developed later due to migrations from the north and eventually displaced Kannada. The implication of this hotly debated[145] thesis is that while the language of the region is an Indo-Aryan language, the people historically belong at least in part to Dravidian ethnic stocks. Franklin C. Southworth (1971) puts forward the hypothesis that Marathi developed through the interaction

between the northern Indo-Aryan settlers and local non-Aryan elements. He suggests that Marathi developed from a creolized form of Prakrit and has its origin in the interaction between the Upper-class Maharashtrian Prakrit and the Lower-class Maharashtrian Pidgin Prakrit; this Pidgin itself is thought to have been derived from an interaction between the Prakrit of the new-comers and the local non-Aryan languages. Additionally, we have many other accounts of "foreign" elements migrating to and settling in Maharashtra at different times. Scythian (*śaka*) kings such as Kṣaharāta and Nahapāna ruled over parts of Maharashtra. There were also Nāgas, Ābhīras, Gurjaras etc. Different Brāhmaṇa communities migrated to this region at different times.

The name *mahārāṣṭra* is most probably a Sanskritized form of some non-Sanskrit expression. Among several etymologies proposed for this name, S.B. Joshi's (1952) derivation from Kannada *mara-haṭṭa* "forest-settlement" seems to be plausible. However, in the course of the history of this region, many peoples proudly considered themselves *māhārāṣṭrika* "Maharashtrian" (Tulpule, 1973: 23-4), and the Sanskritized name *mahārāṣṭra* "the great country" indicates that these Sanskritizers, whoever they were, were proud of this region. This is the first sign of the "felt" pride and unity among the people of this region. This is by no means an indication of any political unity. There were probably several smaller regions within this area which called themselves Maharashtra (Tulpule, 1960: 4).

8. Almost until the end of the first millennium A.D., the region of Maharashtra as such does not emerge as a dominant political unit, though several smaller kingdoms such as Aparānta, Vidarbha and others are mentioned in older sources. This region was a part of the larger kingdoms of the Śātavāhanas, Cālukyas and the Śaka satraps such as Kṣaharāta and Nahapāna, but it is doubtful if we can consider these kings as Maharashtrian kings. None of these kings call themselves particularly Maharashtrian in their inscriptions. The history of Maharashtra as such begins in the second millennium A.D. In general, we may consider the history of the Marathi literature and peoples in five broad divisions: a) Yādava period, b) Bahmani period, c) Maratha period, d) British period, and e) Modern period. Each of these periods shows certain peculiarities of its own, while there are several important features which continue throughout the millennium. These divisions are primarily political, and we shall have to deal with political history in so far it conditions or is conditioned by socio-linguistic notions of unity and disunity.

9. S.B. Joshi (1952) shows that until the rivalry between the Yādava rulers of Devagiri in the upper Godāvarī region and the Yādava rulers of Hoysaḷ in Karnataka became strong, the two languages, i.e. Marathi and Kannada were used generally in the area now known as Maharashtra. Several Old Marathi inscriptions are found in Kannada script, while several Old Kannada inscriptions are available in Devanāgarī. Joshi (1952) argues that with the split between the two seats of Yādava power, there was also a split between the political identity of Marathi and Kannada. The Yādavas of Devagiri came to identify themselves with the local language, i.e. Marathi, and gave official patronage to it. This is probably the first significant official effort in favor of Marathi, though a few smaller kings are known to have used Marathi for their inscriptions (Bhave-Tulpule, 1963: 24ff). It was during the Yādava rule that the famous minister Hemādri Pandit is supposed to have made vigorous efforts to formalize Marathi with Sanskritic expressions and bolster its image as a court language (Bhave-Tulpule, 1963: 24ff).

10. However, as we shall see, in each of these periods, there are certain All-India tendencies within the region which conflict with particular regional tendencies. During this early period, the Brahmanical orthodoxy within the region mostly identified itself with the hieratic Sanskritic traditions which were trans-regional. In general, the orthodox Maharashtrian Brāhmaṇas, like orthodox Brāhmaṇas elsewhere, strongly upheld the Brahmanical traditions and valuations, particularly in such religious centers such as Paiṭhaṇ and Nāśik. As I have discussed elsewhere at length (Deshpande, 1979a: 1-21), the dominant Brahmanical traditions of India held that Sanskrit was the only divine language, created by God or even self-existent, and that only Brāhmaṇas had access to Sanskrit. The Brāhmaṇas also believed that there were no real Kṣatriyas on earth any longer and there were only two social classes, Brāhmaṇas and Śūdras (Deshpande, 1979a: 14ff, 110, 116). For centuries they looked down upon non-Sanskrit languages as "fallen" (*apabhraṃśa*) languages, and criticized Buddhists and Jainas for having used these fallen languages to teach their "perverted" doctrines. These beliefs were upheld by Brāhmaṇas in Maharashtra, as everywhere else in India, and though they used Marathi as their first language, they did not identify with it. In their eyes, Marathi, a Prakrit language, was no less "fallen" than other Prakrit languages rejected by them. This created a wide gap between orthodox Maharashtrian Brāhmaṇas and other peoples in the region. This also

created a gap between those unorthodox Brāhmanas who identified themselves with Marathi for one reason or another and orthodox Brāhmaṇas. Thus we find that in every period of Marathi history, battles were fought between the regional Marathi language and the transregional Sanskrit language. In many ways, this was a continuation of the battles between the orthodox Brahmanism and the "protestant" faiths such as Buddhism and Jainism, both of which had a foothold in Maharashtra (Deshpande, 1978: 40ff). These struggles are not only linguistic, but they are indications of the struggles between the regional and the transregional in many other fields such as religion and politics.

11. Thus we find that Mukundarāj, a Brāhmaṇa, in his *Vivekasindhu*, almost apologizes for having written this philosophical text in Marathi (A.N. Deshpande, 1966: 251). On the other hand, we find that the non-Brahmanical sect of the Mahānubhāvas which prospered in Maharashtra during the Yādava rule exclusively used Marathi for its religious literature. Cakradhar, the founder of this sect was born in Gujarat, and then migrated to Maharashtra. Reportedly, he advised his disciples to live only in Maharashtra and nowhere else (Bhave-Tulpule, 1963: 56-7). The arguments advocated by the Mahānubhāvas for using Marathi exclusively remind one of the Jaina and Buddhist arguments in favor of their respective Prakrit languages (Deshpande, 1979a: 40ff). By the end of the 13th century, Jñāneśvar wrote his famous commentary *Jñāneśvarī* on the *Bhagavadgītā* in Marathi. He totally identified himself with Marathi. He says that his language is the local (*deśī*) Marathi language and yet it can compete with the sweetness of nectar (*Jñāneśvarī* 6.14). He vows to place Marathi and Sanskrit on the same royal throne (Ibid. 12.16; 10.45). Jñāneśvar's father is said to have first become a Sannyāsī and then to have returned becoming a householder. The orthodox Brahmanical society excommunicated the family. One may wonder whether this background of rejection by the orthodox Brāhmaṇas has something to do with Jñāneśvar's intense identification with the vernacular Marathi language.

12. The Marathi identity which strongly developed primarily due to the political support of the Yādavas was shattered by the Muslim invasions in the 14th century. In 1347 A.D., the Bahamani kingdom was established in the Deccan. This led to the wanton killing of thousands of Hindus, the destruction of hundreds of temples and most of all to the destruction of the Hindu, and particularly Marathi, self-respect. With the conclusive loss of their political power, the Hindus gradually came to accept the

domination of the Muslim rulers, and there began the process of Persianization of the Marathi language and culture. Though the Muslim rule in the Deccan had its regional features in contrast with the Muslim rule in the north, as far as the Hindus were concerned, the immediate impact of the Muslim rule was demoralizing. The Hindus gradually "Persianized" themselves in language and outer culture to gain employment with the Muslim rulers. As the Marathi-speaking region was integrated with non-Marathi regions under the Muslim rule, it did not have any political integrity of its own. Eventually though, several splinter Bahamani kingdoms such as those at Bijapur and Ahmednagar adopted Marathi as an official language along with Persian (Deshpande, 1979a: 72-3).

13. While these political upheavals were taking place, many of the old Brahmanical attitudes continued among the orthodox Brāhmaṇas of the region. Thus, we find that the Brāhmaṇa poet-saint Ekanāth (1548-1609 A.D.) was persecuted by the orthodox Brāhmaṇas of Paiṭhaṇ and Banaras for having written a Marathi commentary on the *Bhāgavatapurāṇa*. His manuscript was reportedly thrown into the Ganges, and only a miracle saved it (Abbott, 1927: 173ff; Deshpande, 1979a: 75-77). We are told that his own son, Haripant, disliked his father's Marathi literary activity (Abbott, 1927: 211ff). Despite these problems, it was saints like Ekanāth who preserved some semblance of Marathi regional identity by their literary activities and their wholehearted support of the regional devotional religion. In saluting the older Marathi poet-saints, Ekanāth salutes the Brāhmaṇa Jñāneśvar as well as the tailor Nāmadev.[146] This shows the beginning of a new Marathi identity which cut across caste-lines, and the credit for helping the emergence of this identity must be given to the poet-saints of Maharashtra.

14. Beginning with Jñāneśvar we also see a dominant regional factor emerging in the religious life of Maharashtra. This was the devotional tradition of the Vārkarīs. These were normal Marathi folks from all walks of life who undertook the vow to visit (*vārī*) the God Viṭṭhal twice a year at Paṇḍharpur in the center of the Marathi speaking region. This God was essentially the same as Kṛṣṇa or Viṣṇu, and yet there was more to it. Viṭṭhal is said to have come to Paṇḍharpur to see his devotee Puṇḍalīk, and somehow Puṇḍalīk managed to get the Lord Viṭṭhal to stay there forever. Symbolically, the transregional Viṣṇu appeared in Paṇḍharpur for the benefit of his devotees in this region. Even the Marathi poet saints

acknowledge that Viṭṭhal was originally a God of the Kannada-speaking peoples, and that eventually he became the God of Maharashtra. Marathi poet-saints call Viṭṭhal by the term *kānaḍā*.[147] This may be understood in the light of S.B. Joshi's (1952) theory that Maharashtra was originally a Kannada-speaking region and that Marathi gradually displaced the Kannada language in this region. People from all over Maharashtra focussed their devotion on Viṭṭhal and this was, and still is, one of the most dominant factors unifying the Marathi population. This God was particularly significant for the Marathi-speaking peoples, in that they could approach Him in their own regional language and in their own regional ways of worship. On the face of it this may not appear significant, but we must see this in the context of the hieratic Brahmanical religion which did not allow any great importance to non-Brāhmaṇas, who were considered to be all Śūdras, and which accepted no language other than Sanskrit as divine. Thus the devotion of the Marathi poet-saints to God Viṭṭhal and their constant claims that they relate to Viṭṭhal in Marathi represented a threat to the Brahmanical orthodoxy of the region. How could Viṭṭhal talk to these "fallen" low-castes in their "fallen" Marathi language? This was a crucial theological question. The tradition has it that Lord Viṭṭhal helped his female devotee Janābāī grind grain, helped fetch water in the home of Ekanāth, rescued Dāmājīpant by assuming the form of an untouchable, ate food at the hands of Nāmadev, the tailer, and personally escorted Tukārām, the Śūdra, to heaven. These stories of miracles are historically as good as similar stories in other religions. However, even as claims, they represented a threat to the Brahmanical orthodoxy, which made every attempt to persecute these poet-saints. Like Ekanāth's Marathi *Bhāgavat*, Tukārām's poetic works in Marathi were also thrown into the river Indrāyaṇī by jealous Brāhmaṇas and were reportedly saved from drowning by Lord Viṭṭhal. These poet-saints in turn launched heavy attacks against the orthodox Brāhmaṇas in their poetry, and seem to have won the respect of the majority of the Maharashtrian population. Today they are worshipped by all the people of Maharashtra, non-Brāhmaṇas as well as Brāhmaṇas. Though these poet-saints could not completely destroy the bonds of the caste-system in the region, they indeed helped the Marathi population realize an inherent linguistic and religious unity beyond the divisions of caste. The impact of the poet-saints of Maharashtra on the Maharashtrian society has been discussed in detail by G.B. Sardar (1969).

15. While the poet-saints mentioned above prepared the ground by creating a feeling of Marathi linguistic and religious unity, they them-

selves could not generate a sense of political unity among the Hindus of Maharashtra, nor did they aim at such a political task. During the despotic rule of the Bahamanis, the Marathi people could not see any possibility of a Hindu political revival. Thus the poet-saints, by focussing on the benevolence of their God Viṭṭhal, provided the much needed consolation. This was necessary considering the severity of the anti-Hindu activities of the early fanatical Bahamani rulers.

However, Rāmadās (1608-1681 A.D.), the Brāhmaṇa poet-saint, added a political dimension to the earlier devotional unity. Rāmadās could not stand the wanton destruction of Hinduism at the hands of Muslims and with a desire to create a high degree of militancy in the regional religion he introduced the worship of the warrior God Rāma, another incarnation of God Viṣṇu. According to the epic Rāmāyaṇa, Rāma destroyed the demon-king Rāvaṇa who had troubled gods and sages. Reportedly Rāmadās influenced the young Śivājī, the son of a Maratha warrior who had been in the service of the Muslim ruler of Bijapur. Inspired by Rāmadās and his mother Jijābāī, Śivājī harbored the dream of establishing a Hindu kingdom in Maharashtra. Rāmadās's advice to Śivājī was quite explicit. Out of a mere region, he wanted Śivājī to build a nation. He advised Śivājī to unite all the Maratha people, i.e. the people of Maharashtra, and to try to re-establish the destroyed religion of Maharashtra (*mahārāṣṭra-dharma*).[148]

16. Śivājī (1627-1680 A.D.) followed Rāmadās's advice and gradually succeeded in creating a true "national" feeling in the region of Maharashtra. The core of this new nationality was the linguistic and cultural identity of Maharashtra which the earlier poet-saints had helped to build. Śivājī instilled a new political confidence among the Marathi-speaking people and they responded to his call with a show of strength. With a few exceptions, Śivājī succeeded in uniting the Marathi people and led a continuous fight against the Muslim rulers of the Deccan and the Mughals from the north. In 1676, Śivājī underwent the Hindu ritual of royal coronation. It is interesting to note that while his early correspondence shows only about 14.4 % Marathi words, the rest being Persian, his own correspondence after his coronation shows 66.2 % Marathi and / or Sanskrit words (Gramopadhye, 1941: 11). This de-persianization and re-Sanskritization is an indication of the drastic change in his own socio-linguistic identity. In this change, Śivājī led the region by officially supporting the regeneration of Hinduism in his kingdom (Bendrey, 1943: 64ff; Sardesai, 1957). The use of the term "nation" to refer to this particular phase of Maharashtra is at least as old as the middle of the

nineteenth century. The British editor of the Maratha ballads, Acworth remarked:[149] "It is something higher and nobler than a mere national impulse which his ballads evoke in the breast of a Maratha. ... They recall to him ... great historical deeds and figures which crowded round the nation's mightly development. ... But the fact is that the Maratha, differing herein from evey other native of India, has strong national feelings. ... He has the solid self-respect which true national feeling engenders." Acworth further concludes:[150] "The Marathas are a nation; and from the Brahmin to the Kunbi, they glory in the fact."

17. In this connection, we must mention certain limitations of the concept of "nation" as it developed during Śivājī's reign. This new nation was not a "nation" on the All-India level, but it was primarily restricted to the Marathi-speaking region. Thus, for instance, when Śivājī attacked Surat in Gujarat, he was not attacking the people of his own nation, but he was dealing with an enemy territory. With all respect for Śivājī, we need not make him to be a "nationalist" in the modern sense of the term "nation" in the nation-state of India.

In trying to become a legitimate Hindu king, he had to gain the support of the Brāhmaṇas. Reportedly, the Brāhmaṇas at his court brought with them their Brahmanical hieratic perspectives. Mahīpati, in his narrative on Rāmadās, tells us that the Paṇḍit Gāgābhaṭṭa, who performed Śivājī's coronation, advised him never to read the works of Rāmadās, because they were written in the "fallen" Marathi language (Abbott, 1932: 210ff). If such reports have any validity, this may signify that the orthodox Brāhmaṇas attempted to force a transregional or classical Brahmanical mould on Śivājī. This influence is seen in some of his titles such as "Protector of cows and Brāhmaṇas" (*go-brāhmaṇa-pratipālaka*). He successfully laid the foundation of the regional nationalism in Maharashtra. The later generations followed his ideas and ideals, and their successes and failures stem in part from the virtues and limitations of Śivājī's conception of Maratha nationalism.

18. After Śivājī's death, none of his successors proved to be of the same overall stature. During the reign of Śivājī's grandson Śāhu, the Konkanastha Brāhmaṇa Bāḷājī Viśvanāth was appointed the prime minister or Peshwa. Even Śivājī had Brāhmaṇa ministers and this was by itself not a new move as such. However, the Peshwas gradually became more dominant than the kings at Satara, and the real power shifted to Pune, the seat of the Peshwas. Under the Peshwas, the Maratha rule extended to large

territories in northern and southern India, and gradually the Marathas emerged as the most dominant All-India power. In a sense the British took over India from the Marathas rather than from the Mughals at Delhi, because the Mughals, in their final days, had already been subdeued by the Marathas. In this huge Maratha theatre of power, Marathi became the dominant language of diplomacy and the Brāhmaṇa dialect of Pune Marathi emerged as the standard Marathi language. Though the Marathas thus succeeded in establishing Hindu rule over vast areas of India, we must raise an important question. Did they succeed in creating a new nation in India on a territorial scale larger than the region of Maharashtra? Unfortunately, the answer to this question must be in the negative. Outside the Marathi-speaking region, the Marathas were mainly viewed as conquerers and rulers by the local populations and were not very often welcomed as liberators. The Marathas ruthlessly collected taxes from these non-Marathi regions. Thus the local population in non-Marathi regions was not always comfortable with Maratha rule, and there is sufficient evidence to show that they even hated the Marathas.[151] Several Marathi historians have pointed out this weakness of the Maratha empire as the cause of its rapid collapse.[152] The relations of the Maratha chiefs governing the outer parts of the Maratha empire with the central authority of the Peshwas at Pune were not always conducive to the creation of a nation out of this empire. On several occasions, these Maratha chiefs were at odds with the Peshwas and attacked and looted Pune.[153] Thus the feeling of Maratha nationality and pride remained largely confined to Marathi-speaking areas.

19. After the fall of the Peshwas in 1818, Mountstuart Elphinstone assumed power and was appointed the first governer of the Bombay Presidency. The British abolished the central authority of the Peshwas, but retained several of their chiefs as princes under British paramountcy. This had the immediate effect of destroying the center of Maratha nationalism. Further the Bombay Presidency included areas far larger than the Marathi-speaking region. While many of these areas were part of the Maratha empire in the earlier period, they were viewed merely as "gains". The Marathi language lost its political prestige and had almost no place in the educational system devised by the British for a long time. English had the most dominant place, and next came the classical language, Sanskrit. The Maharashtrian élites turned to English education primarily to gain employment with the British government of India and this employment placed them, along with other Indians, on a subordinate

level. They were deprived of the privilage of making decisions, and had to obey the decisions made for them by their "benevolent" British government. The English-educated Maharashtrian élites, particularly in the early part of the nineteenth century showed little interest in either Marathi or the regional culture, and Lord Macauley's Anglicist plan to produce natives who were Indian in blood and color but English in taste, in opinions and in morals was enforced in Maharashtra (Deshpande, 1979a: 85-89). Thus, as an early effect of the British rule, Maharashtra was stripped of its own identity as a nation and was reduced merely to a region within the British Indian empire.

20. During the last part of the nineteenth century, we see a renaissance of Marathi language and literature. During this period, Marathi begins to function as a weapon against the British government and there is also an upsurge of conflicts between social reformers and orthodox groups. Though Marathi as a language regained its vitality, the direction of the new political movement in the country initiated by the Indian National Congress was quite different from the earlier Marathi political ideas. The concept of "nation" advocated by the Indian National Congress was an All-India level concept in which all the regions were to share equally without any hierarchy among them. This concept of nation was quite different from the concept of nation developed by Śivājī or from the Maratha empire of the Peshwas. The older regional nationalisms had to be given up in order to build an All-India feeling of nationhood. This was a difficult task indeed and posed certain insurmountable problems for politicians in Maharashtra.

21. In order to create a feeling of anti-British self-confidence, leaders like Lokamānya ṬiḶak invoked the powerful memory of Śivājī and initiated the public celebration of his birthday. During such public celebrations, the Maharashtrian leaders of the Indian National Congress gave patriotic speeches and evoked the glories of the pre-British Maratha empire and of the couragous fights led by the Marathas to gain freedom from the Muslim foreigners. This was a politically powerful instrument to stir and provoke the people into anti-British demonstrations. However, this had its own problems, which were at least as significant as the benefits.

22. These were different times and the goals of the Indian National Congress were different from the goals of either Śivājī or the Peshwas. Evoking the memory of the victories of Śivājī against the "foreign"

Muslims did unite the Hindus of Maharashtra, but it obviously alienated the Muslims from the activities of the Indian National Congress. Though Śivājī considered Muslims in India to be "foreigners" who needed to be thrown out, this was no longer the case. The Indian National Congress was aiming at independence for all "Indians" and not just for the Hindus, and evoking past memories turned out to be detrimental. While many Hindu nationalists, particularly the followers of the Hindu Mahā Sabhā, equated the word "Indian" with the word "Hindu",[154] the Muslim leaders could accept that they were Indians, but they would not accept the equation of the word "Indian" with the word "Hindu". Thus, evoking past memories had the effect of uniting the Hindus against the British, but at the same time it divided the Hindus from the Muslims. It is not clear whether the leaders of the Indian National Congress were conscious of this development at the time this was happening. If the Muslims were to accept Śivājī as their "national" hero, would the Hindus agree to accept Aurangzeb also as their "national" hero? Elevating historical personalities like Śivājī to the All-India level created some other problems as well. The Hindus of Maharashtra could accept the exploits of Śivājī and the Peshwas outside the Marathi region as "glorious victories", but why would Indians outside Maharashtra, who often suffered heavily at the hands of the Marathas, accept these humiliating defeats as "glorious national victories"? Thus the historical conceptions of regional nationhood collided head on with the newly emerging concept of All-India nationhood. Using history for political inspiration posed dangers and the eventual hardening of the Muslim demand for the separate state of Pakistan must be viewed in the light of such historical developments.

23. The Indian National Congress, under Mahatma Gandhi's leadership, committed itself to the idea of linguistic states even before India became independent (J. Das Gupta, 1970: 36ff). The regional committees of the Indian National Congress were already organized on the basis of this concept. However, the magnitude of the problems that this conception involved did not become manifest to the leaders at that time, since the entire focus of the Congress movement was on gaining independence from the British. Many promises were made in those days for the sake of political expediency, e.g. that Hindustani would be made the national language of India, without the leaders themselves being fully aware of all the implications (J. Das Gupta, 1970: 36ff). After independence in 1947, the Prime Minister Jawaharlal Nehru kept his promise of reorganizing India into linguistic states and appointed a commission to study the

matter. This commission had to face untold problems because implementing the idea of linguistic states involved administrative partitioning of several regions which were until then part of the same unit. Border regions with bilingual populations posed particularly difficult problems.

24. In the case of Maharashtra, the commission was faced with the problem of what to do with the Bombay city. Though Bombay is situated in the Marathi-speaking region, in the city itself the Marathi population was just a little more than half, while there were large Gujarati and other minorities. The industry in Bombay was by and large in the hands of the Gujaratis and Marwaris, while the labor force was largely from Maharashtra. This posed a problem and finally the commission recommended that both Gujarat and Maharashtra should be put together into a single state. Moraraji Desai became the Chief Minister of this bilingual state in the fifties. As I have stated in the beginning of this paper, a series of organized linguistic riots and demonstrations broke out all over Maharashtra and Gujarat and dozens of people were killed in police gunfire. This movement for independent states for the Marathi-speaking and Gujarati-speaking regions made maximum use of the historical notion of regional nationalism and the name of Śivājī became commonplace as if he were himself fighting for this modern cause.[155] On May 1, 1960, the modern state of Maharashtra was born which included in itself the controversial Bombay city. The Committee for United Maharashtra kept on demonstrating for a while for the inclusion of border towns like Belgaon in Maharashtra, but these demonstrations have been largely unsuccessful. A wave of similar demonstrations showing the same form of regional nationalism swept the region before Goa was "liberated" by the Indian army. The debate over whether Konkani is a dialect of Marathi or is a separate language became a part of political struggle between those who wanted Goa to become part of Maharashtra and those who wanted it to remain separate. Again twisted versions of history were profusely used during these political campaigns.

25. In general, in India today, the question of region and nation is a complex question. The different linguistic states represent not only different administrative regions but they stand for different regional nations. Over and above these regional nationalities exists the newly fostered All-India nationality. While the regional nationalities are more strongly rooted in shared language and common history, the All-India nationality is a matter of the integration and compromise of these regional

nationalities. Today there are at least two distinct levels of nationality in India. The All-India nationality is not really a merger of regional nationalities, but a compromise accepted by the regional nationalities. These two levels of nationality function in different ways at different times. The separatist movements in Punjab, Kashmir and other parts show a tendency on the part of some segments to dissociate from the All-India nationality completely and to promote the region itself as a separate nation-state. On the other hand, the experience in Maharashtra is somewhat different. Even the regionalist party Śivasenā which controls the Bombay city and is making steady inroads into the rest of the state shows no anti-India tendencies. Its slogans show the order of their priorities: *Jai Hind, Jai Mahārāṣṭra.* In these slogans, India comes first and then comes Maharashtra. The stability of India depends on the maintenance of the balance between these different levels of nationality.

VIII

GENESIS OF ṚGVEDIC RETROFLEXION: A HISTORICAL AND SOCIOLINGUISTIC INVESTIGATION

> The text of the *Ṛgveda*, there is reson to suppose, is not quite the same as it was originally. Some *Sūkta*s and *Ṛk*s are found in the other Vedas, and the readings in some cases are different. What the original readings were, will have to be determined, if at all possible, by comparing the variation and taking a good many other facts into consideration. The way has been shown by Oldenberg, and it is quite open to any of us to follow it.
>
> Sir R.G. Bhandarkar
> *Collected Works*, Vol. I, p. 398.

Summary

1) A Perspective on the Problem
2) Plurality of Ṛgvedic Recensions
3) Recensional Variation: An Epistemological Problem
4) *Aitareya-Āraṇyaka* (3.2.6): Its Implications
5) Pre-Ṛgvedic Aryan-Non-Aryan Bilingualism?
6) Emergence of Retroflexion in Prehistoric Indo-Aryan
7) *Brāhmīkaraṇa*: A Gradual Transformation
8) Retroflexion and the Development of the Brāhmī Script
9) Instability of Post-Vedic Retroflexion
10) Irregular Retroflexion in the Vedic Recensions
11) Retroflexion in the *Prātiśākhya*s
12) Aspects of Dravidian Influence on Indo-Aryan
13) Problems in the Reconstruction of the Ur-*Ṛgveda*
14) Other Instances of Alleged Dravidian Influence
15) Conclusions

1. Introduction

1.1. Most modern scholars, if not all, accept that retroflex consonants already appear in the *Ṛgveda* and are seen increasingly in Middle Indo-Aryan. The question for most of these scholars is not whether there is retroflexion in the *Ṛgveda*, but how one is to explain its undisputed presence there. In this chapter, I would like to deal with the prior question: Was there any retroflexion in the Ur-*Ṛgveda*? If there was no retroflexion in the Ur-*Ṛgveda*, how is it that the text of the *Ṛgveda* as we now have it has retroflexion? Before I deal with this question, however, it is important to survey existing views on the question of Ṛgvedic retroflexion.

For some, retroflexion is an independent "well-motivated" process that began in pre-Vedic Indo-Aryan. Others argue that retroflexion in Indo-Aryan is a result of contacts with Dravidians and/or Mundas, and that such influential contacts must have occurred in pre-Vedic times. Bloch (1965: 325) says: "As to the distinction between dentals and cerebrals we have seen that it depends on the adaptation and crystallization of a series of alterations due at first to the action of the pre-historic Aryan *sh* sounds." But he does place a good deal of emphasis on the adaptational aspect of this phenomenon: "The Indo-Aryan innovation is best explained in terms of the use of the two classes in the indigenous languages. This is without doubt the most decisive fact in deciding the earliest Sanskrit texts to be purely Indian" (1965: 56).

1.2. While Katre (1944: 129) thinks that "the action of either Dravidian or Munda substratum is subordinate to the action of the Indo-Aryan" itself, other scholars tend to place equal, if not more, emphasis on the "action of the substratum". Such a trend has been developed in the recent work of Kuiper and Emeneau. Emeneau outlines his main thesis as follows: "The fact, however, that the later in Indo-Aryan linguistic history we go, the greater is the incidence of retroflex consonants and the further fact that most of the Dravidian languages and the proto-Dravidian itself have this type of consonant in abundance, can only lead to the conclusion that the later Indo-Aryan developements are due to a borrowing of indigenous speech habits through bilingualism, and to the well-grounded suspicion that even the early development of retroflexes from certain Indo-European consonant clusters results from the same historic cause."[136] Even if "well-grounded", the theory is still a matter of "suspicion" as far as the early stages of Indo-Aryan are concerned. Kuiper

(1967: 90) raises some important historical-theoretical questions concerning Emeneau's "well-grounded suspicior", but finally accepts it.

1.3. Kuiper points out that there are retroflexes in the *Ṛgveda* which are reflexes of certain Indo-European consonantal clusters, and that there are also some retroflexes in a small number of words of "evidently foreign origin", and explains the contribution of these retroflexed foreign words to the development of retroflexion in Vedic Sanskrit as follows: "It may seem natural to assume that in the same way, pre-historic Indo-Aryan, bilingual speakers who recognized a phonemic contrast between dentals and retroflexes in the foreign language, came to interpret the allophones of proto-Indo-Aryan in terms of the foreign phonetic system. The loanwords with retroflexes which - at least in my interpretation of Ṛgvedic evidence - they must have introduced into Indo-Aryan may have contributed considerably to the spread of this novel phonemic distinction among the speakers of early Indo-Aryan" (1967: 89-90). Kuiper agrees with Emeneau in concluding that pre-Dravidian and pre-Indo-Aryan bilingualism provided conditions which allowed pre-Indo-Aryan allophones to be redistributed as retroflex phonemes. But the fact that there are already retroflexes in the present text of the *Ṛgveda* prompted Kuiper (1967: 97) to derive a "historical implication that the period between the arrival of the Indo-Aryans in the subcontinent and the composition of the oldest Vedic hymns must have been much longer than was previously thought." He also refers to the difference between the "older and more recent" parts of the Ṛgveda to explain the gradual increase in the occurrence of these "innovations of Indo-Aryan" (1967: 93). Relying on the existence of retroflexion and non-Aryan loanwords in the *Ṛgveda* and on the fact that the Dāsas and Dasyus of the *Ṛgveda* are known to the Iranians as Dāhae and Dahyu, Chatterji (1951: 159) claims that the Aryans "did not find any appreciable difference in the non-Aryan people they encountered in India from the non-Aryan people they knew in Eastern Iran. It is also equally likely that racial and cultural fusion (including linguistic influencing) had commenced between the Aryans and the Dāsa-Dasyu people outside the soil of India itself - in Iran in all likelihood."

1.4. Emeneau (1974: 92) refers to Kuiper (1967) and says that this article "spelled out some of the theoretical and chronological implications of the occurrence of retroflex consonants ... in the Ṛgveda, including other matters, that we must accept pre-Dravidian influence upon pre-Indo-

Aryan to explain these full-fledged Ṛgvedic occurrences." The surveys of previous work in Southworth and Apte (1974) and Hock (1975) show that few scholars have doubted the existence of retroflexion in the *Ṛgveda*. Therefore, it is no wonder that Southworth and Apte (1974: 14) remark: "The close contact and wide-spread bilingualism among Indo-Aryan and Dravidian speaking groups in the Vedic period seems well-established by the evidence presented by Kuiper and Emeneau."

Turner has discussed the problem of retroflexion in Indo-Aryan at some length. He takes for granted the existence of retroflexion in the *Ṛgveda*, and also partly seems to favor the substratum argument (Turner, 1975: 226, 240-41, 244, 365). Turner (1924) makes an important distinction between "common Indo-Aryan cerebralization" and "dialectal cerebralization", and tries to reconstruct "the history of the chief waves of cerebralization". Though Turner does not look at the existing Vedic retroflexion as a result of successive modifications of a given oral text under the influence of these waves of cerebralization, he does show that cerebralization is not a monolithic event in the history of Indo-Aryan. He thinks that retroflexion in Indo-Aryan is a combined result of the influence of the Dravidian substratum and of a tendency inherent in Indo-Aryan. According to Grammont (*Mémoires de la Société de Linguistique de Paris*, Vol. 19, pp. 254, 267, 277), the origin of cerebralization in Indo-Aryan must be attributed to a general tendency in Indo-Aryan to relax the pronunciation in favor of articulation in the neighborhood of the palatal arch, a general tendency which, he thinks, is also responsible for other sound changes in Indo-Aryan. One can certainly question the origin of such a tendency in Indo-Aryan. Is it a genetic development within a branch of Indo-European? If so, why is it so unique? Is it possible that the origin of such a tendency lies somewhere in the influence of India as a linguistic area? These are important, but as yet unanswered, questions. Ivanov and Toporov (1968: 48-49) offer some interesting diachronic remarks on Sanskrit retroflexion, but their discussion is by no means conclusive.

1.5. So far I have presented the "other side". In the present chapter I aim to shake up the strong conviction that retroflex consonants form part of the original *Ṛgveda* and to show that they were most probably not a "full-fledged Ṛgvedic occurrence". What was acquired during the long process of pre-redactional oral transmission has been ascribed by most scholars to the original compositions of the *Ṛgveda*. The Ṛgvedic evidence produced by these scholars is clearly from only one of the postredactional versions of the *Ṛgveda* and is not sufficient to let us draw directly any conclusions concerning the original compositions of the *Ṛgveda*. Along with these scholars, I had myself accepted the occurrence of retroflex consonants in the *Ṛgveda* and had used it as an argument in some of my previous work (Deshpande, 1975c: 207). However, since then I have come to different conclusions. Though I realize fully that I cannot prove my case beyond the shadow of a doubt and that I cannot produce evidence from those lost original texts of the *Ṛgveda*, I hope that my arguments are sufficient to raise serious doubts concerning the existence of retroflex phonemes in the Ur-*Ṛgveda*, if not to prove their nonexistence.

1.6. My conclusions, though unorthodox, are by no means entirely new. Grierson (1929) has given a fascinating account of how the Kashmiri text of *Lallā-vākyāni*, originally composed in the latter half of the fourteenth century has been preserved orally to the present day without ever having been written down. Grierson (1929: 74) points out that "save for a few forms that have remained unchanged ... verses are in what is practically modern Kashmiri." However, the text of the *Mahānayaprakāśa* was composed in the fifteenth century and was written down at the time it was composed, and hence its language is preserved without any further change. Grierson describes the "unconscious" change taking place in a precodification oral tradition: "Each hymn [of *Lallā-vākyāni*] was handed down from teacher to pupil through five centuries, care being taken to preserve the text unchanged. But during all this time the languge was insensibly changing, and, as there was no written record of the originals in the form in which they were first uttered, the language of the hymns insensibly changed at the same time. The reciters, it is hardly necessary to point out, were unaware of the change of language that was going on. In each generation that was very slight, and was not noticeable, but the total of the changes at the end of five centuries was very great indeed. ... It was so gradual that no one was ever aware that any change was taking place at all" (1929: 75). Grierson clearly perceived that the same must have happened in the case of the Vedic texts before they were codified by the redactors. He says: "Unfortunately, for the Veda, we have nothing corresponding to the *Mahānayaprakāśa*, i.e. nothing written, and fixed in writing, at about the time that the oldest Vedic hymns were composed, so that we are unable to gauge the difference between the original form of the hymns and the form given to us by the Vyāsa (i.e. the redactor); but the parallel case of the *Mahānayaprakāśa*, is instructive, and shows us that the difference must have been great. In other words, the *Ṛgvada*, as we have it now, is couched in a modernized form of the language in which the oldest hymns were originally composed" (1929: 76-77).

2. Plurality of Ṛgvedic Recensions

2.1. In most recent discussions, a historical fact of utmost importance is often overlooked, namely that the text of the *Ṛgveda* that we have today is not necessarily the original *Ṛgveda.* What we have is only one recension (*saṃhitā*) of the *Ṛgveda* compiled several centuries after the hymns were composed by the Ṛgvedic sages. After the hymns were composed over a period of several generations of sages, they remained for a long time as a kind of floating oral literature preserved through family traditions. At a later time, about 700-800 B.C., several compilers or editors collected these hymns, arranged them according to certain principles, and prepared various editions, along with corresponding "word-by-word texts" (*pada-pāṭha*) by analyzing the words of the orally preserved hymns. The available recension of the *Ṛgveda* is ascribed to the compiler-sage Śākalya and his school. Śākalya is quoted by Pāṇini (8.3.19, 6.1.128, and 1.1.16), the *Ṛgvedaprātiśākhya* (1.16, 1.19, 2.44, 3.7, 3.13, 4.2, 4.5, 6.7-8, 11.10-11, 11.31, and 13.12), and texts such as the *Aitareya-Āraṇyaka* (3.1.1, 3.2.1, and 3.2.6) and *Śāṅkhāyana-Āraṇyaka* (7.3, 7.16, and 8.1-2), and could not possibly have been a mythical figure.

2.2. Other recensions of the *Ṛgveda* did exist but are lost today. We hear of the Bāṣkala recension which had a few more hymns than Śākalya's recension. The *Ṛgvedaprātiśākhya* and the *Śaiśirīya-Śikṣā* belong to the Śaiśirīya recension (*RPR, Vargadvaya,* verse 7). Having studied the treatment of *Abhinihita Sandhi* in the *Ṛgveda* and in the *Ṛgvedaprātiśākhya* by Śaunaka, Rastogi (1957: 29) suspects that "possibly Śaunaka had a text before him which was not totally identical to the extant one." The *Śāṅkhāyana-Āraṇyaka* belongs to the Śāṅkhāyana tradition. There are a few mantras in this text which cannot be traced to Śākalya's recension and belong most probably to the Śāṅkhāyana recension of the *Ṛgveda.*[157] The *Aitareya* and *Śāṅkhāyana-Āraṇyakas* refer to the Māṇḍūkeya recension which preceded Śākalya's recension and differed from it in certain respects.[158] Patañjali speaks of the well made recension (*sukṛtā saṃhitā*) of Śākalya, but also says that there are twenty-one different recensions of the *Ṛgveda* (MB, (M), Vol. I, Sec. I, pp. 54, 292-93). Pointing to a hymn of three verses and three verses of three other hymns which do not have their *pada-pāṭha* prepared by Śākalya, Ghosh (1951: 231) claims that "hymns and verses could have been added to the *Ṛk-saṃhitā* even after the date of Śākalya." We also know of other redactors of the *Ṛgveda* such as Rathītara (Śākapūṇi) and Bharadvāja Bāṣkali (B. Bhattacharya, 1958: 12).

2.3. Several Indologists have expressed doubts as to the originality of the present text of the *Ṛgveda.* Bloch (1970: 1-2) remarks: "The editors of the *Ṛgveda,* as we have it, have partially adapted to their own dialects various religious texts composed in another dialect." Oldenberg (1962: 28) acknowledges that "the study of Śaunaka's work [that is, the *Rgvedaprātiśākhya*] affords us the proof that *from that time on* [author's emphasis] the Vedic hymns, protected by the united care of grammatical and religious respect for letters, have suffered no further appreciable corruptions." However, worth noting are his comments on the preredaction textual transmission: "In some cases, isolated details of the additions of prior epochs were caught and clung to with felicitous acumen; in others, no hesitation was had in wiping out of existence entire domains of old and genuine phenomena to suit half-correct theories, so that the most patient ingenuity of modern science will only be able to restore in part what has been lost" (1962: 27). Oldenberg (1962: 26) reminds us that "the collection was re-corrected on repeated occasions. It is conceivable enough that thus the original structure, yes, even the existence itself of special hymns was often injured, effaced, or destroyed." Basing his conclusions on metrical evidence, Macdonell (1916: 14) inferred that there must have been a period of transition between the original composition and the final redaction of the *Ṛgveda* by Śākalya. Meillet (1912-13) has discussed the changes effected by the editors of the *Ṛgveda* with respect to *h* (—> *bh* and *dh*) and *r* (—> *l*) in accordance with their dialect which preserved the distinction between Indo-European *r* and *l*.[159] Bloch (1970: 2) rightly observes that the editors "could not, however, touch the grammatical forms without seriously modifying the aspect of the religious language borrowed by them." *Thus, most of the changes which occurred during the early natural oral transmission were euphonic and phonetic and were mostly unconscious changes, not deliberate alterations.* Recently, Esteller has devoted a number of publications to the question of the reconstruction of the original *Ṛgveda.*[160] He calls the text of Śākalya a "palimpsest", a written-over text, and remarks: "The bamboo-curtain of a *Ṛgveda-Saṃhitā* palimpsest was woven twenty-five centuries ago by the skillful and well-meaning but deformingly reforming, updatingly defacing (and thus palimpsesting) paṇḍita-mentality of the Saṃhitākāra agency in the *Śākala-śākhā* tradition" (1968: 16; 1969: 17). It is quite natural that not every scholar would agree with Esteller, for example Abhyankar (1969). Particularly when he alleges that the redacters made "conscious" grammatical changes and changes in the word order, etc., we must reject his views. For a comprehensive critique of Esteller's theories, see Mehendale (1975).

3. Recensional Variation: An Epistemological Problem

3.1. We must, at this stage, face up to certain important epistemological questions. It must be said that all our knowledge about the *Ṛgveda* rests primarily on the recension of Śākalya as we have it preserved today. To what extent can we say that Śākalya's text exactly represents the phonology of the original *Ṛgveda*?

Let us consider a simple example. The *Ṛgveda* as we have it changes intervocalic *ḍ* and *ḍh* into *Ḷ* and *Ḷh*. The retroflex *Ḷ* is not known to the classical Sanskrit. Many scholars have considered *Ḷ* as forming a genuine part of the original *Ṛgveda*. However, Bloch (1970: 156), with his characteristic caution, says: "Does it go back directly to the Vedic language? We dare not affirm it." Concerning the *l/Ḷ* variation in Prakrits, he remarks: "Paiśācī is the only dialect which is shown as normaly converting the intervocalic Skt. *l* into *Ḷ*. But it should also be noted that the rules concerning the same date from Hemacandra, that is to say from a very late epoch. The texts, written in other dialects, do not have a uniform sign. Thus, as could be expected, the meridional manuscripts have *Ḷ*, while those of the North keep *l*" (1970: 154). Burrow (1971: 556) refers to the continuation of *Ḷ* into Pāli. However, that also could very well be a result of Dravidian influence on the Sinhalese text-transmission of Pāli, and we do not know whether the "Indian Pāli" had this sound before being transported to Ceylon. In this connection, then, it is important to note Vaidya's remarks concerning the text-transmission of the *Ṛgveda* as we know it. He points out that the Ṛgvedic Brāhmaṇas at present are to be chiefly met with in the Deccan and the Koṅkaṇ and in some parts of southern India. The *Ṛgveda* is the most important and the oldest of all the Vedas, and yet its adherents are so few and found only to the south of the Vindhyas. Vaidya (1930: 56) attributes the existence of the retroflex sounds *Ḷ* and *Ḷh* in the present text of the *Ṛgveda* to this predominantly southern (or rather Dravidian) tradition of oral transmission and suggests that these sounds "are not to be found in the recitation of the Black Yajurveda and probably not in the recitation of the other Śākhās of the Ṛgveda itself now extinct." I value Vaidya's remarks more as a caution. I shall try to show later that substitution of the sounds *Ḷ* and *Ḷh* in the available recension of the *Ṛgveda* for intervocalic *ḍ* and *ḍh* originated most probably in the oral traditions in northeastern India and did not exist in the Ur-*Ṛgveda.*

3.2. How far can we say that the distribution of retroflex sounds and their statistics in the Śākalya text represent the reality of the original *Ṛgveda*? Let us consider the example of different recensions of the Yajurveda which are fortunately available to us. As Hoffmann (1960: 176-77) shows, the Maitrāyaṇī text has the reading *páṇyāt páṇyatarā*, while the Kāṭhaka text reads *pányāt pányatarā.* One may note that the Kāṭhaka text itself has *páṇyāt páṇyatarā* besides *pányāt pányatarā* without cerebrals (Bloomfield and Edgerton: *Vedic Variants*, Vol. 2, p. 87). This helps us realize that in a chaste epistemology we must begin with all these variant readings of different recensions and then reconstruct the original reading as best as we can. The important point is that the original - preredactional original - is not given to us but must be reconstructed from what is given to us. After comparing a few passages from the Kāṭhaka, Kapiṣṭhala-Kaṭha and Maitrāyaṇī recensions, Kuiper (1958: 350) concludes: "The parallel texts [Kāṭhaka and Kapiṣṭhala-Kaṭha] leave no doubt that *krūḍayati* is a variant of the rather rare verb *kūḍayati* or *kūḶayati*, for which the Maitrāyaṇī version has substituted the current synonym *vidahati.*" This example brings forth various different issues. We not only have phonological alternation, but occasionally a recension subsitutes a "current synonym" for an archaic expression. By the same token, it is perfectly logical to argue that after a lapse of several hundred years, the received product of the precodification oral tradition may exibit rather more "current" phonological features.

3.3. Comparing the identical hymns in the Śaunakīya and the Paippalāda recensions of the *Atharvaveda*, one finds the same principle of recensional variation:[161]

1. *tanvo adya dadhātu me* (*Ś-AV*, 1.1.1)
2. *tanvāmadhyā dadhātu me* (*P-AV*, 1.6.1)
3. *vidmo ṣvasya mātaram* (*Ś-AV*, 1.2.1)
4. *vidmo hyasya mātaram* (*P-AV*, 1.3.1)
5. *apo devīrupa hvaye* (*Ś-AV*, 1.4.3)
6. *apo devīrupa bruve* (*P-AV*, 1.2.3)

Thus, we cannot consider either of the two recensions as automatically representing the original *Atharvaveda*. With respect to this variation, Acharya (1971: 97) says: "As has been rightly pointed out by Hoffmann (*IIJ*, XI, 1968, pp. 1-10), these variations should be regarded as authentic in as much as they are taken to form the peculiarities of the particular *śākhā* to which they belong." Quite instructive is Edgerton's (1936: 507-8) discussion of the two recensions of the *Saddharmapuṇḍarīka*.

3.4. Coming back to the *Ṛgveda*, we have the biggest hurdle to overcome. The fact that one recension is all that we have creates an illusion that this is THE *Ṛgveda*. However, even the existing exegetical literature on the *Ṛgveda* indicates that there must have been serious differences in various text-traditions. Apart from differences in wording (as we have seen in the two recensions of the *Atharvaveda*), the different recensions and oral traditions must have differed in the pronunciations of sounds, too. Uvaṭa, the commentator of the *Ṛgvedaprātiśākhya*, says that while some traditions pronounced an anusvāra in the sequence *māṃścatve*, other traditions pronounced a nasal vowel, i.e., *mā̃ścatve*.[162] As I have discussed elsewhere, the *anusvāra* varied from a voiced consonant-or-vowel pronunciation to an unvoiced nasal spirant according to the testimony of the *Ṛgvedaprātiśākhya* itself.[163] The *Ṛgvedaprātiśākhya* (13.15-16) refers to the variation in the pronunciation of the diphthongs *e*, *o*, *ai* and *au* in the different schools of reciters.[164] It is extremely important to note that the so-called dental series *t*, *th*, *d*, *dh*, *n* is in fact *danta-mūlīya* 'produced at the roots of the teeth' or alveolar, according to the *Ṛgvedaprātiśākhya* (1.9), while for most other known traditions, including Pāṇini, these are dental (*dantya*) sounds. The *Prātiśākhya*s vary on the pronunciation of *r*, *ṛ*, the *k*-series and several other sounds. It may be noted that the *Ṛgvedaprātiśākhya* (1.11) quotes the view of Vedamitra that *ḍ* and *ḍh* were in fact palato-velars (*jihvā-mūlaṃ tālu ca*) and not retroflexes.[165] This brings these sounds closer to the Iranian *zd* and *zdh*. The more we study these variations, the more ignorance we must confess concerning our knowledge of the exact original sound system of the Vedic texts. In terms of our epistemology, whatever Vedic literature is given to us is already in the form of various sectarian recensions of a relatively late period, a period in which variation of pronunciation existed among different regions and different Vedic schools. We do not have a presectarian recension of any of the Vedic texts, let alone the prerecensional original compositions of the Vedic poets.

3.5. The strength of retroflexion in Indo-Aryan has always varied in different periods of Indian linguistic history and in different regional and social dialects. Based on a study of modern Indian languages, Southworth (1974: 211-12) concludes that the strength of retroflexion was greater in the northwest and in the South and that it was weaker in the northeastern regions. However, that may not have been the case for all periods of Indian linguistic history. Patañjali shows that the local Prakrit had words like *goṇī, yarvāṇa, tarvāṇa, āṇapayati, diṇṇa*, etc. for the Sanskrit words *gauḥ, yad vā naḥ, tad vā naḥ, ājñāpayati*, and *datta.*[166] These are examples from the eastern part of the country during the immediate post-Mauryan period. Looking at the Aśokan inscriptions, one finds that the eastern region shows a higher frequency of cerebrals as compared to the western region. Bloch (1970: 6) points out that *r* plus dental gives a dental in the west, and a cerebral in the east, but while we find "*ṇ* in the west, in the east there is no cerebral *ṇ* nor a palatal *ñ*." This is confirmed by the extensive work of Mehendale, who says: "The dentals under the influence of *r* or *ṛ* are cerebralised in all inscriptions of Aśoka, save those in the West (only *rdh* is cerebralised so early as that in the West). The influence is observed in the West mostly from the beginning of the Christian era. The dentals *t* and *th* in combination with *ṣ* are, however, cerebralized at all places since the earliest times" (1948: xxiii); and, "It will be observed that the Western dialect is the least affected by cerebralisation" (1948: 18).

3.6. Even within the same region of northwestern India, there were variations. Thus, while the Prakrit Dhammapada knows the distinction between *n* and *ṇ*, Konow (1936: 607) remarks: "It is, however, remarkable that the Kurram casket inscription which contains a quotation of a canonical passage written in practically the same language as Dhp. [i.e., Dharmapada], has no trace of the Dhp. distinction between *n* and *ṇ*. We are left with the impression that Dhp. in this respect represents a normalization which may be due to the influence of another literary Prakrit, or belongs to a limited territory within the area, where the treatment of *n* was different." While the Aśokan inscriptions do show regional variation in the strength of retroflexion, one may contrast the treatment of literary Prakrits by the Prakrit grammarians. The cerebralization of dentals under the influence of *r, ṛ* or a sibilant is noticed by the grammarians as a feature common to all Prakrits, without any dialectal variation (Mehendale, 1948: xxxi).

3.7. Very often the orthography of documents is misleading. With respect to literary Prakrits, Ghatage (1941: 23) points out: "By a convention the editors write *ṇ* everywhere in purely Mahārāṣṭrī works. But the practice of the Jaina scribes to write initially *n* is followed in editing works in AMg [i.e., Ardhamāgadhī] and Jain Mahārāṣṭrī. It has been suggested that initial *n* became alveolar and was felt by some as dental and by others as cerebral." In the Kharoṣṭhī inscriptions "*n* is cerebralised both initially and medially ... *n* is also preserved in many cases" (Mehendale, 1948: 304). With respect to this variation, Konow (1929: ciii-civ) writes: "The impression left by this state of affairs is that intervocalic *ṇ* and *n* had the same sound, at least over the great part of the territory, and that the sound was probably a cerebral. The significance of the two letters was consequently lost sight of, the traditional writing acting as a check on the development of a consistent orthography." This is quite comparable to Grierson's (1906: 18) remarks on the modern Paiśācī languages: "Cerebral and dental mutes appear to be interchangeable ... So far as I can ascertain ... there is no real distinction between these two classes of mutes, and there is only one class ... a semi-cerebral ... To some, these sounds appeared to be dentals and were recorded as such; and to others they appeared to be cerebrals and were recorded as such. ... Identical words are quite frequently recorded with cerebral letters by one and with dental letters by the other."

3.8. Along with these perceptual and orthographic problems, we must also bear in mind certain other difficulties. We find that one passage of *Samayasāra* has the reading *hodi* (<— *bhavati*), while the other has *havadi.*[167] The meter is not affected by either reading. This is also true of retaining or dropping the intervocalic voiced stops and of inserting or not inserting the euphonic weak *y*. For example, while the printed text of Kundakunda's *Pañcāstikāya* (verse 49) reads *egattappasādhagam* (<— *ekatvaprasādhakam*), the commentary *Tātparyavṛtti* of Jayasenācārya has the reading *eyattapasāhagam.* The morphology of the two readings is the same, but they represent two different phonological states. Similar other variants are: text *pagāsagā*, commentary *payāsagā* (verse 51); text *padhāṇā*, commentary *pahāṇā* (verse 53); text *hoi*, commentary *havadi* (verse 54); text *bhaṇidam*, commentary *bhaṇiyam* (verse 54).[168] These are variations of the same text. These are all phonological variations of the kind which does not seriously affect the morphological or the syntactic content of the text or its metrical form, and hence they seem to have been tolerated with ease by the reciters, scribes, and readers. But this creates an intolerable situation for a critical historical understanding of what the exact phonology of the original text might have been, and such a picture of the original phonology often remains a matter for scholastic reconstruction. What is important is the fact that such variations as those mentioned above did exist and were treated as a matter of little concern, and were not normally viewed as seriously altering the basic text.

3.9. In the oral transmission of Vedic texts, there are two important historical periods. The first is the period of their composition and scattered retention by the early Vedic families. This is a "natural" period of oral transmission. The second is the scholastic period of recension-making and also of the growing formalism concerning the magical potency of the exact pronunciation. The text of the Vedic compositions must have been quite fluid, in both the synchronic and diachronic sense, in the prerecensional oral traditions. Otherwise we would not be able to explain the vast differences between the various recensions of Vedic texts. But the post-recensional period of oral transmission must be clearly distinguished from this early fluid state. In this later period, monumental intellectual efforts have been made to preserve the recensions in tact in the form given them by the various sectarian schools. These schools devised meticulous methods of oral recitation like the *pada-pāṭha* and textual permutation-combinations (*vikṛti-pāṭha*). Particular sectarian phonetic treatises (= *Prātiśākhyas* and *Śikṣās*) were written to "freeze" the then existing sectarian pronunciation. These traditions of formal recitation have been kept up until recent times, and they maintained an "idealized text" more or less intact. I call it an idealized text because, in fact, the pronunciation of the same Vedic text in Kashmir, Bengal, and Tamilnadu was never exactly the same. Regional variation in Sanskrit pronunciation has been ably described by Chatterji (1960a). I shall take up the concept of fluidity of the preredactional oral traditions later in detail.

4. *Aitareya-Āraṇyaka* (3.2.6): Its Implications

4.1. Scholars who have attempted reconstructions of the original *Ṛgveda* have not paid enough attention to discussions of the various redactors and editors of the *Ṛgveda* found in the *Aitareya* and *Śāṅkhāyana-Āraṇyakas*. Though it is true that many of these discussions on the notion of *saṃhitā* are somewhat mystical and mythological, there still are a very significant number of linguistic discussions. The participants in these discussions, such as Śūravīra Māṇḍūkeya, Hrasva Māṇḍūkeya, Mākṣavya, Śākalya, and others, represent the first generation of scientific linguistic thinkers who are quoted directly as respected authorities by the *Prātiśākhyas* and by Pāṇini. Below we shall examine certain passages related to the question of retroflexion found in these texts.

4.2. How far are the retroflexes in the existing *Ṛgveda* historically authentic? In my view, they are authentic only in that they represent the sounds in the text as it was preserved in the Śākala school at the time of the formation of this particular recension. Beyond this point we are entering the field of reconstruction. If we know that at a certain point there had been doubts and differences concerning Ṛgvedic retroflexion, then we should be less categorical about ascribing retroflexion existing in the present text to the original. Such an indication is to be found in the *Aitareya-Āraṇyaka* (3.2.6):

> Now Kṛṣṇahārīta proclaims this secret doctrine, as it were, regarding speech to him. Prajāpati, the year, after creating creatures, burst. He put himself together by means of the meters, therefore it is the *saṃhitā*. Of that *saṃhitā* the letter *ṇ* is the strength, the letter *ṣ* the breath, the self. He who knows the *saṃhitā* and the letters *ṇ* and *ṣ*, he knows the *saṃhitā* with its breath and its strength ... If he is in doubt whether to say it with an *ṇ* or without an *ṇ*, let him say it with an *ṇ*. If he is in doubt whether to say it with an *ṣ* or without an *ṣ*, let him say it with an *ṣ*. . . . Hrasva Māṇḍūkeya says: "If we repeat the verses according to the *Saṃhitā*, and if we recite (according to) the teaching of Māṇḍūkeya, then the letters *ṇ* and *ṣ* are obtained for us". . . . Sthavira Śākalya says: "If we repeat the verses according to the *Saṃhitā*, and if we recite (according to) the teaching of Māṇḍūkeya, then the letters *ṇ* and *ṣ* are obtained for us".

This is an extremely important passage. Regarding the doctrine, which is repeated twice, Keith (1909: 257, fn. 9) comments: "The sayings are identical and apparently this is intended to denote that the doctrine received universal acceptance." I do not quite agree with Keith's interpretation. The passage does indeed emphasize and preach the doctrine of *ṇ* and *ṣ*, but it also implies at the same time that there were others who did not accept this doctrine and doubted the correctness of this practice.

4.3. The word *saṃhitā* could theoretically mean either a *sandhi* "joint, euphonic combination, juncture", or it could mean the whole "continuous, undivided" text, as contrasted with the later scholastic *pada-pāṭha*.

If the word *saṃhitā* refers only to the "joints", then the passage would refer only to *ṇ* and *ṣ* produced at the joints or boundaries of contiguous words. This would imply that while Śākalya and Māṇḍūkeya recensions read *mo ṣu ṇaḥ* (<— *mā* + *u* + *su* + *naḥ*), there were other traditions which doubted the existence of *ṇ* and *ṣ* in such cases and perhaps read **mo su naḥ*. However, in this interpretation of *saṃhitā*, the dispute would not refer to those instances of *ṇ* and *ṣ* which are in some sense "internal" or intrinsic to the words and do not depend on word junctures. However, whether internal or external, the sounds *ṇ* and *ṣ* in the present *Ṛgveda* passage *mo ṣu ṇaḥ* and in words like *viṣṇave* or *vidatheṣu* are produced by the same basic historical rules which cover both the internal and external sandhi. The word *saṃhitā* is frequently used for "whole" texts, and we know that Śākalya and Māṇḍūkeya collected these "continuous texts" and then subjected them to a scholastic analysis. The analytical "word-by-word text" (*pada-pāṭha*) was not given by the early oral tradition. The creation of the "word-text" is the very first attempt to analyze and explain the orally received texts. As I shall demonstrate later, during the preredaction period, these Vedic texts were passed down as unanalyzed sequences and were split into words later by scholars like Śākalya. But the historically significant fact that different redactors disagreed even on the words in a given sequence clearly indicates the manner in which these "continuous texts" were transmitted. Many phonetic changes took place in these continuous sequences at a time when there was no clear awareness of word boundaries, and hence the distinction between "internal" and "external" is somewhat irrelevant with respect to the pre-*pada-pāṭha* oral transmission. For instance, it seems that the original sequence **āpṛṇosi* diverged later into *āpṛṇosi* and *āpṛṇoṣi*. Then the sequence *āpṛṇosi* was analyzed as *āpṛṇaḥ* + *asi*, and the sequence *āpṛṇoṣi* was looked upon as a single verbal form from the root *pṛ*- (*Vedic Variants*, Vol. II, p. 152).[169] In my view the above passage gives an indication of how the phonologies of orally preserved continuous texts had diverged. But even in the limited interpretation of *saṃhitā* as "juncture", the passage indicates that there were people who considered the *saṃhitā* text to be *mo su naḥ* rather than *mo ṣu ṇaḥ*. I shall demonstrate later that this latter kind of retroflexion is irregular even in the existing Vedic recensions.

4.4. We have to examine this passage carefully. Contrary to Keith's suggestions, I see in this passage an indication that even at this stage, there were some people who suspected that the original *Ṛgveda* might have been *aṇakāra* "without *ṇ*" and *aṣakāra* "without *ṣ*". The very phrase "*if* we say [i.e., follow in recitation] the teaching of Māṇḍūkeya, *then* the letters *ṇ* and *ṣ* are obtained for us" seems to indicate that if the teaching of Māṇḍūkeya were not followed, then these sounds were not to be obtained in the *Ṛgveda*. This would be parallel to the statement: "If we accept the Maitrāyaṇī tradition, then the forms *páṇyāt páṇyatarā* are with *ṇ*, but if we follow the tradition of the Kāṭhaka reciters, these forms could be without *ṇ*." Thus the presence or absence of *ṇ* is not absolute with respect to the Ur-text of the *Yajurveda*, but is definitely a recension-specific phenomenon. Kuiper (1958: 350) claims that *krūḍayati* of the Kāṭhaka text is replaced by the "current synonym" *vidahati* in the Maitrāyaṇī text. One could similarly argue that the nonretroflexed forms *pányāt pányatarā* of the Kāṭhaka text (which occur beside the retroflexed forms *páṇyāt páṇyatarā*) are uniformly replaced by the more current retroflexed forms in the Maitrāyaṇī text. Thus one could claim the following probable development: The Ur-*Yajurveda* had **pányāt pányatarā*. By the time of the Kāṭhaka recension, retroflexion had made its way into the oral tradition, but was still quite unstable. Thus, the Kāṭhaka text has retroflexed forms beside nonretroflexed forms. By the time the Maitrāyaṇī recension was codified, or in the region where it was codified, the process of cerebralization had advanced further, and hence the Maitrāyaṇī text shows only the retroflexed forms. Considering that Kāṭhaka tradition comes from the northwestern regions and that the Maitrāyaṇī tradition is found in Gujarat, the possibility of reconstructing such an evolution cannot be denied.

4.5. The *Aitareya-Āraṇyaka* passage indicates that not every school accepted the teachings of the Māṇḍūkeya tradition. At any rate, the *Aitareya-Āraṇyaka* was known to Pāṇini, who also quotes Śākalya (Keith, 1909: Intro., pp. 25, 73). The Māṇḍūkeya tradition preceded Śākalya, who accepted its prescription of *ṇ* and *ṣ* in the recitation of the *Ṛgveda*. We must recognize the fact that whatever the statistics of any retroflex sound that we collect from Śākalya's text, they do not directly represent the Ur-text of the *Ṛgveda*. They only reflect the phonology of Śākalya's recension.

4.6. What is the intention in saying that *ṇ* is the strength and *ṣ* is the breath of the *saṃhitā*? I have discussed this issue in another article (Deshpande, 1976: 177, fn. 12). Briefly stated, we may ask why only these sounds posed a doubt in the minds of some of the reciters. The answer to this question requires a careful study of the *Prātiśākhyas* and the Indo-Iranian sources of the Sanskrit retroflexes. The only retroflex sounds known to the *Prātiśākhyas* are the retroflex series *ṭ, ṭh, ḍ, ḍh*, and *ṇ*, and the sibilant *ṣ*. Occurrence of *Ḷ* and *Ḷh* as intervocalic allophones for *ḍ* and *ḍh* in the present text of the *Ṛgveda* is a recension-specific phenomenon, as is certainly the case with the different recensions of the *Yajurveda.*[170] The vowel *ṛ* is not retroflex, but either *jihvāmūlīya* 'produced at the root of the tongue' velar or uvular? or alveolar; and *r* is either dental or alveolar.[171] It seems quite conceivable that *r* and *ṛ* (that is, *ə rə*), which are also found in Iranian, continued from Proto-Indo-Iranian to the *Prātiśākhya* period in their non-retroflex form. We see that *ṇ* and *ṣ* are relatively more unpredictable in their distribution, while *ṭ, ṭh, ḍ*, and *ḍh* are more stable by this time. One conceivable reason for this is that sounds such as *ḍ* and *ḍh* are often reflexes of the Proto-Indo-Iranian clusters such as *zd* and **zdh*. Since **z* did not exist in Indo-Aryan developments, there was no question of confusing *ḍ* and *ḍh* with any existing **z* clusters. Similarly, the operation of Fortunatov's Law reducing IE **l* plus dental to a Sanskrit retroflex was complete by the pre-*Prātiśākhya* period, leaving only very few examples of such clusters behind, e.g., Vedic *gáldā-* beside *gárdā-* However, *n* —> *ṇ* and *s* —> *ṣ* are changes which have numerous exceptions and spontaneous occurrences (see sections 9.1-5). Though the statement of the *Aitareya-Āraṇyaka* directly relates only to the sounds *ṇ* and *ṣ* (which are peculiarly involved in mechanical metrical retroflexion), the historical source of this concern must be related to the entire question of retroflexion at an earlier period of the language. It is difficult to accept a stage in the history of ancient Indo-Aryan at which the phonemes *ṭ, ṭh, ḍ* and *ḍh* had emerged, but *ṇ* did not exist, since the shifts caused by principles like Fortunatov's Law should apply equally to *ṇ*. Though the Prakrit languages show different stages in the distribution of *ṇ* in different times and regions, it is hard to separate the general emergence of *ṇ*, from that of the other retroflex consonants. The case of *ṣ* is slightly different, since there are many Prakrits known to us which had other retroflexes but which did not have *ṣ*. This sound is found only in the northwestern Prakrits and Dardic. Emergence of *ṣ* is predominantly due to a partial modification of the Indo-European *ruki* rule in Sanskrit, and apparently did not cover all the Indo-Aryan dialects. These points will be discussed in detail later.

4.7. If at a late period, such as that of the *Aitareya-Āraṇyaka* (about 700 B.C.), retroflexion of *ṇ* and *ṣ* was being debated among various schools of Ṛgvedic recitation, what kind of a phonetic picture can we reconstruct for the Ur-*Ṛgveda*? The methodological problems in such an attempt are numerous. We not only have to follow a method similar to "internal reconstruction", but perhaps must also go beyond it, since we are dealing with purely Aryan compositions in a form which was fixed and handed down to us after Aryan-non-Aryan convergence was well advanced. Thus, we have to figure out the impact of such convergence on the oral text transmission and try to eliminate those features which are most probably results of this convergence. It is difficult to accept the view that retroflex phonemes existed in the Ur-*Ṛgveda* composed before the Aryan-non-Aryan convergence, and that several centuries later, when in fact Aryan-non-Aryan convergence was well developed, a dispute arose among the traditional reciters about the authenticity of these sounds. Theoretically, either we have to accept the hypothesis that retroflexion existed in the Ur-*Ṛgveda*, and then was lost or retained in different recensions, or we accept a nonretroflexed Ur-*Ṛgveda* with the development of retroflexion in particular recensions and the retention of a less retroflexed or nonretroflex text by certain "conservative" schools of Vedic recitation.

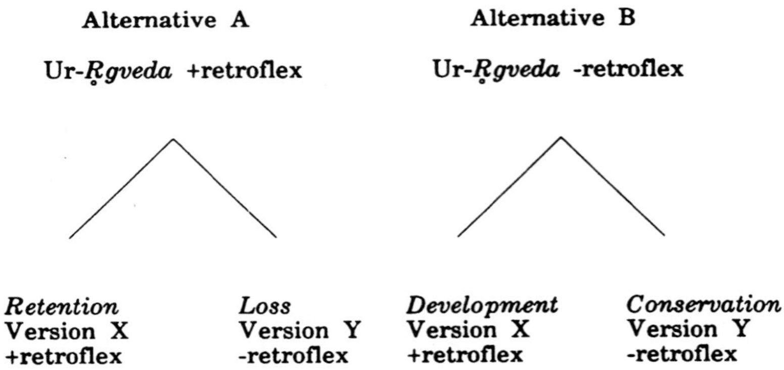

Of these two alternatives, alternative B is more logical and suits the historical situation in India as we know it from various sources. It also resembles previous attempts by Mehendale (1968: 96-97, 101) to reconstruct certain "pre-Sanskrit" stages. In his analysis, Mehendale depends primarily on the formal linguistic method of "internal reconstruction", and hence calls the reconstructed stage "pre-Sanskrit". In my view, we have the additional sociolinguistic complexity of Aryan-non-Aryan convergence to consider, and I find that his "pre-Sanskrit" stage often closely resembles my concept of "preconvergence" Sanskrit in which the original *Ṛgveda* was composed.

4.8. In the period between the composition of the hymns (1500-1200 B.C.) and the work of the compilers of the various recensions (about 700 B.C.), the retroflex sounds had developed in Sanskrit and had become an organic part of it. Since the Vedic hymns were being preserved and transmitted orally, often without awareness of word boundaries in continuous sequences, the phonology of the language of the reciters naturally had an impact on the transmitted recensions. We may compare this with the different pronunciations of Pāli texts in different countries of Southeast Asia. Thus, at a later time the dispute arose quite naturally as to whether the orally transmitted texts should or or should not, and did or did not, have these retroflex sounds, the "innovations of Indo-Aryan" as Bloch calls them. Known variations in the different recensions of the *Atharvaveda*, *Yajurveda*, and even within the text of the *Ṛgveda* as we have it, are definitely a result of this natural instability of oral literature before it is codified. I shall discuss examples of such variation later on.

4.9. It is extremely important to note that the present recension of the *Ṛgveda* is based on the northeastern recension of the Māṇḍūkeya tradition which had established itself in Magadha. The Aryan character of groups like the family of Māṇḍūkeyas is a matter of suspicion (Kosambi, 1947, 1950). There is even some question concerning the origin of the Aitareya and the Kauṣītaki traditions. While the tradition considers Aitareya to be the son of a Dāsa woman (*dāsī*), there is a possibility that the founder of the Kauṣītaki tradition was a purified *vrātya*, a non-Vedic Aryan (Banerjea, 1963: 164ff). We also know from other sources that there were severe disputes over the question of retroflexion in Magadha in ancient times. Rājaśekhara informs us in his *Kāvyamīmāṃsā* (p. 50) that the king of Magadha, Śiśunāga banned retroflex sounds in his harem. Specifically he banned the following eight sounds: *ṭ*, *ṭh*, *ḍ*, *ḍh*, *ś*, *ṣ*, *h*, and *kṣ*. It has been suggested that Śiśunāga was a non-Indo-Aryan person. Deb (1922, 1925) argues that he was an Elamite, while A. Banerji Shastri (1936-37) contends that he was a Nāga prince. Whatever the origin of the Śiśunāgas, it is extremely significant that there were poignant disputes over retroflexion in Magadha even up to the fifth century B.C.

5. Pre-Ṛgvedic Aryan-non-Aryan Bilingualism?

5.1. The postulation of the Ur-*Ṛgveda* without any retroflexes may at first seem to be a radical departure. However, if we properly interpret the facts known about the *Ṛgveda* and its transmission - as well as the history of the development of religion, mythology, and social structures - in the light of what we have learned from studies of contemporary bilingualism, then we find support for such a hypothesis.

5.2. We cannot deny that the incoming Aryans came in contact with certain non-Aryan people in India. There is ample evidence for such contacts. Though in most cases the Ṛgvedic Aryans are seen as generally hating the non-Aryan (i.e., the Dāsas, Dasyus, and Paṇis), occasionally we find that some Aryans did enter into political and military alliances with some non-Aryans, as evidenced by the War of Ten Kings. We may also agree that some of the Vedic sages like Kavaṣa Ailūṣa had non-Aryan sounding names and were a sort of Aryanized non-Aryans (Kuiper, 1967: 87). Moreover, one may perhaps agree with Kosambi (1965: 82-83) that the unorthodox birth account of Vasiṣṭha indicates his non-Aryan origin. One may perhaps also accept that there is grafting of an Austroasiatic myth onto one of the Indra myths (Kuiper, 1967: 87). On rare occasions, the Ṛgvedic poets praise gifts from certain non-Aryans kings like Bṛbu. I am not sure exactly how to interpret and evaluate these "sporadic reports" of Aryan-non-Aryan contacts, but even if one were to accept them all as reflecting historical facts, the general picture in the *Ṛgveda* is still one of Vedic Aryans in this early period hating non-Aryans and despising their religion and speech. Apart from "implications" and "assumptions", there is not the slightest evidence in the *Ṛgveda* of any large-scale bilingualism or social or religious convergence of Vedic Aryans with non-Aryans. For a critique of Kosambi's views on such early non-Aryan influence in the *Ṛgveda*, see Brough (1953: xiv ff).

5.3. Emeneau (1974: 93) not only proposes that there was "extensive bilingualism", but that "Sanskrit was handed down at some early period by a majority of speakers who learned it as a second language, their first language being Dravidian. In their first language, there were contrasting dentals and retroflexes; in Sanskrit, or we had better say pre-Indo-Aryan, there were only dentals and some allophones of dentals 'backed' toward the Dravidian retroflex position. Assignment of these backed allophones to their own Dravidian retroflexes was easy for native Dravidians."

Emeneau himself begins this statement with "we must postulate", and it must be said that there is no positive evidence to turn this postulation into a historical assertion, particularly with respect to the period of the composition of the *Ṛgveda*. *It is impossible to believe that the composers of the Ṛgveda had Sanskrit as their second language and had some Dravidian language as their first language.*

5.4. However, the sociolinguistic "process" suggested by Emeneau is quite significant, and I shall try to demonstrate in this chapter that this process must have taken place in the text transmission of the *Ṛgveda*, rather than prior to the original composition of the Vedic hymns. Emeneau himself and others have adduced strong evidence for the socioreligious and linguistic convergence of the Indo-Aryans with indigenous populations at a somewhat later period.

5.5. Brown (1953: 131) describes the Vedic Aryans as being "more like their linguistic and religious kinsmen, the Iranians, than like their eastern Indian contemporaries." Even by the time of the composition of the *Ṛgveda*, the Vedic Aryans had hardly moved to the east of the *sapta-sindhu* "land-of-the-seven-rivers" region, i.e., Punjab. Chakladar, (1928: 161-62) claims that the Vedic culture originated in the eastern region and that the Ṛgvedic Aryans had "occupied" the eastern lands during the composition of the *Ṛgveda*. This is absolutely untenable. The attitude of the Vedic Aryans toward the non-Aryans as seen in the *Ṛgveda* is also significant. The general attitude is characterized by a strong hatred toward the non-Aryans, whether they are Paṇis, Śabaras, or Dāsas; very rarely are there any references to them as friends.[172] The battles with the non-Aryans are called *dasyu-hattyā* "slaughter of the Dasyus".[173] The non-Aryans are hated for being *mūradeva* 'with dummy gods', *śiśna-deva* 'phallus-worshippers', *adeva* 'godless', etc., and are particularly accused of being *mṛdhra-vācaḥ* 'with obstructed speech'.[174] It is unreasonable to think that such attitudes prevailed when the Aryans entered India and yet did not continue up to the composition of the *Ṛgveda*. These are the attitudes of the Ṛgvedic poets themselves. How could the Ṛgvedic poets expressing these attitudes, in the very latest parts of the *Ṛgveda*, be Sanskrit-speaking Dravidians, assuming that some of the non-Aryans mentioned in the *Ṛgveda* are in fact Dravidians?

5.6. This does not contradict the existence of several words in the *Ṛgveda* which can only be explained as loanwords from Dravidian and Munda languages. The loanwords do indicate contact with non-Aryan peoples, something known even from Ṛgvedic descriptions and which cannot be doubted. But at the same time, these loanwords are not sufficient to indicate the degree of intensity of Dravidian or Munda influence on the Vedic language which Kuiper would like to see in them. Even if one accepts the entire lists of Ṛgvedic loanwords provided by Kuiper and Burrow,[175] the total number of these words in the *Ṛgveda* is still not as great as the number of Indo-Aryan loanwords in Tamil or in Southeast Asian languages. S. Vaidyanathan has put together a list of Indo-Aryan loanwords in old Tamil, and not only do those words show clear signs of Tamilization, but the oldest Tamil grammar, *Tolkāppiyam*, has explicit rules for changing Sanskrit sounds into Tamil sounds.[176] Rarely did Tamil sounds change because of Indo-Aryan loan words. Ganesan (1971: 152) has discussed in detail the sound-changes involved in Sanskrit loanwords in Tamil. He remarks: "This [Tamil] phonemic system, which has been fairly well stabilised by the corresponding phonemic orthographic system, makes substantial changes inevitable in words which are borrowed from other languages, especially from a language like Sanskrit, which has a much different phonemic system. Practically, whenever a word is borrowed, a phonological change is almost obligatory and the word gets a new form." (Also see Miranda, 1977: 264).

5.7. Ananthanarayana (1970: 66) basically accepts the concept of bilingualism as proposed by Emeneau and Kuiper, but derives a slightly different conclusion: "It is suggested that in the first period of this contact bilinguals were recruited chiefly from the native population. Support for such an assumption is provided in the greater number of Sanskrit loans as opposed to an insignificantly small number of Dravidian words in Sanskrit." This would mean that more Dravidians accepted Aryan words than Aryans accepting Dravidian words. This also suggests that the initiative for adoption was more prominent on the part of the native non-Aryan than on the part of the incoming Aryan.

5.8. Kuiper's account of the specific role of bilingualism in the development of retroflexion is somewhat less convincing. He says that the Aryans - bilingual Aryans - recognized a phonemic contrast between dentals and retroflexes in the *foreign language*, and then they - the Aryan bilinguals - interpreted allophones of their Aryan language in terms of the *foreign phonemic system*. Early Aryans, even if there were bilingual Aryans, most probably did not reinterpret allophones of their own Aryan language in terms of a *foreign phonemic system*. On the contrary, they would have adapted foreign loanwords to their own native Aryan phonology. Kuiper himself (1958: 351) says that there were such "Sanskritizations": "Sanskritization of foreign words by substitution of *tr, dr* (or *rt, rd*) for *ṭ, ḍ* is well attested in the classical language." He (1958: 352) carries this tendency further into the *Ṛgveda*: "The explanation of *kartá-* as a Sanskritization of *kāṭá-* would seem to be rather the only one that is phonetically admissible according to our present knowledge." If one accepts Kuiper's explanation of *kartá-* <— *kāṭá-*, which is by no means certain,[177] it would appear that the Ṛgvedic Aryans did think of *rt* as being more native to the Aryan tongue, and *ṭ* as being somewhat foreign.

5.9. Further support for the implausibility of Kuiper's view may be gained by examining the British treatment of retroflexes in loanwords from Indian languages. "It is no wonder", says G.S. Rao (1954: 39), "that he (i.e., an Englishman) wrote and spoke each Indian word as he heard it with his English ears." He points out (p. 47) that "the laws of English phonetic usage operated in the transition of Indian words into English." The British had to use hundreds of local Indian words in English. However, they did not pick up the retroflex sounds, but rather approximated them to other English sounds. Thus, the Marathi place name *puṇe* became "Poona" and *khaḍkī* came to be called "Kirkee". Similarly, the presence of non-Aryan loanwords in the *Ṛgveda* is insufficient to indicate that the intensity of contact with the non-Aryans was sufficient to cause phonetic and phonemic alterations in the Aryan language in that early period. W.J. Gedney's extensive work on "Indic Loan-words in Thai" also indicates that, despite the existence of hundreds of loanwords and a living tradition of Pāli texts, the Thai language did not adopt Indian sounds and that the same is true of Cambodian and Burmese.[178] It may be noted that several words in the *Ṛgveda* claimed by Southworth to be Dravidian loanwords have no retroflexes in their Ṛgvedic form, but their supposed Dravidian cognates do have retroflexes.[179] This appears to me to be the expected direction of change.

5.10. On the other hand, a study of Indian English and English loanwords in Indian languages reveals the other side of the process. When native speakers of Indian languages heard English with their "Indian ears", English alveolars were naturally felt to be closer to Indian retroflexes and were approximated to Indian retroflexes. For example, English 'table' becomes *ṭebal* in Marathi. Also compare other English words in Marathi: 'government' *gavharmeṇṭ*, 'bottle' *bāṭlī*, 'taxi' *ṭaeksī*, 'post' *posṭ*, etc. T. Grahame Bailey (1938: 109) says: "The modern Indian hearing alveolar *t* and *d* considers them cerebrals." Thus, the adoption by Indian speakers of English as a second language has caused changes in English in India, but hundreds of loanwords in British English from Indian languages have not altered the phonemic structure of English as spoken by the British. "The historic statement of the problem of loan phonology is that a speaker of LT [= target language], in perceiving and reproducing the sounds of LS [= source language], substitutes for them those that he takes to be 'closest' in his own language" (Lovins, 1974: 240).

5.11. However, Emeneau recognized this problem. Instead of saying that Aryans interpreted allophones of Proto-Indo-Aryan in terms of the foreign Dravidian phonemic system, he considers it more logical to assume that the Dravidians interpreted allophones of Proto-Indo-Aryan in terms of their native phonemic system in the process of adopting the foreign Aryan language. In his excellent paper "Bilingualism and Structural Borrowing", as early as 1962, Emeneau (1962a: 434) points out that "the evident Dravidianization of Sanskrit in some of its structural features must lead to the partial conclusion that a sufficient number or proportion of certain generations of Sanskrit speakers learned their Sanskrit from persons whose Dravidian linguistic traits were translated into Indo-Aryan and who provided the model for succeeding generations." Ananthanarayana (1970: 60, 67) essentially agrees with Emeneau and points out that, numerically, more Dravidians than Aryans must have participated in the transmission of the Aryan language, and he refers to the example of retroflexes in Indian English.

5.12. In his 1962 article, Emeneau proposed an essentially correct sociolinguistic process for the development of retroflexion in Sanskrit, but he was not sure of the exact chronology or of the intensity of this process with reference to the early Vedic texts. Were Dravidians participating in a significant proportion in the use of Sanskrit in the pre-Vedic times? In 1962 Emeneau (1962a: 434) was not sure: "Nothing is known of the Indian social and political structure into which the Sanskrit-speaking invaders made their way or of the changes brought about by incursion, or of the numbers of the invaders, or even how many bands were involved; was there intermarriage of the invaders and the aborigines, or concubinage, or the use of aboriginal nurses? And above all, who were the bilinguals - a significant number of the invaders or of the aboriginals, or of both? We shall never know the answers to these questions in detail." In 1974, making essentially the same sociolinguistic argument, Emeneau (1974: 92) claims more confidently that such a process must have taken place before the composition of the *Ṛgveda*, and agrees with Kuiper that retroflexion in the existing *Ṛgveda* is an indication of pre-Ṛgvedic Dravidianization of the Aryan language.

5.13. In my view, this is the beginning of confusion. I entirely agree with Emeneau that retroflexion in the existing *Ṛgveda* can and must be explained by the Dravidianization of the Aryan language. However, the fact that the present text of the *Ṛgveda* has retroflexion does not at all prove that there must have been retroflexion in the original compositions of the *Ṛgveda*, and hence does not prove that the original compositions of the *Ṛgveda* must also be posterior to Aryan-Dravidian convergence. The totality of evidence provided by Kuiper for pre-Ṛgvedic "convergence" is, in my opinion, still insufficient to prove that the original *Ṛgveda* was composed by Sanskrit-speaking Dravidians. Even two hundred loanwords, if we accept the entire list of Kuiper, a few non-Aryan sounding names, and an Austroasiatic myth grafted onto the Indra myth, do not prove that the composers of the *Ṛgveda* were already Aryanized Dravidians. Kuiper (1967: 87) mentions the Vedic sage Kavaṣa Ailūṣa as a non-Aryan accepted by the Aryans. However, this is not the norm. The *Aitareya-Brāhmaṇa* (2.8.1) shows that initially the Vedic Aryans rejected him by saying: "How could this bastard born of a *dāsī*, a cheat who is not a Brāhmaṇa be initiated into the sacrifice with us." He was accepted only when he "saw" a hymn. The Southeast Asian languages would definitely compete and fare better in all these respects. Those languages have hundreds of Indic loanwords, entire Hindu and Buddhist religious and cultural systems, and also the living continuity of Pali texts, and yet these languages did not develop retroflexion. This is a very strong counter-example to Kuiper's claims.

5.14. The difference between the sages who composed the original hymns of the *Ṛgveda* and the editor-redactors of the later Vedic recensions is quite considerable. Oldenberg (1896, 1973: 39) points out that "in the ancient times for instance, the Aryans of the Northwestern part of further India had not yet entered deep into the borderland by the use of force and were still the brothers and almost neighbours of the Zarathustrian Aryas of Iran, or rather of the Aryans who were opponents of Zarathustra.

The situation changed in later times. Hinduism spread all along the peninsula with the Aryan character ever weakening, with the blood of the natives mingling in their blood stream in a never-ceasing continuity and with an infinite series of shades of complexion, ranging from the fair to the dark, observable in the populace. ... It will not do to mix up the old times with the modern times." He further differentiates the Ṛgvedic Aryans from the later bearers of the Hindu cultures: "The linguistic affinities between the Veda and the Avesta ... have been compared with the dialectal refinements of the inscriptions of Aśoka; or, if, on the other hand, compare the Vedic gods with the Avestic gods, or if we compare the Vedic sacrifice, the priests and the special designations of priests with their counterparts in the Avesta, and then, on the other side, if we observe what revolutionary changes have been introduced in the gods and in the sacrifices by the cult of Viṣṇu or Śiva ... and how the externals as well as the inner meanings of religion have been profoundly changed ... we can say that there has been here a development corresponding to that between the script of the Aśokan rock-edicts and the present Devanāgarī script" (Oldenberg, 1973: 34-40). Nothing that Kuiper has come up with can change the picture thus depicted by Oldenberg and turn the composers of the original Vedic hymns into Sanskrit-speaking Dravidians.

5.15. In order to be able to evaluate the arguments put forward by Kuiper to establish "bilingualism" between the Vedic Aryans and Dravidians, we must take into account a recent analysis of bilingualism by Nadkarni (1975: 681), who points out that "structural borrowing at all levels of language, including syntax (the so-called 'deepest' level), can take place irrespective of the factor of social prestige, but solely as a consequence of 'intensive and extensive' bilingualism with a certain time-depth. ... By 'extensive' bilingualism, I mean a situation in which bilingualism is coextensive with the entire community, as in the case of K[annad] S[arasvat] K[onkani] speakers. By 'intensive' bilingualism, I mean a situation in which a community whose mother tongue is language A is not merely conversant with language B, but actually uses it for a wide range of purposes in the course of normal, everyday living. Extensive bilingualism, in particular, seems necessary for structural borrowing to be stabilized, since it renders all the members of the community more or less equally receptive to influences and traits of the non-native language - which, first randomly, and gradually more and more regularly, find their way into their mother tongue. A linguistic innovation has a strong chance of stabilizing itself in a language if it attracts no notice, and therefore no resistance from speakers, particularly in the early stages. This is possible only in situations of extensive bilingualism."

5.16. A more recent study of Konkani loan-phonology by Miranda (1977: 264) asserts: "Konkani dialects in the Dravidian area have been under the influence of the local Dravidian languages not only with respect to vocabulary but also with respect to phonology and syntax. However, they have succeeded to a large extent in molding the Dravidian loan words to their phonological and morphological patterns." This is an important conclusion. With Nadkarni's precise definitions and with Miranda's conclusions, we must question Kuiper's theory of loan-phonology in the *Ṛgveda.* We must say that the non-Aryan languages were not only not prestige languages for the Aryans, but that the Aryans, by referring to their obscure language (*mṛdhravācaḥ*) as they did, hated the non-Aryans. There indeed were contacts and alliances of convenience, and yet no love lost. There is no evidence that there existed "extensive" or "intensive" bilingualism with the non-Aryans. Kuiper's data can at best indicate "sporadic" bilingualism, but it is insufficient to indicate extensive or intensive bilingualism as defined by Nadkarni. Without making distinctions between the different kinds of bilingualism and the differences in their impact, the concept of bilingualism as used by Kuiper remains vague and leads to misleading conclusions which are not supported by the cases of loan-phonology referred to earlier.

5.17. The Ṛgvedic Aryans were always conscious of the Aryan-non-Aryan distinction (*ārya-varṇa* versus *dāsa-varṇa*). The unity among Aryans as Aryans does not refer to any objective racial unity, since the Indo-Europeans must have mixed with the local populations of Iran and other regions before they reached India. This unity is more a matter of cultural perception. However, things changed in later times. The original Vedic Aryans settled in northwestern India and gradually expanded to the east and to the south. The original non-Aryan population underwent Aryanization, and the non-Aryan religion and culture were gradually "Sanskritized".[180] Eventually the earlier distinctions lost their value.

5.18. Already in the Brāhmaṇa texts, we hear of dark-complexioned Brāhmaṇas proving themselves academically superior to the fair-complexioned Brāhmaṇas (Chatterji, 1962: 69-70). The author of the *Mahābhārata* is the dark-complexioned (*kṛṣṇa*) Vyāsa, who is also said to be the progenitor of the Kauravas and Pāṇḍavas, and has himself a non-

Aryan mother. It is to him that the Indian tradition attributes the beginning of the process of editing and redacting the Vedas. With the prominence of Kṛṣṇa, the "dark" Lord, the *Mahābhārata* shows the emergence of dark Aryanized non-Aryan personalities in religious and political life.[181]

5.19. The Māṇḍūkeya tradition had reached Magadha in the east by the time Śākalya compiled his recension.[182] Looking at this drastically different sociolinguistic situation, it is not at all surprising to see that the reciters of the *Ṛgveda* at this late "post-convergence" period were influenced by the retroflexion in their own post-Vedic speech. What is in fact more surprising is that, even after such a long time, there were at least some people who doubted the existence of retroflexion in the original text of the *Ṛgveda.*

5.20. Based on the references in the *Brāhmaṇa* and *Āraṇyaka* literature, we may be able to speculate on the possible reasons for this divergence of opinion on the authenticity of retroflexion in Sanskrit. As the Indo-Aryans entered India and moved eastward, it seems that some of them always thought of the "good old days" in the "golden age in the northwestern homelands", while others gradually accepted the changes that were taking place in their life while they were moving eastward. Thus, in terms of purity of speech, some Aryans kept looking back to the northwestern trails from which they had come. This is clearly supported by the *Brāhmaṇa* statements that those who want to learn the best speech go to the north (west), since the best known speech is spoken in the north(west).[183]

5.21. On the other hand, there were traditions such as that of Māṇḍūkeya, which had moved eastward as far as Magadha, and which were fighting for the recognition of "new" or more eastern features such as retroflexion as a part of the orally transmitted *Ṛgveda.* We know now that Śākalya accepted the tradition of the Māṇḍūkeyas in the matter of retroflexion; and hence, in the text of the *Ṛgveda* as we have it today, the retroflex sounds are there as an integral part of it. It is also important to note that Śākalya did not accept all the conventions of the Māṇḍūkeya tradition and introduced some new changes. The text of the Māṇḍūkeya recension of the *Ṛgveda* was perhaps somewhat closer to the original *Ṛgveda* than was Śākalya's recension.[184] Figure 1 shows the geography of these shifts.

FIGURE 1

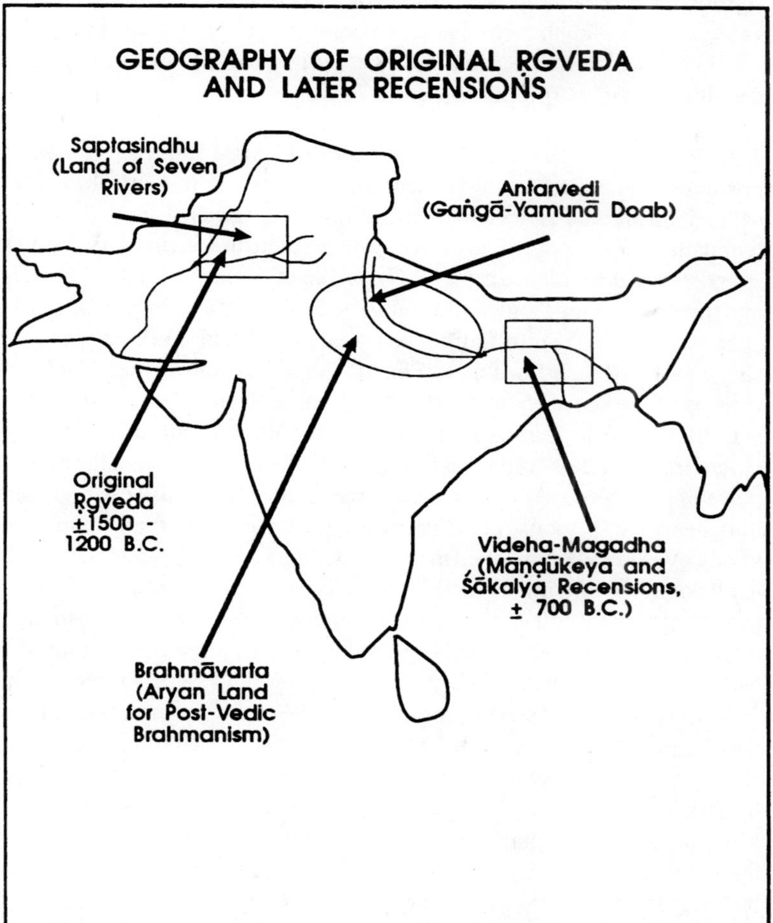

6. Emergence of Retroflexion in Prehistoric Indo-Aryan

6.1. The fact that the pre-Śākalya tradition of the Māṇḍūkeyas, upon which Śākalya relied for his retroflex sounds, had already reached

Magadha in the east, and the fact that the *Kauṣītaki-Brāhmaṇa* (7.6) considers the northwestern dialect to be relatively purer are of great significance to the linguistic history of ancient India. At this point, one has to consider the theory of successive migrations of Aryans into India. As I shall demonstrate, this theory is quite relevant to the historical development of retroflexion in Indo-Aryan.

6.2. Hoernle (*A Grammar of the Eastern Hindi*, 1880, pp. xxx-xxxii) postulated the existence of two early Aryan groups in North India, the Māgadhan and the Śaurasenī, representing two waves of Indo-European language speakers, of which the Māgadhans were the older. This idea was supported by Grierson (*Imperial Gazetteer of India*, Vol. 1, pp. 353-59) and given an ethnological footing by Risley (*The People of India*, London, 1915, p. 55). In addition to social institutions and languages, the shape of the skull, according to Chanda (1916: 59) shows that "the Indo-Aryans of the outer countries originally came from an ethnic stock that was different from the stock from which the Vedic Aryans originated."[185] However, Chanda's "inner" and "outer" are different. For him the second wave of post-Vedic Aryans bypassed the "inner Vedic Aryans" and went into the "outer" regions. For Chakladar (1928, 1961-62), the second wave of post-Vedic Aryans pushed the Vedic Aryans into the "outer" lands and itself occupied the "inner" lands. To me, Burrow's conception of the west to east movement of the two waves of Aryans seems to be more reasonable than the other theories. Oldenberg also supported and elaborated this idea and pointed out that "probably the first immigrants, and, therefore, the farthest forward to the east ... are those tribes ... the Aṅga and Magadha, the Videha, the Kosala and Kāśī."[186] He (1890, 1882: 9) also claims that it was the second wave that produced the Vedas. This theme has been linguistically upheld by Meillet who shows that the Vedic dialect, like the Iranian, is an *r*-only dialect in which the Indo-European *l* merged into *r*, but the dialect of the redactors of the Vedas was an *r* and *l* dialect, where the original Indo-European **r* and **l* were retained; the redactors of the Vedic texts have put this *l* back into some of the Vedic words, where the original Vedic dialect had an *r*(Meillet, 1912-13; Bloch, 1070: 2). In later Prakrits we clearly see the eastern Prakrit, Māgadhī, developing into a pure *l*-only dialect; whereas the western and particularly the northwestern dialects, almost devoid of *l*, represent the early *r*-only dialect (Mehendale, 1948: 297).

6.3. The difference between the *r*-only dialect, the *r-l* dialect (and possibly an *l*-only dialect) is quite significant. Burrow (1972: 535) says that "the *r*-dialect prominent in the early Ṛgveda shares a common change (of *s* —> *ś*) with Iranian. It is unlikely to have undergone this change independently and consequently we must assume that it took place when a group of Indo-Aryan migrants were still in contact with Iranians. ... On the other hand, those Indo-Aryans who preserved the distinction between *r* and *l* had already departed to India, and so they were unaffected by it. The speakers of the *r*-dialect were the latest comers on the Indian scene and there ensued a mixture of the two dialects."

6.4. The significance of the *r-l* dialect moving earlier into the interior of India and eventually on to eastern areas like Magadha (where dialectally all *r* —> *l*) is further enhanced by its connection with the operation of Fortunatov's Law. The law states that in the group IE **l* + dental in Sanskrit, the *l* is dropped and the dental is changed to a cerebral (cf. Skt. *paṭa-* 'cloth', OSlav. *platino*, Russ. *polotno*). Here an original Indo-European cluster yields a single retroflex, while *r*+ dental in Middle Indo-Aryan always results in a cluster, dental as well as retroflex (cf. Skt. *vartate*, Pkt. *vaṭṭaï* beside *vattai*) (Burrow (1972: 531)). The particular connection of Fortunatov's Law with *l*-clusters means that this Law cannot apply in dialects such as Iranian and Ṛgvedic Sanskrit, where every IE **l* —> *r*. Burrow (1972: 531) has admirably defended Fortunatov's Law against all the objections raised by different scholars and has tried to date the beginning of its operation on the basis of the Ṛgvedic word *gáldā-* 'dripping, flow', beside the *r*-dialect form *gárdā-*. The fact that *gáldā-* is still found in the *Ṛgveda*, while later Sanskrit has the derived root *gaḍ*, implies, according to Burrow (1972: 542), that "the change according to Fortunatov's Law took place during the period of early *Ṛgveda*, so that it was possible for one form antedating that change to be preserved in that collection."

6.5. One could argue in a slightly different way. The Ṛgvedic dialect, as pointed out by Meillet and by Burrow himself, is an *r*-only dialect, like the Iranian, and hence was not logically subject to Fortunatov's Law. Thus, the retroflexes in the existing *Ṛgveda*, which can only be accounted for by Fortunatov's Law, may be viewed as a part of "normalization" by the later redactors belonging to the *r-l* dialect in tandem with the replacement of the Ur-Vedic *r* by *l* from their own dialect. This further separates the Ur-*Ṛgveda* dialect from the direct impact of Fortunatov's Law.

6.6. The fact that the *r*-only dialect of the northwest and the *r-l* dialect (and possibly the *l*-only dialect) of the northeast underwent different developments with respect to retroflexion can be demonstrated by referring to early inscriptional Prakrits. In particular, Mehendale's monumental *Historical Grammar of Inscriptional Prakrits* throws a flood of light on this problem. Mehendale (1948: 18) points out that the cerebralization of dentals in the environment of *r* is predominant in the eastern inscriptions, but "it will be observed that the western dialect is the least affected by cerebralisation." Bloch (1970: 6) and Burrow (1936: 419, 421) also emphasize this point. Burrow (1936: 421) further points out that even within the northwestern region, the Niya Prakrit in the further west preserved *r*+dental clusters better than the northwestern Aśokan inscriptions. He concludes that phonologically the language of Niya presents a pronouncedly more archaic aspect than that of Aśoka, namely, by better preserving consonant combinations such as *rt*, *rdh*, etc. Burrow (1936: 422) draws a significant conclusion:

> Obviously we cannot derive the Niya Prakrit from the language of Aśoka, and the most natural conclusion to draw from the fact that phonetically it is better preserved is that its home is to be sought further to the west. Because it seems clearer (then as now) that the more remote a language was in the direction of the north-west, the less liable it was to phonetic decay.

In an interesting way, Burrow's conclusion coincides with the passage from the *Kauṣītakī-Brāhmaṇa* (7.6) discussed earlier.

6.7. It is obviously not the case that a dialect is better preserved just by being in the west. The reason lies primarily in the dialectal division of ancient Indo-Aryan and the fact that laws like Fortunatov's Law and the *ruki*-rule applied to different dialects of Indo-Aryan. It is thus clear that Fortunatov's Law applied to the *r-l* dialect (or the *l*-only dialect) of pre-Vedic Aryans who moved into eastern India, and not to the *r*-only dialect of Iranians and Vedic Aryans of northwestern India. Oldenberg discusses in detail the question of the non-Vedic eastern Aryans and says that they confronted the non-Aryans long before the Vedic Aryans did.[187] At this point a discussion of the *Vrātya* Aryans becomes quite relevant. For a detailed discussion of the *Vrātyas* and their eventual assimilation into the later Aryanized society, I shall only refer to the treatment by K.A. Nilakanta Sastri (1967) and Banerjea (1963: 81ff), but I shall quote an important observation by Kimura (1927: 26ff): "The *Vrātyas* being

Aryans outside the Vedic circle always fought against the Vedic Aryans. Therefore, their sympathy naturally tended towards other tribes beside the Vedic Aryans." The *Baudhāyana-Dharma-Sūtra* (1.1.32-33) gives us a clear idea of how the "Vedic Aryans" viewed the "mixed Aryans" of the "outer" regions: "The inhabitants of Ānartta, of Aṅga, of Magadha, of Saurāṣṭra, of the Deccan, of Upavṛt, of Sindh and the Sauvīras are of mixed origin. He who has visited the countries of the Āraṭṭas, Kāraskaras, Puṇḍras, Sauvīras, Vaṅgas, Kaliṅgas or Pranūnas shall offer a Punastoma or Sarvapṛṣṭhī sacrifice [for purification]." Thus, the early Aryan dialect of the *Vrātyas* came into closer contact with non-Aryans and this gives us the necessary sociolinguistic motivation for the operation of Fortunatov's Law in their dialect. But it must be remembered that this development is essentially different from the history of the Vedic *r*-dialect. In later times, there occurred an obvious dialectal mixture which is reflected in Classical Sanskrit.

6.8. The evidence of Prakrit inscriptions is significant in another respect as well. It has been claimed by Burrow (1971: 557), quite rightly, that "the cerebral sibilant *ṣ* is differentiated from the other cerebrals in that its ultimate origin goes back to a much earlier date. The development of *s* to *ś* (whence Indo-Aryan *ṣ*) is common to Indo-Aryan and Iranian." It may be observed that despite a few cases of *ṣ* as a spontaneous retroflex (cf. Burrow, 1971: 557) and a few cases to be derived by Fortunatov's Law (Burrow, 1971: 543-44), the sound *ṣ* in Sanskrit is primarily an extension of the Indo-Iranian palatal *ś*, itself derived from the Indo-European **s* by the *ruki* rule, and is generally not in any way connected with Fortunatov's Law. This Law applies to the *l*-dialect of the pre-Vedic eastern Aryans, while the development of the Indo-European **s* into the Indo-Iranian *ś* by the *ruki* rule, essentially a development within the Indo-Iranian *r*-dialect, is preserved in the northwestern inscriptional Prakrits.

6.9. It has been pointed out by many a scholar that of all the Prakrits, only those of the northwest preserve the triple distinction between *ś*, *ṣ*, and *s* (Mehendale, 1948: 297; Konow, 1936: 609; and Burrow, 1936: 419). It may be hard to determine whether or not the phonetic development of [*ṣ*] by an extension of the *ruki* rule had already taken place by the time of the Ur-*Ṛgveda*, though it is certain that it took place after the division between the Iranian and the Indo-Aryan branches of Indo-Iranian had already taken place. It seems probable that the western *r*-dialect of the Vedic Aryans had allophones of *s* and *ś* which were interpreted later, after the dialect mixture, as a separate phoneme *ṣ* parallel to the retroflexes *ṭ*, *ḍ*, etc., derived by Fortunatov's Law in the eastern dialect. In the same way, the later Sanskrit rule *n*—> *ṇ* due to preceding *r*, *ṛ* or *ṣ* has its origin in the western dialect. This may be one of the reasons why the early western Prakrit inscriptions have *rt*, *rd*, etc., for eastern *ṭ*, *ḍ*, etc., but have ṇ corresponding to eastern *n* (Bloch, 1970: 6).

6.10. However, at the time of the composition of the original *Ṛgveda* the western dialect of the Vedic Aryans most probably had nothing more than cerebral allophones of *ś* and *n*, and also perhaps of *t*, *d*, etc., in clusters with *ś*, which were later identified with eastern retroflexes and interpreted as phonemes by the later mixed population. Thus, *ṣ* in the word *deveṣu* comes from an extension of the *ruki* rule in the western Aryan dialect, while *ṣ* in *bhāṣate* is the result of the operation of Fortunatov's Law from an Indo-European cluster **ls*, cf. Lith. *balsa-* 'voice'. While in early stages of Indo-Aryan, these two instances of *ṣ* seem to have had two different origins in two different dialects, in later Sanskrit they are interpreted as belonging to the same phoneme.

6.11. A study of inscriptional Prakrits also helps us clear another problem with respect to the existing recension of the *Ṛgveda*. This is the problem of the origin of the retroflex sounds *Ḷ* and *Ḷh* for intervocalic *ḍ* and *ḍh* in Śākalya's recension of the *Ṛgveda*. Most scholars take for granted the existence of these sounds in the *Ṛgveda*. I have already referred to Vaidya's view that these sounds developed in the southern *Dravidian* recitational traditions. I disagree with this view. I think that like other eastern retroflexes, *Ḷ* developed when the Ṛgvedic recitational traditions moved eastward in North India. Evidence to support this possibility comes from inscriptional Prakrits. Mehendale (1948: 11) points out that, in inscriptional Prakrits, the "change *-ḍ-* —> *-Ḷ-* occurs in the non-Western groups." His detailed statement is as follows (1948: 272-73):

> Medially the change *-ḍ-* —> *-Ḷ-* or *-l-* is found in the East and North (and perhaps in the Center) in the days of Aśoka. It is next noticed in the Western inscriptions in the 1st cent. A.D. and in the Southern group in the 2nd cent. A.D. The change, therefore, seems to have gone from E (and N) —> C —> W —> S.

This is an extremely important statement. This shows that the change of *-ḍ-* to *-Ḷ-* did not occur in the northwestern regions of India at the time of Aśoka. Pāṇini, who comes from the northwest and precedes Aśoka by about two centuries, does not have the sound *Ḷ* in his Sanskrit. It is also a matter of great significance that his rules concerning the Vedic language do not have any indication of the existence of the sound *Ḷ* in the Vedic texts known to him. In fact, in his rules like P.6.3.113 (*sāḍhye sāḍhvā sāḍheti nigame*) and P.8.3.54 (*iḍāyā vā*), he refers to Vedic usages such as *sāḍha* and *iḍā* without *Ḷh* and *Ḷ* for the intervocalic *ḍh* and *ḍ*, but commentators like Bhaṭṭoji Dīkṣita quote the examples *sāḶhā* and *iḶā* (*Siddhāntakaumudī*: 340, 348). Pāṇini obviously knew Śākalya's *padapāṭha*, and hence it is quite surprising to find him not recording the existence of *Ḷ* in that text. The *Ṛgvedaprātiśākhya* also does not ascribe the sounds *Ḷ* and *Ḷh* to Śākalya, but it attributes them to Vedamitra.[188] It is then conceivable that the version of Śākalya's *Ṛgveda* itself originally did not have the sounds *Ḷ* and *Ḷh*, and that what we have is not the original version of Śākalya, but a modified version of Śākalya.

The other possibility is that the northwestern version of Śākalya's *Ṛgveda* available to Pāṇini did not have the sounds *Ḷ* and *Ḷh*, but the original eastern version of Śākalya's *Ṛgveda* did have these sounds. Yāska is not too far removed from the *pada-kāras* like Śākalya, and he often doubts their *pada* divisions and proposes his own. Mehendale (1965: 13) has given a convincing argument to prove that Yāska had the sounds *Ḷ* and *Ḷh* in his own dialect:

> In *Nirukta* 7.16, Yāska cites Rv. 1.1.2 and in N. 8.8 he cites Rv. 10.110.3. In both these verses occurs the word *īḍyaḥ* which shows *ḍ* since it does not occur between the two vowels. But while paraphrasing it in his commentary, Yāska uses the form *īḶitavyaḥ* with *Ḷ* since here it occurs between two vowels. Had Yāska not used *Ḷ* in his speech, he would have paraphrased the Vedic word by *īḍitavyaḥ*.

If this argument is valid, and I think it is, then one may advocate a similar argument to indicate a possibility that Śākalya's own dialect also had the sounds *Ḷ* and *Ḷh*. Sköld (1926: 46) has indicated that Śākalya's word text for the *Ṛgveda* word *vīḍvagam* (1.118.9) is *vīḶu-agam*. This raises a strong possibility that Śākalya's own dialect had these sounds. The *Aitareya-Āraṇyaka* passage discussed earlier shows that the Śākalya tradition followed the Māgadhan tradition of the Māṇḍūkeyas. The *Bṛhadāraṇyaka-Upaniṣad* (3.1-9) has clear indications that Brāhmaṇas from the Kuru-Pañcāla region in north-central India were migrating to the eastern regions like Videha, and that a Vidagdha Śākalya was at the court of the king Janaka of Videha. Though the question of identity of this

Vidagdha Śākalya with Sthavira Śākalya of the *Aitareya-Āraṇyaka* and the redactor of the *Ṛgveda* is a matter of dispute (see *Aitareya-Āraṇyaka*, Keith: 239ff; and *Vedic Index of Names and Subjects*, Macdonell and Keith: Vol. 2, 368-69), the available information is sufficient to place the Śākalya tradition in the eastern regions of Videha and Magadha. Considering the above arguments it seems unlikely that the Ur-*Ṛgveda* of the northwestern region had the sounds *Ḷ* and *Ḷh*. Even in later times, there must have been other recensions of the *Ṛgveda* which did not have these sounds. For instance, while the available recension of the *Ṛgveda* (10.90.5a) reads *tasmād virāḶajāyata*, the *Yajurveda* version of the same hymn in the Mādhyandina recension (31.5a) reads *tasmād virāḍajāyata*. It is conceivable that the Mādhyandina reading represents a pre-Śākalya stage in the evolution of the Ṛgvedic oral traditions.

6.12. Whatever we know about Vedic, pre-Vedic, and Iranian from other independent sources fits well with the regional distribution of sounds in the early North Indian Prakrit inscriptions. One may reasonably suspect that this is not by accident but is the result of natural development. It seems interesting that the inscriptional Prakrits known from the third century B.C. should reflect a natural development of what we know to have been true of pre-Vedic and Vedic Indo-Aryans, and Iranians of a much earlier period. One of the reasons could very well be that after arrival of the Indo-Aryans, this region was not seriously disturbed by any peoples other than Iranians until the invasion of Alexander the Great. Figure 2 sums up the results of the preceding discussion of the development of Indo-Aryan retroflexes.

7. *Brāhmīkaraṇa:* A Gradual Transformation

7.1. The passage from the *Aitareya-Āraṇyaka* also appears with slight differences in the *Śāṅkhāyana-Āraṇyaka* (8.11). It contains a significant additional statement which throws some new light on the process of editing and redacting the older texts that had just begun in this period. After saying that some people have doubts about the existence of *ṇ* and *ṣ* in the Saṃhitā, and after advising that these sounds must be pronounced - as is done in the traditions of Māṇḍūkeya and Śākalya, the *Śāṅkhāyana-Āraṇyaka* (8.11, p. 315) says:

> Similarly, one should recite whatever else there is, namely any speech, historical traditions and *Purāṇa* texts, as if after having them transformed into the *Brāhma* [system].[189]

FIGURE 2

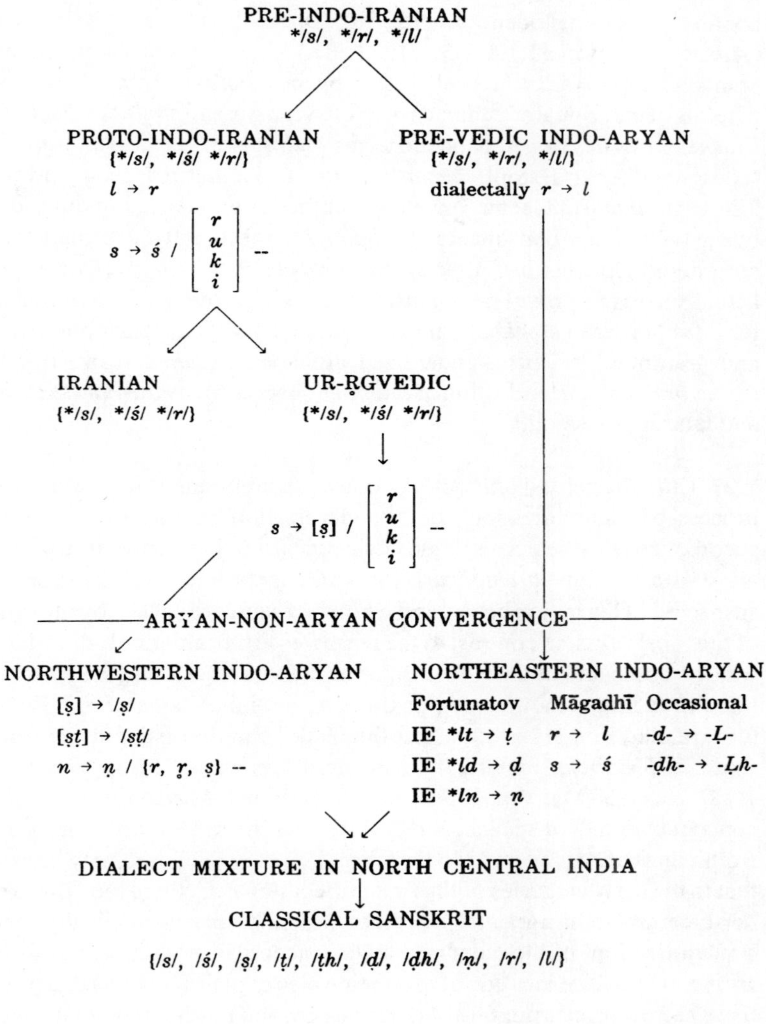
PRE-INDO-IRANIAN
*/s/, */r/, */l/
PROTO-INDO-IRANIAN
{*/s/, */ś/ */r/}
l → r
s → ś / [r u k i] --
PRE-VEDIC INDO-ARYAN
{*/s/, */r/, */l/}
dialectally r → l
IRANIAN
{*/s/, */ś/ */r/}
UR-ṚGVEDIC
{*/s/, */ś/ */r/}
s → [ṣ] / [r u k i] --
ARYAN-NON-ARYAN CONVERGENCE
NORTHWESTERN INDO-ARYAN
[ṣ] → /ṣ/
[ṣṭ] → /ṣṭ/
n → ṇ / {r, r̥, ṣ} --
NORTHEASTERN INDO-ARYAN
Fortunatov
IE *lt → ṭ
IE *ld → ḍ
IE *ln → ṇ
Māgadhī
r → l
s → ś
Occasional
-ḍ- → -Ḷ-
-ḍh- → -Ḷh-
DIALECT MIXTURE IN NORTH CENTRAL INDIA
CLASSICAL SANSKRIT
{/s/, /ś/, /ṣ/, /ṭ/, /ṭh/, /ḍ/, /ḍh/, /ṇ/, /r/, /l/}

What is the process that is signified by the gerund *brāhmīkṛtya*? The compound verb *brāhmī-kṛ*, according to the standard rules of Sanskrit, should refer to a process of transforming something which is not *brāhma* into something which is *brāhma.*[190] The word *brahman* is often used in the contexts where its identity with *vāk* 'speech' is clearly expressed (*Aitareya-Āraṇyaka* 1.1.1, 1.3.1, 1.5.1, etc.). The concrete manifestation of this *brahman* = *vāk* = 'speech' is seen by the *Aitareya-Āraṇyaka* (2.3.6) in terms of individual sounds such as stops (*sparśa*) and sibilants (*ūṣman*). This text uses developed phonetic terms such as *svara* 'vowel', *vyañjana* 'consonant', *sparśa* 'stop', *ūṣman* 'sibilant' and *antaḥsthā* 'semi-vowel'. The term *antaḥsthā* 'semi-vowel' which literally means 'standing between [vowels and consonants?]', possibly suggests that the formation of an ordered alphabet had already taken place. The *Aitareya-Āraṇyaka* actually uses the term *akṣara-ṣamāmnāya*, which is the standard technical term for "ordered alphabet" in systematic works on Sanskrit phonetics and grammar.[191] This standardized alphabet, *akṣara-samāmnāya*, is called *brahma-rāśi* 'collection of *brahman* (= speech)' by the *Prātiśākhyas* and later by Patañjali.[192]

7.2. Thus, the gerund *brāhmī-kṛtya* most probably stands for the gradual process of "normalization" or "standardization" of the oral texts in accordance with the norms of the Gangetic basin. The connection of this word with the name *brahmāvarta* for the Gangetic basin may be strongly suspected. This region becomes the home of standard speech by the time of the *Āraṇyakas*, in contrast to the northwestern frontier of India which was the homeland of the Ṛgvedic Aryans. Even Yāska seems to use the word *ārya* in a somewhat regional sense, i.e. inhabitants of *Āryāvarta* (often called *Brahmāvarta*), whose linguistic habits he distinguishes from those of *Kamboja* 'eastern Iran, Western Punjab', *Surāṣṭra*, etc. (*NR* 1.127-28; *MB* (M), Vol. I, Sec. I, p. 54). Patañjali also discusses the concept of standard speech, and defines it as the speech of the learned Brāhmaṇas of Āryāvarta (*MB* (M), Vol. II, p. 882). Thus, it may be said that in the early centuries of the first millennium B.C. there took place in north-central India a gradual process of *brāhmīkaraṇa* 'normalization and standardization' of the older oral texts in accordance with the norms of *Brahmāvarta*. The location of this region also explains how, by this time, there had occurred a mixture of northwestern and northeastern dialects in an essentially north-central region.

7.3. This process of "normalization" or "standardization" of orally preserved ancient texts is quite similar to what happened to the originals of the Sangam works which were composed in Ancient Tamil during the first three centuries after Christ, but which had their language altered and are now found in Cen-Tamiẓ redactions which must date from about 600 A.D. and later. Chatterji, who talks about this normalization, also speaks of a similar normalizing transformation in the case of the Vedic literature from its composition to its present preserved form and mentions several other cases of such transformations in the process of oral transmission.[193]

8. Retroflexion and the Development of the Brāhmī Script

8.1. In the context of the process of *brāḥmī-karaṇa*, it is important to look at the origin and development of the Brāhmī script. Bühler (1895: 84-85) has convincingly demonstrated the derivation of the Brāhmī script from Phoenician signs, and recently this has been supported by Dani and Mahadevan.[194]

8.2. The highly probable Phoenician origin of the Brāhmī script raises some interesting questions. The *Ṛgveda* speaks of a non-Aryan community called Paṇi, which is hated by the Aryans for being foolish, faithless, having obstructed speech and not worshipping the Aryan gods like Indra. But at the same time they are described as being well established merchants who were rich and went in caravans and who undertook sea voyages for trading and gain (Rahurkar, 1974: 43ff). Some scholars have identified the Paṇis of the *Ṛgveda* with the Phoenicians (Rahurkar, 1974: 45-46; S.R. Rao, 1972-73: 6). At present, there is not sufficient evidence to establish such an identification, but the plausibility of the identification cannot be easily denied. In any case, the Phonecian language did not have retroflexes and hence could not have affected Aryan speech directly in that respect. The Phoenician language does have a contrast of emphatic and non-emphatic dental stops and sibilants, but the development of the Brāhmī script shows that Indians did not look upon these emphatic dentals as retroflexes.

8.3. It is interesting to see how the retroflex Sanskrit sounds could have been gradually represented through modifications of the Phonecian signs for dentals. Sir Alexander Cunningham remarks that "it seems not improbable that this old Indian alphabet, when it was framed or adopted, did not possess any retroflex letters."[195] The Phoenician *Samech* is the origin of the signs for both *s* and *ṣ* in the Brāhmī script. Bühler (1895: 66) points out that a single sign probably served in the beginning to express both *s* and *ṣ* and that two separate signs were developed later out of this original representative of the Phonecian *Samech.* Similarly, the signs for the sounds *ṭ*, *ṭh*, *ḍ*, *ḍh* and *ṇ* in the Brāhmī script are derived from the dental signs in the Phoenician alphabet (Bühler, 1895: 73). While the Brāhmī *ḍ* comes from *d* (*dh* Phoenician *daleth*), the sign for retroflex *Ḷ* is a further modification of the sign for *ḍ* (Bühler, 1895: 77). The following chart shows the derivation of the Brāhmī retroflex signs (Bühler, 1895: 82-83):

Phoenician		**Brāhmī**		**Brāhmī Derivatives**
Daleth	——>	*dh*	——>	*d*, *ḍ*, [*ḍh*, *Ḷ*]
Theth	——>	*th*	——>	*ṭh*, *ṭ*
Nun	——>	*n*	——>	*ṇ*
Samech	——>	*ṣ* (Bhattiprolu type)	——>	*s*, *ṣ*

Even if we do not believe in the Phoenician origin of the Brāhmī script, still the relatedness of its retroflex and dental signs is significant in itself.

8.4. The fact that the same sign was earlier used for *s* and *ṣ* and that two different signs were later developed from this common sign is interesting. As the Sanskrit grammarians teach, the sound *s* changes to *ṣ* under the influence of the preceding *i*, *u*, *ṛ*, *e*, *ai*, *o*, *au*, *k*-series, *r*, or *l* (cf. P.8.3.57, *iṇ-koḥ*). It is quite possible that originally *ṣ* was looked upon only as an allophone of *s* and was not distinguished from *s* in writing. Gradually as *ṣ* became phonemically different from the original *s* through changes in its distribution, *s* and *ṣ* came to be distinguished in writing. The derivation of the Brāhmī *ṣ* from *s* perhaps goes hand in hand with the phonemic evolution of *ṣ* from *s*. The derivation of the Brāhmī sign for *Ḷ* from *ḍ* may indicate a similar evolution.[196] Bühler has amply demonstrated that Indian grammarians and phoneticians must have been involved in the formation of the Brāhmī script. Since the formation of an *akṣara-samāmnāya* 'standard alphabet' had already taken place before the *Aitareya-* and *Śāṅkhāyana-Āraṇyakas* and since this very *Śāṅkhāyana-Āraṇyaka* speaks of the process of *brāhmī-karaṇa*, we may be able to conclude with some justification that the process of *brāhmī-karaṇa* referred to here was the gradual process of "normalizing and standardizing" the orally preserved ancient Vedic texts. The earlier phase of this process may have been primarily an oral realignment, and in its later phase it may have involved orthographic standardization.

8.5. In terms of the development of ancient Indian scripts and retroflexion, it may be interesting to refer to S.R. Rao's attempts to decipher the Harappan script. While most of the recent Western attempts (cf. Parpola, 1975) presume that the Harappan language is an old Dravidian language. S.R. Rao's alphabetical interpretation of the late Harappan inscriptions is interesting in that, according to his findings, the Harappan script, like the later Brāhmī script, is derived from the Phoenician alphabet, and the Harappan language turns out for him to be a form of (pre-Vedic?) Indo-Aryan. According to him, there are no signs for the retroflex sounds *ṭ*, *ṭh*, *ḍ*, *ḍh*, and *ṇ*, but there are signs for the sounds *r*, *ṛ*, and *l*.[197] This surprisingly resembles the phonetic system of the pre-Vedic Indo-Aryans which I have already discussed. While I am not convinced of the accuracy of S.R. Rao's, or for that matter anyone else's decipherment of the Indus script, Rao's statements quoted above are linguistically significant in the context of the possible history of retroflexion in Indo-Aryan.

9. Instability of Post-Vedic Retroflexion

9.1. Coming down to post-Vedic times, one finds that the sounds *ṇ* and *ṣ* continue to be intriguing even after the time of Śākalya. Pāṇini, who refers to Śākalya as an authority, has rules dealing with *ṇ* and *ṣ*, in particular, which show us that these sounds were still among the least predictable in Sanskrit. The whole distinction of *ṇopadeśa* and *ṣopadeśa* verbs in Pāṇini testifies to this complexity.[198] In simple terms, the distinction worked in this way: the sound *n* of roots sometimes changed to *ṇ* after *r*, *ṛ*, and *ṣ* in the prefix (*upasarga*), but sometimes it did not change. Pāṇini knew where the change took place and where it did not, but he could not find any general phonological or morphological condition that would distinguish these two classes of verbs from each other. In fact, he had to identify every such item which underwent this change individually. For example: *nṛtyati/pranṛtyati*, but *namati/praṇamati*. The same situation existed in roots with *s*. This either changed to *ṣ* or remained *s*. For example: *sīdati/viṣīdati*, but *sarpati/visarpati*. Even Patañjali could provide only a partial generalization for these cases.[199]

9.2. An instance of "right" and "wrong" speech given by Patañjali shows that retroflexion was fluid in the speech of even upper-caste learned people. He narrates the story of sages who were called Yarvāṇastarvāṇa (*MB* (M), Vol. I, Sec. I, p. 56). They were called so because instead of pronouncing the Sanskrit sequences *yad vā naḥ* and *tad vā naḥ* correctly, they used to pronounce these as *yarvāṇa* and *tarvāṇa* in everyday speech, but as *yad vā naḥ* and *tad vā naḥ* when they were either teaching or sacrificing. This story illustrates how, in these post-Vedic times, even learned Brāhmaṇas were involved in diaglossia.

9.3. In order to explicate further the relationship of retroflexes to dentals and palatals in Sanskrit, it may be observed that there is a hierarchy of phonological features. The following examples illustrate the presence and absence of such hierarchies. In Sanskrit, a voiced stop, followed by an unvoiced consonant, becomes unvoiced across the word-boundary, e.g., *d+t —> tt.* However, an unvoiced stop, followed by a voiced consonant, becomes voiced, e.g., *t+d —> dd.* This general rule, which operates only in the specified direction, indicates that the features of [+ voice] and [- voice] are of equal strength in the context of assimilation. On the other hand, the dental, palatal, and retroflex sounds show a clear hierarchy. Pāṇini's rule 8.4.40 (*stoḥ ścunā ścuḥ*) says that a dental stop or sibilant is replaced by the corresponding palatal stop or sibilant if *followed or preceded* by a palatal stop or sibilant, e.g., *tat+ca —> tacca.*[200] A palatal never becomes a dental. Pāṇini's rule 8.4.41 (*ṣṭunā ṣṭuḥ*) says that a dental stop or sibilant is replaced by the corresponding retroflex stop or sibilant *if followed or preceded* by a retroflex stop or sibilant, e.g., *rāmas+ṭīkām —> rāmaṣṭīkām, ṣaṭ+nagaryaḥ —> ṣaṇṇagaryaḥ.* A retroflex consonant never becomes dental. Similarly, there are rules to change palatals into retroflex consonants, e.g., *viś+ta —> viṣṭa, rāj+bhiḥ —> rāḍbhiḥ,* but no retroflex consonant is ever changed into a palatal. This gives us a hierarchy of dental —> palatal —> retroflex, such that there are no changes in the reverse direction.

9.4. The first half of this hierarchy is to some extent part of the Indo-Iranian heritage, while retroflexion is the added "marked" higher feature of Indian origin. Actually the Indo-European *ruki* rule which yields the Indo-Iranian *ś* from the Indo-European **s* has been partly extended in Sanskrit to *ṣ*. The *ruki* rule says that the Indo-European **s* is changed to *ś*, if preceded by *r, u, k,* or *i.* This particular rule ceases to be productive in Indo-Aryan, except as an extension to the derivation of retroflex *ṣ*. Pāṇini's rules 8.3.57 and 8.3.59 (*iṇ-koḥ, ādeśa-pratyayayoḥ*) say that *s* which is either a substitute or a part of an affix is replaced by *ṣ*, if it is preceded by *i, u, ṛ, ḷ, e, o, ai, au, h,* semi-vowels, or one of the *k*-series, e.g., *deve+su —> deveṣu.* The statement of the rule by Pāṇini is basically the same as the *ruki* rule if we understand the following relationships between different sounds:

$$s \longrightarrow ṣ \;/\; \begin{bmatrix} r \\ u \\ k \\ i \end{bmatrix} \;\text{—}$$

r covers *ṛ* (and perhaps *ḷ*, *l*)
u covers *o*, *u*, and *v*
k covers the *k*-series of stops
i covers *e*, *ai*, and *y*

For several of these conditioning sounds, there are no examples found in Sanskrit, and in the Pāṇinian group-symbols *i-Ṇ* and *kU*, several "unused" sounds are included. But the basic structure is the same as the *ruki* rule. This shift of the same basic *ruki* rule to retroflexion, a partial shift producing a split between *ś* and *ṣ*, shows the process of realigning the original Indo-Iranian non-retroflex sounds in terms of Dravidian influence on Indo-Aryan. This shift was by no means either complete or regular even by the time of Pāṇini (8.3.57ff).

Indo-European *s
↓
Indo-Iranian *s, *ś
↙ ↘
Iranian *s, *ś — Ur-Vedic *s, *ś
↓
*s, *ś, [*ṣ]
↓
Recensional Vedic after Aryan-Dravidian Convergence
/s/, /ś/, /ṣ/

9.5. Though Hans Hock (1975: 101-2) points out that retroflexion is "a natural phonetically well-motivated phenomenon, found, at least dialectally, in the majority of the sub-branches of Indo-European", I would still agree with Kuiper (1967a: 104) that "the assumption of retroflex phonemes for proto-Indo-Iranian is fully unwarranted. In old Iranian such retroflexes are entirely lacking, and in Indo-Aryan the genesis of these phonemes is in all likelihood a comparatively late process which must have taken place in the separate branch owing to foreign influence in the Indian linguistic area." At the same time, it must be emphasized that such foreign influence cannot be evidenced for the *Ṛgveda* (also see Hock, 1975: 113-14) apart from some loanwords. Extension of the *ruki* rule to yield retroflex *ṣ* marks the beginning of *ṣ* in Sanskrit, but this extension had not begun by the time of the Ur-*Ṛgveda*. As we shall see in the following sections, the same must be true of Fortunatov's Law and Burrow's "spontaneous cerebrals" (Burrow, 1972).

10. Irregular Retroflexion in Vedic Recensions

10.1. An examination of the present text of the *Ṛgveda* reveals certain aspects of retroflexion in that text which could come about only through unconscious shifts and mechanical application of the retroflexion rules by the early preredaction reciters and preservers of the Vedic texts. A few examples will suffice to clarify this point.

10.2. In classical Sanskrit as codified by Pāṇini, the change of *n* to *ṇ* and *s* to *ṣ* is specifically limited to occurrences of both the conditioning sound and the substituendum *n* or *s* within the same *pada* 'inflected word'. For instance, we can have **rāmena—> rāmeṇa* because both *r* and *n* are parts of the same inflected word, but we cannot have the sequence of the two words *tatra na* changed to **tatra ṇa*, because the sounds *r* and *n* belong to two different inflected items. The same is true of the change of *s* to *ṣ* when preceded by *iṆ* sounds (i.e., all vowels, except *a* and *ā*, *h*, and semivowels) and the *k*-series of stops. For instance, in *rāme+su* the sound *s* changes to *ṣ* and we get *rāmeṣu*; but we cannot get this change in cases like the sequence *rāme supte*, where *e* in one word is followed by *s* in another word. Thus, these rules in the normal language are not simply conditioned by the "absolute sound sequence", but by further morphological considerations. This seems to be quite natural; for instance, the Indo-European *ruki* rule is conditioned by sound sequence and morphology both, and not simply by the sound sequence.

10.3. However, if we look at the present text of the *Ṛgveda*, we find changes like the ones mentioned above taking place even when the conditioning sound belongs to a different word. All that seems to matter is the sound sequence within a metrical foot (*pāda*). A metrical foot is looked upon as if it is a continuous sequence, and the awareness of word boundaries is dispensed with in making changes like *n* —> *ṇ* and *s* —> *ṣ*. We find compounds in Vedic illustrating this kind of change, i.e., *agnī-somau*—> *agnī-ṣomau*. One may perhaps understand the "psychological propinquity" involved in a compound, though this propinquity is not exhibited in classical Sanskrit. However, in Vedic even words which are uncompounded undergo changes of this type quite often, i.e., *mo ṣu ṇaḥ* (from *mā u su naḥ*).[201] Pāṇini himself is aware that the metrical foot, not the word, is the unit used as the basis of these changes (*antaḥ pādam*).[202] If we were to say that this kind of change, based on metrical units and their assumed indivisibility, rather than on word units, was quite normal in the real Vedic spoken language, then we are faced with a precarious situation. We would have to assume that the scope of retroflexion in the real spoken Vedic language was far greater than in classical Sanskrit. This would be quite contrary to the generally seen pattern of steadily increasing strength of retroflexion, along with the increasing intensity of the Aryan-Dravidian convergence.

10.4. To me it appears that this kind of retroflexion appearing in the preserved Vedic recensions must be ascribed to the effect of recitation. There was a gradual development of conditioned and spontaneous retroflexion in the spoken language of the reciters. The rules which in the real language were conditioned by particular sound sequences and limited in scope to the grammatical word were mechanically applied by these preserver-reciters to the orally preserved archaic texts wherever the sequence conditions were met. The metrical units of the Vedic recensions were viewed by the early reciters as undivided continuous units, and along with this notion of continuity, the increasingly archaic nature of the texts helped such unconscious mechanical application of retroflexion rules. Ghatage (1962: 93) says: "The sentence or word-group as the basis of *sandhi* explains the change of *n* to *ṇ* and of *s* to *ṣ* even when the retroflex sound is found in another word, (*ni ṣasāda, pra ṇa āyūṃṣi*)."

10.5. Thus, a majority of the cases of retroflexion seen in the preserved Vedic texts must be ultimately ascribed to the gradual unconscious change in oral recitation. Such mechanical application of retroflexion rules was again not uniform.[203] That the emergence of retroflexion itself was not uniform can be seen from Pāṇini's retroflexion rules. Pāṇini himself notes that some of the retroflexion rules applied only as unconditioned options in certain Vedic texts. Thus, the same Vedic text shows *agnis tvā* and *agnis te*, but also *agniṣ ṭvā* and *agniṣ ṭe*.[204] Once personalities like Śākalya and Māṇḍūkeya had fixed the texts of their respective recensions, the orally preserved texts were as if quickly frozen with all the changes that had taken place so far, and then texts like *Prātiśākhya*s were composed to describe in detail the features of these "frozen" texts. Staal (1967: 17) rightly points out that the *Prātiśākhya*s were "not interested in the Vedic language as such, *but in the utterances handed down*" by the oral tradition. However, phenomena like retroflexion had set in before the process of "text-freezing" had begun. The same phenomenon is seen in the application of other *sandhi* rules in the preserved recensions.

10.6. In order to emphasize the point that the Ṛgvedic hymns were preserved for a long time as "continuous" archaic sequences and not as spoken sentences, I shall give a few examples which indicate that Śākalya, Yāska, and other ancient Vedic scholars who received the ancient "unanalyzed" continuous texts from the older oral traditions often could not agree on what the words were in a given sequence. All these instances are discussed by Bishnupada Bhattacharya (1958: 9-23):

R̥gveda Sequences:

1.	*vāyaḥ*	Śākalya	*/vā/yaḥ/*
		Yāska	*/vāyaḥ/*
2.	*māsakr̥t*	Śākalya	*/mā/sakr̥t/*
		Yāska	*/māsa-kr̥t/*
3.	*mehanā*	Śākalya	*/mehanā/*
		Gārgya	*/mā/iha/nā/*
4.	*tr̥ṣṇaje*	Śākalya	from *tr̥ṣṇa-ja-*
		Yāska	dative of *tr̥ṣṇaj-*

5\. Śākalya's analysis: */katham/rasāyāḥ/antaraḥ/*
Yāska's analysis: */kathaṃ-rasā/yā/antaraḥ/*

These examples show clearly that Śākalya, Gārgya, Yāska, and other ancient Vedic scholars were all dealing with orally preserved continuous texts and therefore the "words" in these "continuous texts" were essentially a matter of scholastic analysis and reconstruction. Twenty-eight pages of "false divisions and patchwords" in the second volume of *Vedic Variants* (3.66-94) substantially prove that preservation of the Vedic literature in the preredaction and preanalysis period was anything but perfect. All the austere methods of oral preservation like *krama-pāṭha*, *ghana-pāṭha*, etc., depend upon the *pada-pāṭha* 'the word-text'. If the words in a given sequence are *xyz*, then the later permutation-combinations could be produced giving us patterns like *xy*, *zy*; *xyyxxy*, *yzzyyz*, etc. But all these variations depend on first having the "continuous" text split into *x*, *y*, and *z*. If an editor-redactor felt that a certain sequence as a whole was a single word and was not to be split into *x*, *y*, and *z*, then there cannot be further recitational variations. If Śākalya, Yāska, and Gārgya often could not agree with each other on what the exact words in the orally preserved continuous texts were, we can hardly imagine that the early oral traditions had the same austerity. Rather, they were very much "natural" ways of passing on an oral text from generation to generation. Therefore, the later austere methods could not have preserved what was lost before those methods themselves came into being.

10.7. Irregular, indeed, is retroflexion in the *Ṛgveda* sequence *mo ṣu ṇaḥ*. However, it is irregular not only with respect to the classical language, it is irregular within the *Ṛgveda* itself as it has been handed down to us. Below I shall mention instances of irregular "spontaneous" *n/ṇ* variation within identical texts. These cases are collected from *Vedic Variants* (Vol. 2, pp. 444ff.).

Texts:[205]

RV, AV, TS, TB	*pra ṇo*	beside	*pra no*
SV, MS, AB	*pra ṇa*	beside	*pra na*
MS	*nakir ṇu*	beside	*nakir nu*
TS	*svar ṇa*	beside	*svar na*
KS	*indra eṇam*	beside	*indra enam*
VS, MS	*pari ṇo*	beside	*pari no*
MS	*uruṣyā ṇo*	beside	*uruṣyā no*

Similar cases of "spontaneous" *s/ṣ* variation occur in Vedic (*Vedic Variants*, Vol. 2, pp. 447ff.):

Texts:

RV	*dhanuṣ ṭanvanti*	beside	*dhanus tanvanti*
SV	*svasuṣ ṭamaḥ*	beside	*svasus tamaḥ*
TS	*agneṣ ṭvāsyena*	beside	*agnes tvāsyena*
KS, TA	*tābhiṣ ṭvām*	beside	*tābhis tvām*
SV	*prabhoṣ ṭe*	beside	*prabhos te*
TS, TB	*bṛhaspateṣ ṭvā*	beside	*bṛhaspates tvā*

These are only a few cases cited from the long list of variants in *Vedic Variants*. The only explanation which Bloomfield and Edgerton (1932: 444) could come up with is that "the greater the degree of psychological propinquity between the alterant sound and *n*, the greater is the likelihood of lingualization." But free variation within the same texts and between different texts only suggests that this "psychological propinquity" was very much a matter of the reciter's psychology and unconscious phonological inclinations.

10.8. We also have occasional free variation of spontaneous retroflexes in the Vedic texts (*Vedic Variants*: Vol. 2, pp. 87ff):

Texts:

SV	*avatasya*	beside	*avaṭasya*
HG	*manthakālo*	beside	*maṇḍakālo*
KS	*panyāt panyatarā*	beside	*paṇyāt paṇyatarā*
ApS	*padbhiḥ*	beside	*paḍbhiḥ*
KS	*rāvat*	beside	*rāvaṭ*
KS	*vikirida*	beside	*vikiriḍa*

When it comes to such unconditional variation in the same text, Bloomfield and Edgerton (1932: 444) remark: "The school tendencies which appear are capricious and unstable; one sometimes has a feeling as if Taittirīya texts, in particular, took a perverse delight in violating their own general principles." I believe I have given sufficient evidence to prove my point that the pre-redaction oral traditions were extremely irregular, imperfect, flexible and, therefore, ironically, more natural to ancient oral literature, and that a major amount of the phonetic information which we find in the existing Vedic recensions can hardly be considered to represent the original compositions.

10.9. This discussion agrees well with Burrow's excellent demonstration of the gradual increase of "spontaneous cerebrals" in Sanskrit. As Burrow (1971: 558-9) convincingly claims: "Spontaneous cerebralization has taken place in Sanskrit on quite a massive scale. Previously the view had been that cerebrals arose in Indo-Aryan only as a result of combinatory changes (though a few cases of spontaneous change had been admitted as exceptions), but it is now clear that this development has frequently taken place without the presence of any such influence." However, as Bloch (1970: 128) points out, the spontaneous cerebrals are extremely rare, if any, in the *Ṛgveda*, but the "list starts getting longer the moment we reach the ancient most period of classical Prakrit." We can compare several *Ṛgveda* words with later Sanskrit words:

Ṛgveda	Classical Sanskrit
dī-	*ḍī-*
āti-	*āṭi-*
atati	*aṭati*
cat-	*caṭ-*
udumbara	*uḍumbara*
methi	*meḍhi*
nada	*naḍa*
suvenī	*suveṇī*
bhanati	*bhaṇati*

As Abhyankar points out, the Taittirīya reciters occasionally pronounce *ṇ* in the place of *n* "without any reason" (cf. *enāḥ/eṇāḥ* and *agniḥ/agṇi*), and that this practice was noticed by Bhartṛhari as early as 400 A.D. This process of unconscious and spontaneous cerebralization was noticed by Patañjali (*MB* (M), Vol. I, Sec. I, p. 62) when he said that one must make a complete listing of all nominal stems so that one may know the correct pronunciation and not mispronounce the correct words *śaśa* and *palāśa* as **ṣaṣa* and **palāṣa*.

10.10. As Emeneau (1974: 97) points out, Burrow's spontaneous cerebrals can be best explained on the sociolinguistic assumption of the increasing adaptation of Indo-Aryan by native Dravidian speakers to their own phonological system. This process is much more evident in the development of Prakrits, and Ananthanarayana (1970: 67) rightly says that "retroflex consonants become much more frequent in the Prakrits as compared to Sanskrit which may have happened due to deeper contact of

Dravidian with them." A gradual conversion of a large Kannada-speaking region to Marathi, without any shifting of the original Dravidian population, has been discussed by S.B. Joshi (1952).

11. Retroflexion in the *Prātiśākhyas*

11.1. As has been noted earlier, no *Prātiśākhyas* consider *r* and *ṛ* to be retroflex sounds (*mūrdhanya*), and to find them classified as retroflexes we have to come down to such late texts as the *Pāṇinīya-Śikṣā* (verse 17). What is of interest is the fact that even those texts which do not classify *r* and *ṛ* as retroflexes still have the rule which says that a dental *n* becomes retroflex *ṇ* if preceded by *r* and *ṛ*. If we look at the late texts such as the *Pāṇinīya-Śikṣā*, where *r* and *ṛ* are explicitly classified as retroflexes, the rule

$$\text{(A)}\quad \text{dental } n \rightarrow \underset{\cdot}{n} \;/\; \left[\begin{array}{l} r \\ \underset{\circ}{r} \;\; \text{all three retroflexes} \\ \underset{\cdot}{s} \end{array}\right] \text{—}$$

appears to be a phonologically natural rule of contiguous or noncontiguous assimilation as the case may be.[206] But if we look at the older classifications of *r* and *ṛ* in the *Prātiśākhyas*, the rule, at first glance, does not seem to be as natural as it appears in later times. The *Ṛgvedaprātiśākhya* (1.8, 10) classifies *ṛ* as a *jihvā-mūlīya* 'produced at the root of the tongue, i.e. velar' and *r* as *danta-mūlīya* 'produced at the root of the teeth (alveolar)'. Thus, the rule for the *Ṛgvedaprātiśākhya*, considering that the *t*-series for the *Ṛgvedaprātiśākhya* is alveolar, may be stated as follows:

$$\text{(B)}\quad \text{alveolar } n \rightarrow \underset{\cdot}{n} \;/\; \left[\begin{array}{l} r \;\; \text{alveolar} \\ \underset{\circ}{r} \;\; \text{velar} \\ \underset{\cdot}{s} \;\; \text{retroflex} \end{array}\right] \text{—}$$

The *Ṛktantra* (2.1.4, 7, 8) classifies *ṛ* as *jihvā-mūlīya* 'velar', and *r* as either a *dantya* 'dental' or *danta-mūlīya* 'alveolar' sound. The *Taittirīya-Prātiśākhya* (2.18, 41) classifies *ṛ* as being produced at the upper back gums and jaws, while *r* is an alveolar. For the *Śaunakīyā Caturādhyāyikā* (1.20, 28) and *Vājasaneyī-Prātiśākhya* (1.65, 68), *ṛ* is velar and *ṛ* is alveolar. However, for all these texts, the *t*-series is a dental series, in contrast to the *Ṛgvedaprātiśākhya*. Thus, we may write a rule to cover all these classifications:

$$\text{(C)}\quad \text{dental } n \rightarrow \underset{\cdot}{n} \;/\; \begin{bmatrix} \text{velar } \underset{\circ}{r} \\ \text{upper back gums } \underset{\circ}{r} \\ \text{dental } r \\ \text{alveolar r} \end{bmatrix} \;\_\_$$

11.2. Looking at all these nonretroflex classifications of the sounds *r* and *ṛ*, and the fact that all of these texts do have the rule prescribing the change of *n* —> *ṇ*, one must conclude that this is phonologically an unnatural process at least on the surface. How can a nonretroflex sound such as *r* or *ṛ* cause the change of a dental *n* to a retroflex *ṇ*? We may hypothesize that even though different texts do not exactly consider *r* and *ṛ* to be retroflexes, still there must be something in common between a strict retroflex sound and alveolars and velars. It may be that in all variant classifications of *r* and *ṛ*, there is some degree of tongue-raising involved, if not retroflexing in the strict sense, and this tongue-raising may be considered to be the factor leading to the change of *n* to *ṇ*. Thus, this case of assimilation may be natural not so much in terms of "the point of articulation", but in terms of a somewhat similar manner of tongue-raising producing a somewhat similar acoustic quality.

11.3. This point needs some elaboration. In the ancient Sanskrit phonetic texts, we find that the Indian phoneticians considered articulatory process, as well as acoustic quality, while explaining interrelations of sounds. According to them, there was definitely something common to *r* and *ṛ*, despite the difference of the point of articulation as described by them. This common factor is designated as *ra-śruti* 'sound heard as *r*' by Patañjali.[207] Similarly, the consonant *l* and the vowel *ḷ* were said to have a common *la-śruti* 'sound heard as *l*'. The term *śruti* 'heard sound' makes it clear that these statements refer to the acoustic common factor between *r* and *ṛ*, and *l* and *ḷ*. These statements of Patañjali are based on the older statements of the *Prātiśākhyas* where the constitution of the vowel *ṛ* is explained as *ə rə*, a sequence of a vocoid plus a consonantal *r* followed by a vocoid. For instance, a text such as the *Ṛgvedaprātiśākhya* (13.14) classified *ṛ* as a velar vowel and *r* as an alveolar consonant, but it maintains at the same time that *ṛ* contains an *r*. The close relationship between *r* and *ṛ* may explain the common functional load of these two sounds in conditioning the change of *n* to *ṇ*.

11.4. It is important to realize that despite the variations in the phonetic classifications of *r* and *ṛ* in different texts, these sounds had the same functional load in all the known grammatical systems of Sanskrit, and this functional load was shared in common with the sibilant *ṣ*, which is classified by all the known Sanskrit phonetic treatises as a retroflex. Thus, we may say that there was all along a kind of phonological retroflexion shared by *r*, *ṛ*, and *ṣ* in all the known grammatical texts, despite the differences in exact phonetic classifications. As far as the change of *n* to *ṇ* was concerned, this phonological retroflexion was the most dominant factor.

11.5. This "phonological retroflexion" may be viewed in a functional sense in that all three sounds *r*, *ṛ*, and *ṣ* are "cerebralizers", if not all cerebrals themselves in the view of the *Prātiśākhyas*. In later texts such as the *Pāṇinīya-Śikṣā*, both *r* and *ṛ*, along with *ṣ* are classified as retroflexes, and thus all of them become cerebralizers and cerebrals. This development may be viewed as a phonetic development, but at the same time one may speculate that the phonological behavior of these sounds, i.e. their phonological or functional retroflexion, may have at least partially contributed to this phonetic shift. Thus, we find that the phonological requirements in Pāṇinian grammar are greatly facilitated if we assume that *r* and *ṛ* had the same point-of- articulation classification (Bare, 1976: 171). We may trace the development of retroflexion in *r* and *ṛ* in the following sequence:[208]

Indo-Iranian
r*, **r̥* (ərə*)

↓

Ur-R̥gvedic
**r*, **r̥*
(not cerebrals)

↓

Prātiśākhyas
r, *r̥*
(not cerebrals, but cerebralizers)

↓

Pāṇinīya-Śikṣā
r, *r̥*
(cerebrals and cerebralizers)

11.6. The phonetic description of *r* and *ṛ* in the Prātiśākhyas is perhaps more significant in understanding the history of retroflexion than it first appears. Fortunatov's Law connects the Indo-European clusters of **l* + dental with Sanskrit retroflexes, but in the later periods of Indo-Aryan, we find *r* and *ṛ* emerging as cerebralizers and have to connect clusters like *rt, rd, rn* with *ṭṭ, ḍḍ, ṇṇ,* and *ṭ, ḍ,* and *ṇ* in later Indo-Aryan. Emeneau speculates that in Proto-Indo-Aryan there were backed allophones of dentals, which were interpreted as retroflexes by the mixed Aryan-Dravidian bilinguals. If we observe closely the *Prātiśākhya* description of *r* and *ṛ,* we can see a phonetic motivation for Emeneau's comment in the role of these sounds as "cerebralizers". The sound *r* is rarely classified as dental. It is mostly alveolar. The vowel *ṛ* is mostly velar, and occasionally alveolar. Thus, both of these sounds may be described as "backed" with respect to dentals. This may phonetically explain why sequences such as *rt, rd, rn,* etc. would develop an assimilatory "backward" pull. Thus, a cluster of an alveolar *r* and dental *t* could easily produce an alveolar *t.* This alveolar stage would then be interpreted by the Aryan-Dravidian bilinguals as retroflexion. According to the *Ṛgvedaprātiśākhya* (1.9), the *t*-series is not dental, but alveolar. It is true that the dental/alveolar variation is not phonemic. But this precisely offers the documentary evidence for the existence of what Emeneau calls the "backed" allophones of dentals. The Indo-Iranian clusters like *zd* and *śt* may be viewed in the same light, where the palatals *z* and *ś* must have exerted a similar "backing" influence on *t* and *d.*

12. Aspects of Dravidian Influence on Indo-Aryan

12.1. With respect to the influence exerted on the early Aryan speech by the Dravidian languages of North India, I shall touch upon a point which has been left out of consideration by many previous studies. Referring to *Tolkāppiyam* (*Piṟappiyal,* verse 9), P.S. Subramanya Sastri (1930: 13) remarks: "These two sounds, *ṭ* and *ṇ,* are alveolar according to Tolkāppiyaṉar, but at present they are pronounced by rounding the tongue and allowing it to touch the uppermost part of the hard palate exactly in the same way as *ṭ* and *ṇ* are pronounced in Sanskrit. Hence, it is worth investigation whether the Sanskrit *ṭ* and *ṇ* were borrowed from the Dravidian languages." He argues that retroflexes in Sanskrit are independent of Dravidian influence and that Fortunatov's Law could have worked independently in producing Sanskrit retroflexes (P.S. Subramanya Sastri, 1934: 58-60). He quotes Jespersen in support of this "natural development" theory, and takes the existence of retroflexes for granted in the *Ṛgveda*. With this he argues that the *Ṛgveda*, even though it has retroflexes, was composed before Sanskrit had been influenced by Dravidian languages.

12.2. If all Dravidian languages had a triple contrast of dental/alveolar/retroflex, e.g., *t*, *ṯ*, *ṭ*, then at first it would appear unnatural that Dravidian influence would accelerate the change of Proto-Indo-Aryan dental *t*, *d*, *n*, or even *rt*, *rd*, *rn* to retroflex *ṭ*, *ḍ*, and *ṇ*. It would seem more natural that a dental *t*, under the influence of *r*, would shift to an alveolar *ṯ*. Thus, we might expect in Sanskrit, under Dravidian influence, an alveolar series, rather than a retroflex series.

However, Subramanya Sastri's argument is based only on one interpretation of Tamil, and does not take into account other Dravidian languages. In fact, while discussing Dravidian influence on the early phases of Indo-Aryan, consideration of Tamil is somewhat irrelevant, as early Indo-Aryan was definitely not affected by a southern Dravidian language, but must have been affected by northern Dravidian languages. Even a casual glance at the tables of phonetic correspondences given by Burrow and Emeneau (1961: xii-xiii) and Andronov (1970: 38-39) show us an astonishing picture of Dravidian alveolar sounds. The northern Dravidian languages, i.e., Brahui, Malto, and Kurukh have no alveolar sounds. Among the central and south-central Dravidian languages, only Old Kannada, Old Telugu, Gondi, and Konda have a single alveolar sound, i.e., *ṟ*, while the other languages have no alveolar sounds. Toda in the south has the maximum number of alveolar sounds, i.e. *ṯ*, *ḏ*, *ṟ*, *s̱*, *ẕ*, and *ṉ*, while Malayalam and Kolami have only some: *t*, *d*, *ṟ*, and *n*. Kolami does not have *ṟ*. Old Tamil had the alveolar sounds *ṯ*, *ḏ*, *ṟ*, and *ṉ*, but Andronov (1970: 34) points out that "in Modern Tamil alveolar sounds (and phonemes) as well as the liquid retroflex sonant *ẓ* do not exist."

12.3. We have no clear historical evidence that the southern Dravidians of modern times are the ancient northern Dravidians pushed downwards by the Aryans. Brahui, Kurukh and Malto share some common innovations, and Emeneau (1962c: 62ff.) argues for the existence of a northern Dravidian family which included these languages. "Having also words in common not known from other Dravidian languages, they may be considered as remnants of a large north Dravidian dialect area, which was subsequently overlaid and assimilated by the Aryans" (Parpola, 1975:

191). Thus, it seems natural to assume that the Aryans confronted and gradually intermingled with the northern Dravidians who did not have alveolar consonants, but, like all Dravidians, had markedly retroflex consonants.

12.4. This is quite interesting. Existence of alveolar *ṟ* in some of the central Dravidian languages may explain to some extent why the Sanskrit *ṟ* of the *Prātiśākhya* period could vary from dental to alveolar, and could stay an alveolar for some time, despite the emergence of *ṭ*, *ṭh*, *ḍ*, *ḍh*, and *ṇ*. The central Dravidian languages, Old Kannada and Old Telugu show retroflex *ṭ*, *ḍ*, *ṛ*, and *ṇ*, but they do have the alveolar *ṟ* as well. However, under the influence of the existence of retroflex *r* in all the Dravidian languages, and internal phonemic leveling, the alveolar *ṟ* of the *Prātiśākhya* period seems to have shifted later to the retroflex *r*, as is seen in the *Pāṇinīya-Śikṣā* and other later treatises. In the development of retroflexes from dentals, there must have been an alveolar or "backed dental" stage, but this stage must have been quite unstable, since the northern Dravidian languages did not have alveolars. The existence of this unstable alveolar Sanskrit series is further supported by the fact that the *Ṛgvedaprātiśākhya* considers the *t*-series to be alveolar rather than dental. This variation is clearly allophonic, but its existence as recorded by the *Ṛgvedaprātiśākhya* is significant nonetheless.

12.5. Northern Dravidian languages do not have *ṣ*, and it is absent from Old Kannada, Old Telugu, and Old Tamil. This makes it harder to link emergence of *ṣ* in Sanskrit with any direct Dravidian influence. This corroborates the view expressed by Burrow (1971: 554) and Ivanov and Toporov (1968: 49) that the development of *ṣ* in Sanskrit, by a special modification of the *ruki* rule, was a somewhat different process from the emergence of *ṭ*, *ṭh*, *ḍ*, *ḍh*, and *ṇ*. However, later phonemicization of *ṣ* is indirectly connected with the general leveling of all retroflex sounds. Thus, northern Dravidian languages substantially explain the phonetic and phonemic transformations of the ancient Indo-Aryan. Since northern and central Dravidian languages show the most influence by Indo-Aryan (Zvelebil and Svarny, 1955: 379- 80), we may look to these languages for early Dravidian influence on Indo-Aryan, rather than to the remote languages of extreme south India.

12.6. With respect to the argument given above in this section, Professor Emeneau suggests (in a personal communication) that Proto-Dravidian had a set of alveolars and most probably even the early North Dravidian languages had alveolars at the time they met the Indo-Aryans. Not being a Dravidianist myself, I can only gratefully accept Professor Emeneau's suggestion, without any further questions. If this is indeed the case, it would lead to a reconsideration of the explanation given above.

One could argue that in a situation of language contact, the phonetic or phonemic polarities are more distinctly noticeable than the intermediate positions. Thus, it is quite conceivable that Dravidians perceiving the Aryan language viewed dentals and their backed allophones in terms of this polarity principle. Therefoie, the backed allophones of dentals shifted to the polar position of retroflexion rather than stabilizing at the intermediate position of alveolars. Eventually, as the dental-retroflex polarity became dominant in Indo-Aryan, the Dravidian languages in the North, which were encircled by Indo-Aryan, themselves adopted this dominant polarity, and hence the North Dravidian alveolars were eventually lost. As an example of this polarity principle, one may point out that despite the presence of alveolars in the South Dravidian languages today, the English alveolars are still percieved and pronounced by the speakers of these languages as retroflexes. This is the only explanation I can come up with at present. This explanation fits very well with the concept of "maximal differentiation" advocated by André Martinet (1966: 191-92).

I have retained my previous explanation simply because both of these explanations are, coming from a non-Dravidianist as they do, no more than suggestions.

13. Problems in the Reconstruction of the Ur-*Ṛgveda*

13.1. Though it may be concluded with a fair degree of probability that the language of the Ur-*Ṛgveda* could not have been far removed from the ancient Iranian, the process of actual linguistic reconstruction is full of extreme difficulties, some of which we may never be able to overcome. Chatterji (1960: 58-59) says that the present text of the *Ṛgveda* (1.1.1a) *agnim īḷe purohitam* may have been originally *agnim izdai purazdhitam*. Going back from *ḷ* or *ḍ* to **zd* takes us from a single consonant to a cluster. This would also lead us to assume perhaps the lengthening of *i* to *ī* (cf. **nizda —> nīḍa*). Thus, it is important to realize that restoring the non-retroflex originals of the Ur-*Ṛgveda* would also perhaps require vocalic changes, if we go all the way back to the Proto-Indo-Iranian clusters. Fortunately this does not alter the number of syllables in the text and hence would not harm the metrical form. We must also realize that the sound change from *zd* to *ḍ* or *Ḷ* is not a direct change of one sound into another sound, but implies a whole range from *zd* to *ḍ* or *Ḷ*. It seems probable that the cluster *zd* would pass through a phase of being reduced to a geminate or an emphatic single consonant before being reduced to a single retroflex *ḍ* or *Ḷ*. Śākalya's own word-text *duḥ-dabha* for the *Ṛgveda* word *dūḶabha* (7.86.4c), shows that he is aware of a probable development such as *durdabha* —> *dūḍabha* —> *dūḶabha*. It is quite possible that the Ur-*Ṛgveda* had some kind of geminates or emphatic backed allophones of dentals. However, in the present state of our knowledge, we cannot be more precise about the exact nature of these Ur-*Ṛgveda* sounds. Mehendale (1963: 41) shows that a palatal pronunciation of the retroflex *ṣ* continued dialectally in Sanskrit even during the period of the Upaniṣads. This makes the prospect of an exact reconstruction quite difficult.

13.2. I shall discuss only a few problems in the linguistic reconstruction of the original nonretroflex sounds. For instance, if we remove *ṣ* from the text of the present Ṛgveda, where do we go back to? The retroflex *ṣ* in Sanskrit corresponds to various sounds in different Prakrits, e.g., to *s* in Pāli (Skt. *puruṣa* / Pāli *purisa*); to *ś* in Māgadhī (*puliśe*); to *kh* in some branches of Yajurveda (*purukha*), and to *ch* (Skt *ṣaṭ* / Pāli *cha*). This may indicate the complexity of the problem. Alfred Master's description of *ṣ* and its features raises complex historical problems. He remarks: "Now *ṣ* is a cerebral by convention only. It is, like *r*, a cerebralizer and has been differentiated from the palatal *ś*, its fellow hush-sound, partly for graphical, partly for phonetic reasons. So we find *aṣṭau* 'eight', but *aśītiḥ* 'eighty' *pṛṣṭa* 'asked', and *praśna* 'question'. The phoneme is not carried into Middle Indian and for *ṣaṣ* we find *cha*, which seems to show that *ṣ* is a graphic variant of *kṣ*, regular predecessor of *ch* or *kh* in Middle Indian. The later confusion of *ṣ* and *kh*, both phonetically and graphically (the Gujarati *akṣara* for *kh* is a form of Nāgarī *ṣ*) points to the same conclusion" (Master, 1960: 261). Existence of *ṣ* in the ancient northwestern inscriptional and non-inscriptional Prakrits complicates the issue of *ṣ* to a great extent. The sound *ṣ* is distinctly preserved in the Niya Prakrit, in the Prakrit Dharmapada, in northwestern Aśokan dialects and in Dardic languages (Konow, 1936: 609; Burrow, 1936: 419). Niya Prakrit, which presents a pronouncedly more archaic aspect than the northwestern Aśokan dialect, better preserves the cluster *rṣ* (Burrow, 1936: 422). Like Niya Prakrit, occasionally later Kharoṣṭhī inscriptions of the northwestern region have *ṣ* even in those contexts where Sanskrit shows *ś* or *s*, e.g., *śr*—> *ṣ* in *ṣamana* (from *śramaṇa*); in Niya, *śmaśru*—> *maṣu* and *śrayate* —> *ṣayati*; the Kharoṣṭhī Dharmapada shows it, and also a similar treatment of *sr* in which *anavaṣuta* is equated with *anavasruta* (Burrow, 1936: 422). These examples would suggest that there indeed was a distinction between *ṣ*, *ś* and *s*, and they show the role of *r* as a cerebralizer even for clusters with *ś* and *s*.

13.3. Mehendale's occasional reconstructions of some of the "pre-Sanskrit" stages also raise some interesting issues. He says: "I had suggested that such an extension of I[nternal] R[econstruction] can be done on the basis of Sanskrit past passive participle morpheme, where we can see the alternation *t/ṭ* (*ga-ta/tuṣ-ṭa*). On internal evidence this *ṭ* can be reconstructed as **t*, because *t* never occurs after *ṣ* in Sanskrit. ... But once this is done, we make use of this information and always remember the possibility of reconstructing *ṭ* as *t* in other non-alternating items where *ṭ* occurs in the same environment (after *ṣ*) in which it alternates with *t* in the paradigm. Hence, the possibility of reconstructing Sk. *aṣṭa-* as **aṣta* should not be lost sight of when we are comparing Sanskrit with Avesta which shows the cognate *aśta*" (1968: 88). Referring to the forms *gata-* and *tuṣṭa-*, he says: "We have every right to assume that the morpheme of the pre-Sanskrit stage had the phonetic shape **ta*, and not **ṭa*. The implication of our choice is that in the history of Sanskrit **naṣta* —> *naṣṭa*, and not **gaṭa* —> *gata*. In this illustration, I do not think anyone will feel satisfied if we were to say that from the Sanskrit alternation *t/ṭ*, it should be possible to reconstruct 'one original morpheme, *ṭa*'" (1968· 96-97).

13.4. I largely agree with Mehendale's analysis, but would like to point out some differences. I would rather consider his "pre-Sanskrit" stage as closely corresponding to what I think to be the state of the original compositions of the *Ṛgveda*. Another point is that I doubt if one can reconstruct forms like **tuṣta* and **naṣta*, as different from the Indo-Iranian **tuśta* and **naśta*, implying that there was a stage in the history of Indo-Aryan when the phonetic contrast between *ś* and *ṣ* had developed, but the phonetic contrast between *t* and *ṭ* had not developed. In my opinion, the initial allophonic divergence between *ś* and ṣ on the one hand, and *t* and *ṭ* on the other, leading eventually to a phonemic split, went on side by side.

13.5. Mehendale has another interesting discussion of the emergence of *ś* from *s*. He says: "In Sanskrit, *s* alternates with *ṣ*, some of the environments being when the former is preceded by *i, u, e, o.* The first two of these vowels have closeness as the common feature, but while *i* is a front vowel, *u* is a back vowel. The first and the third are both front, but *i* is close while *e* is an open vowel. Now on some other evidence if it is possible to reconstruct Sk. *e* and *o* as **ai* and **au,* then we discover closeness as a feature common to all the four (*i, u, ai* and *au*) environments. Therefore it should be possible for us to say that the change **s* —> *ṣ* is two stages removed from the attested stage, while **ai* —> *e* is one stage removed" (1968: 101). This is an interesting discussion and would indicate one possible way of reconstructing a pre-*ṣ* stage in the pre-history of Sanskrit. It shows the possibility of certain vocalic changes being necessary for such a reconstruction. I shall not go into a detailed discussion of Mehendale's analysis at this point, but I may point out that he is taking into account only the vowels in the *ruki* rule and that basically the *ruki* rule yields a palatal *ś* from Indo-European **s,* and that this rule is partially extended in Sanskrit to *ṣ.* Even within Sanskrit, the rule as stated by Pāṇini (8.3.57, 58) incorporates more conditioning sounds than just *i, u, e,* and *o* (cf. the examples: **dik-su* —> *dikṣu, *pitṛ-su* —> *pitṛṣu, *a-kār-sī-t* —> *akārṣīt*). The question as to how, if at all, the sounds *i, u, r,* and *k* can be considered a natural class has been the subject of considerable investigation by Andersen (1968) and Zwicky (1970), although no entirely satisfactory solution has as yet emerged.

14. Other Instances of Alleged Dravidian Influence

14.1. If the retroflex sounds do belong to a post-Ṛgvedic period, this would lead to a reconsideration of other elements such as gerunds and particular uses of *iti* 'thus', which are ascribed by some scholars to Dravidian influence (Kuiper, 1967). There is no reason to rule out all foreign influences from the original speech of the Ṛgvedic poets. The very fact that there are loan-words in the *Ṛgveda* obviously indicates that there was some give and take even at that early period. However, as discussed in this paper, there is no evidence of extensive pre-Ṛgvedic convergence with non-Aryans. This opens up several new possibilities for consideration. If the Ṛgvedic gerunds and the use of *iti* cannot be traced back to extensive pre-Ṛgvedic convergence, what kinds of contacts may be considered to be sufficient for such borrowings of new patterns? Could these elements be traced back to some other source?

14.2. In fact, in both the cases, i.e., gerunds and the use of *iti,* we are not even talking about large-scale lexical borrowing. Kuiper (1967: 91) notes that the word *iti* is an inherited word.[209] Similarly, in the case of gerunds in the *Ṛgveda*, we have to accept that they are not borrowed lexical items, but are developments of inherited roots, or, as Kantor and Jeffers (1984) point out, the Sanskrit gerund-endings reflect regrammatized instrumental (*-tvā*, *-yā*, *-tyā*) or locative (*tvī*) verbal noun suffixes, and that they are to be associated etymologically with Old Indic infinitives in *-tu*, *-ti*, and *-i*. In this case, one would be seeking an explanation of a development of an inherited set of items in terms of foreign influence.

14.3. Can we say on the basis of any general principles that the contact with the non-Aryans which was insufficient to produce large-scale phonological changes could have been sufficient to promote new morphological and syntactic developments of inherited items? Weinreich (1953) has studied such theoretical issues concerning languages in contact.[210] However, the total inventory of known linguistic and extralinguistic facts about early Aryan- Dravidian contacts is not sufficient to let us derive any conclusions which are in any real sense beyond doubt. Kuiper (1967: 90) himself has raised several important doubts concerning the extension of methods based on later periods of history to early periods of prehistory. It may be noted that several scholars have expressed their disbelief concerning Dravidian influence in the development of Sanskrit gerunds (Kuiper, 1967: 83). A better approach here would be to investigate whether Ṛgvedic gerunds are rare and /or used differently than in Dravidian.

14.4. While considering retroflexion in Sanskrit and the question of Dravidian influence on early Indo-Aryan phonology, another instance ascribed by some scholars to Dravidian influence deserves mention. Chattopadhyaya (1974: 194ff.) says that in the days of Pāṇini the short *a* in Sanskrit was an open (*vivṛta*) sound like long *ā*, and that in post-Pāṇinian times this open short *a* became a close short *a* due to Dravidian influence. I have discussed this question in detail elsewhere (Deshpande, 1975c) and have shown that there is no evidence to indicate that Sanskrit short *a* was an open sound in the days of Pāṇini and none to indicate that Dravidian influence on Sanskrit began only after Pāṇini. From the evidence in the *Aitareya-Āraṇyaka*, we know that retroflexion had already made its way into standardized Sanskrit speech before Śākalya, who precedes Pāṇini. Thus, if the Sanskrit short *a* became close due to Dravidian influence, it would probably have become close before the time of Śākalya. Actually, Macdonell (1916: 14) claims that short *a* was open at the time of the composition of the *Ṛgveda*, but had become close by the time the Vedic recensions were put together. This may, then, parallel the case of retroflexion. However, the evidence presented by Macdonell is not quite conclusive for a determination of the change in phonetic quality of *a*, and there is no evidence yet to conclude that North Indian Proto-Dravidian had indeed a close short *a*. If Old Tamil is any indication, according to *Tolkāppiyam*, there is no quality distinction between Old Tamil *a* and *ā* (Subbiah, 1968: 253). Max Walleser (1927: 195ff.), on the other hand, argues that the short *a* in Sanskrit has always been close, and he connects it with the Indo-European schwa (ə). If that is the case, we have no reason to suspect Dravidian influence in this respect.

15. Conclusions

15.1. In conclusion, it must be emphasized that the aim of this paper is not to discount the contacts of non-Aryans with Aryans in Ṛgvedic times; but we must carefully differentiate between contacts, conflicts, confrontations, coexistence, and convergence. In the *Ṛgveda* we have evidence for contacts, conflicts, and confrontations with non-Aryans, but certainly there is no evidence for convergence with them. The Aryan speech at this time could not have been phonologically affected by foreign speeches. I think that Emeneau (1974) has come up with the correct linguistic process. Later speakers of Sanskrit, a mixed Aryan-non-Aryan community, interpreted allophones of Proto-Indo-Aryan in terms of their native Dravidian system. However, the convergence of Aryan-non-Aryan peoples required to support this process can be evidenced not for the Ṛgvedic times, but only for later times, and Emeneau himself, among others, has given significant evidence for later convergence in terms of the development of caste terminology.

15.2. Hock (1975: 114) considers all the available evidence and concludes: "While it is thus unlikely that there was early convergence of Indo-Aryan with Dravidian, this should not be understood to imply that there is proof against such a convergence." Burrow (1955: 387) cautiously says: "The main influence of Dravidian on Indo-Aryan was concentrated at a particular historical period, namely between the late Vedic period and the formation of the classical language." On the basis of comparisons of caste terminology in Sanskrit and Dravidian languages, Emeneau (1974: 113) argues that "the invading Aryans did not bring this social structure with them. They either met it in India and adopted it in their process of Indianization, or they and those they met it in India developed it together to produce the India we know now." However, the elaborate lists of caste terms on which Emeneau's argument for convergence is based are first found in the *Mahābhārata* and not earlier. From a study of Agnicayana, Converse (1974) comes to a conclusion that post-Ṛgvedic Aryans adopted the elaborate brick altars from non-Aryan communities and this shows that such a convergence took place in the post-Ṛgvedic period. Hart (1975) arrives at similar conclusions through a study of the literary history of Indo-Aryan and Dravidian. He claims that the principle of poetic suggestion (*vyañjanā*) is of Dravidian origin, and that it makes its headway in Sanskrit literature after the *Mahābhārata*, but is clearly seen in the *Rāmāyaṇa*.

15.3. Even after accepting the arguments for Dravidian linguistic influence at the time of the *Ṛgveda*, Trautmann (1974: 84) shows that the ancient North Indian literature does not show signs of cross-cousin marriage, which is a marked feature of Dravidian communities: "... had cross-cousin marriage obtained among the dominant Aryan group, its literature would have so testified." Thus, the Indo-Aryans did not borrow everything that was Dravidian from the first day of their arrival in India, and it is quite reasonable to assume that the non-Aryan influence on the language and culture of the early Indo-Aryans was not of equal strength at all times. Weinreich (1953: 67) discusses various views concerning relationships of foreign influence in different linguistic domains such as vocabulary, sound system, morphology, syntax, proper names, etc., and points out that it is still very premature to say that we can predict priorities and proportions of influences among these various domains in a given situation of language contact.

15.4. This discussion makes us aware of the fact that explaining the emergence of a feature like retroflexion involves many complex elements. After stating that "Indic acquires Dravidian retroflex apicals", Bailey and Gardens (1974: 16) remark: "To analyse such typical cases in the history of languages as natural sound changes would of course be as theoretically profitless as to formulate umlauted German noun plurals or apophonic English verbs (e.g., *sing*, *sang*, sung) in terms of natural phonological rules." This indicates that features which are due to linguistic convergence cannot be reconstructed as part of texts belonging to a preconvergence stage, and it also warns us against pure genetic explanations of such features. Though features like retroflexion are unnatural from the point of view of purely genetic evolution within the

Indo-Aryan family, recent studies indicate that such features can be explained in terms of naturalness of loan phonology. Lovins (1974: 240, 244) explains that the historic statement of the problem of loan phonology is that a speaker of a given language, substitutes for them those that he takes to be "closest" in his own language. This further suggests that a feature like retroflexion, not genetically evolved, is a product of the process of phonetic approximation (Lovins, 1974: 240) of the phonic material of a given nonretroflexed language by the speakers of a retroflexed language. Thus, even in theory, it is hard to assume that speakers of a non-retroflexed language adopted the foreign feature of retroflexion without its phonetic approximation to their own system. Thus, to explain the development of retroflexion, we have to posit a sociolinguistic process of adaptation of a nonretroflexed Indo-Aryan tongue by the speakers of a retroflexed language. In the early stages, the principle of *phonetic approximation* must have affected the linguistic perception as well as the linguistic production of these people who adopted a nonretroflexed language as their second language. This process of linguistic adaptation guided by the principle of phonetic approximation can, then, be used to explain what happens in a preliterate oral tradition.

The orthodox Indian tradition has greatly respected the relationship of a teacher and his disciple and has continued to believe that nothing ever changed in this oral transmission. It is believed that the oral text has been handed down from one generation to the next without any changes. However, we must view a preliterate oral tradition with a fresh linguistic and analytical approach. We must distinguish a "pseudo-connection" from a "real connection" between two successive synchronic states of a preliterate oral text. For this purpose, we may compare the model of linguistic change given by Andersen (1973: 767):

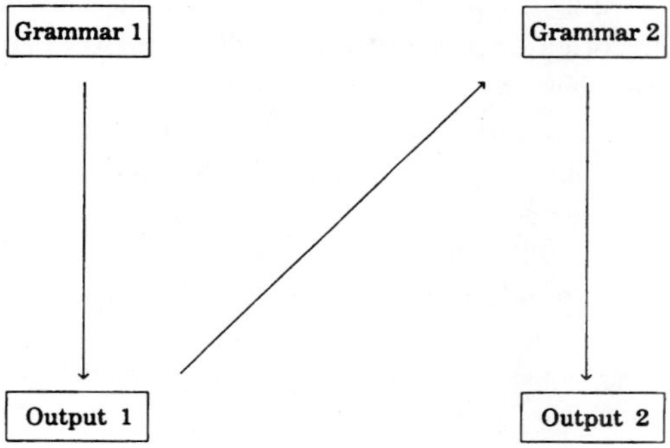

With respect to this model, Ebert (1976: ix) says: "The crucial process in language transmission - and the one that plays a central role in language - is the learner's formulation of his grammar (Grammar 2) on the basis of the output of speakers from whom he learns (Output 1). An analysis of Output 1 by the learner which differs from Grammar 1 can lead to an observable change in usage."

By using this analysis of language change and language learning, we may construct a model for gradual change in a text orally transmitted from a teacher to a student in a preliterate society. The following is an attempted model:

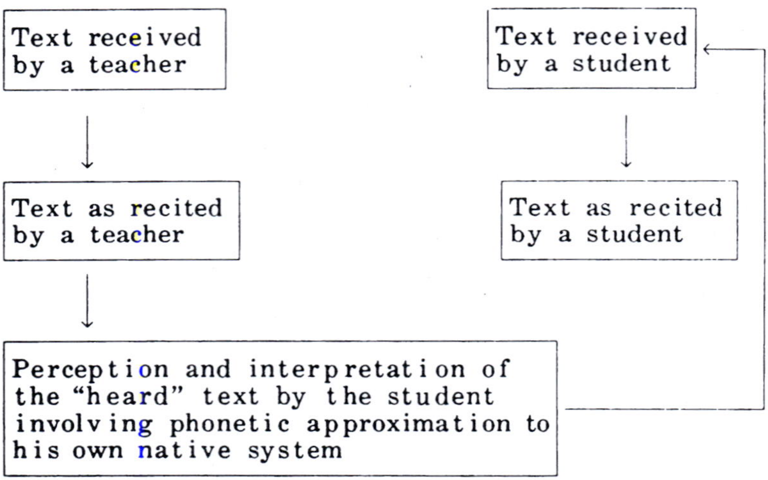

We must realize that only such dynamic models will explain the actual complex processes involved in the development of the nongenetic features like retroflexion in orally transmitted Indo-Aryan texts. With the above model in view, we may further sharpen our analytical tools.

Lovins (1974: 244) talks about how context-sensitive processes determine one's perception of one's own native language and also of foreign sounds: "When we speak, we apply allophonic processes 'forwards' to produce contextual variants; when we listen to someone else, we apply them 'backwards' to relate the allophones to their associated phonemes. ... Likewise, in listening to unfamiliar foreign sounds, we try to relate what we hear to possible surface forms in our own language. These

FIGURE 3

MODEL OF AN ORAL TRADITION

"A student of the previous generation becomes a teacher of the next".

$$(S\text{-}T)_1 \longrightarrow (S\text{-}T)_2 \longrightarrow (S\text{-}T)_3 \longrightarrow (S\text{-}T)_n$$

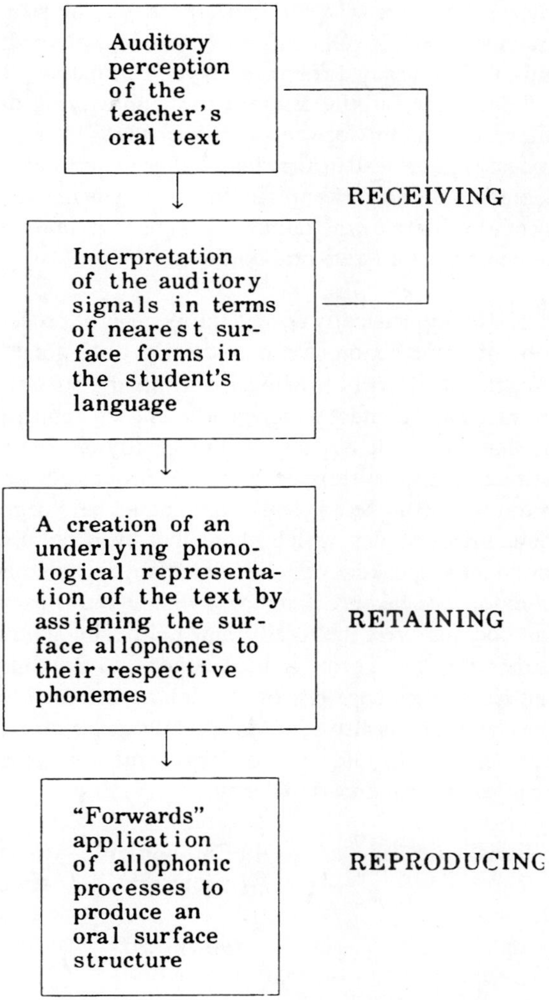

(S-T) = Student of one generation, teacher of the next.

surface forms may already be acceptable underlying representations, or related to such by backwards-derivation of an allophonic process." Thus, one can say that when a teacher recites a "received text", he is applying allophonic processes "forwards" to produce an oral text. When a disciple hears this oral text, he applies the allophonic processes "backwards" to relate the heard allophones to "appropriate" phonemes in his own phonological system. When he recites the text, he applies the allophonic processes "forwards" to the "received text". This received text must now, obviously, exist in full conformity with his native phonological system. Thus, if there is any difference between the native phonological systems of the teacher and the disciple, these underlying differences, plus the differences in the "forwards-and-backwards" application of allophonic processes, must lead to a gradual change in the transmitted oral text. This theoretical framework explains in a most clear manner the inner functioning of a preliterate oral tradition. Figure 3 is an attempt to schematize the nature of a pre-literate oral tradition.

15.5. Having basically accepted Emeneau's "process" for the development of retroflexion, we may clearly distinguish between language contact that allows borrowing of vocabulary, but not transfer of phonetic contrasts, and contact which generates such contrasts. How far can we say that the Vedic Aryans, who originally did not have retroflexion in their language, developed this feature through contacts with non-Aryans whom they conquered, hated, dominated, and segregated? There are abundant examples which show that even culturally and politically dominating speakers of retroflexed languages could not transmit retroflexion to speakers of languages without retroflexion. For example, the Cambodians were culturally and politically dominated by an Indo-Khmer empire. Through these Hindu and Buddhist contacts, the Old Cambodian language borrowed a large number of Sanskrit/Pali words. The Cambodians also adopted several aspects of Indian culture, but not retroflexion. In Old and Modern Cambodian, the Sanskrit and Pālī retroflexes are reduced to dentals:[211]

Sanskrit-Pālī		Old Cambodian	Modern Cambodian
t	—>	*t* (voiceless)	*t* in clusters, otherwise *d*
th	—>	*th* (voiceless)	*th*
d	—>	*d* (voiced)	*t*
dh	—>	*dh* (voiced)	*th*

n	—>	*n* (voiceless?)	*n*
ṭ	—>	*t* (voiceless)	*d*
ṭh	—>	*th* (voiceless	*th*
ḍ	—>	*d* (voiced)	*d*
ḍh	—>	*dh* (voiced)	*th*
ṇ	—>	*n* (voiced)	*n*

The same phenomenon takes place in Old and Modern Siamese:

Sanskrit-Pālī		Old Siamese		Modern Siamese
t, ṭ	—>	*t*	(voiceless)	*t*
th, ṭh	—>	*th*	(voiceless)	*th*
d, ḍ	—>	*d*	(voiced)	*th*
dh, ḍh	—>	*d*	(voiced)	*th*
n, ṇ	—>	*n*	(voiceless?)	*n*

Burmese does have separate characters for retroflex sounds, which are used only in writing Pālī words, but the Burmese pronounce them exactly as the corresponding alveolars.[212] Assamese, an Indo-Aryan language which is historically almost a dialect of Bengali, shows convergence of dentals and retroflexes into alveolars, an event which can be explained as the result of the predominance of a Tibeto-Burman substratum in the Assamese population.[213] There is retroflexion in Javanese, but it can be argued that it is not due to the influence of Sanskrit phonology.[214]

15.6. Thus, simple contacts and even cultural and political domination do not seem to have caused the development of retroflexion in a nonretroflexed language. On the other hand, with respect to the occurrence of some retroflex sounds in eastern Iranian languages like Pashto, Parachi, and Ormuṛi, one can speak of Indian linguistic influence. Geiger and Kuhn (1895-1901: 206-7) consider this point under "Fremde Elemente im Afghanischen", and speak of the influence of Sindhi. Morgenstierne speaks of Indic, and particularly Dardic, influence on Pashto.[215] Bloch (1965: 56) thinks that "the presence of cerebrals in Afghan probably points to an Indian substratum", and a Dravidian element may be suspected on the basis of the nearby presence of Brahui.

15.7. In the case of Sanskrit, the origin of retroflexion lies not so much in the Aryans borrowing this trait from Dravidians in early times as in Dravidians adapting Aryan speech to their native phonology. As we can see from the cultural history of India, by the time of the Brāhmaṇa period, the speakers of the Sanskrit language were not ethnically pure ancient Vedic Aryans, but were already a mixed people. The development of the caste system shows to what extent the non-Aryan elements were Aryanized in the historical development of Hinduism.[216] Non-Aryans and non-Vedic Aryans were raised to the status of Brāhmaṇas and Kṣatriyas, and the Ṛgvedic enemies such as Paṇis seem to have been absorbed into the Vaiśya caste.[217] This makes one wonder if the descendents of the original Aryans were numerically not a minority in this mixed Aryanized society (Panikkar, 1961: 31). In the words of Dandekar (1967: 28-29): "In the long and continual history of Hinduism, the age of the Veda must be said to have occurred more or less as an interlude."

15.8. In classical Hinduism, the pre-Aryan Proto-Hinduism regained its strength in an Aryanized form, so much so that the Vedic gods like Indra and Varuṇa and their elaborate fire-sacrifices almost became extinct, while Kṛṣṇa, Śiva, and host of other gods and goddesses came to dominate the field, with the claim that they still represented the essence of the Vedas.[218] This process gradually changed the constitution of the Sanskrit-speaking community in such a way that the ethnic non-Aryan segment of this Aryanized community steadily increased in proportion. In such circumstances, speakers of Sanskrit were essentially bilinguals, with Sanskrit as their second language, and a local language as their first language. The particular process involved in the development of retroflexion as described by Emeneau applies clearly to this post-Ṛgvedic period. Steadily increasing retroflexion in Indo-Aryan is a significant index of this sociolinguistic and religious transformation of the Sanskrit-speaking community. However, to the speech of the Ṛgvedic poets, retroflexion was almost certainly still a foreign habit.

NOTES

1. Besides Deshpande (1979a), sociolinguistic issues have been discussed in other publications: Deshpande (1978), (1982b), (1985a), (1985b) and (1985c).
2. *ābhirādi-giraḥ kāvyeṣv apabhraṃśa iti smṛtāḥ / śāstreṣu saṃskṛtād anyad apabhraṃśatayoditam //*, *Kāvyādarśa* I. 36.
3. *brahma vā idam agra āsīt / tad ekaṃ san na vyabhavat / tac chreyo-rūpam atyasṛjata kṣatraṃ yāny etāni devatrā kṣatrāṇīndro varuṇaḥ somo rudraḥ parjanyo yamo mṛtyur īśāna iti / tasmāt kṣatrāt paraṃ nāsti / tasmād brāhmaṇaḥ kṣatriyam adhastād upāste rājasūye kṣatra eva tad yaśo dadhāti saiṣā kṣatrasya yonir yad brahma /*, *Śatapatha-Brāhmaṇa*, XIV, iv, 2, 23.
4. *sa hovācājātaśatruḥ pratilomaṃ caitad yad brāhmaṇaḥ kṣatriyam upeyād brahma me vakṣyatīti /*, *Bṛhadāraṇyaka-Upaniṣad*, 2.1.15.
5. *ehi tvaṃ brāhmaṇa yena bhagavā tenupasaṅkama / upasaṅkamitvā mama vacanena bhagavato pāde sirasā vandāhi / evaṃ ca vadehi - "rājā bhante māgadho ajātasattu vedehiputto vajjī abhiyātukāmo," Mahāparinibbānasutta, Dīghanikāya, Mahāvaggo*, Nalanda Edition, p. 58.
6. *rājā bho gotama ... /*, Ibid, p. 58.
7. *dāni mayaṃ bho gotama gacchāma, bahukiccā mayaṃ bahukaraṇīyā ti /*, Ibid, p. 61.
8. *yassa dāni tvaṃ brāhmaṇa kālaṃ maññasī ti /*, Ibid, p. 61.
9. *Ambaṭṭhasutta, Dīghanikāya*, Nalanda Edition, Vol. I, pp. 84ff.
10. *iti kho ambaṭṭha yadā khattiyo parama-nihīnattaṃ patto hoti tadā pi khattiyā va seṭṭhā, hīnā brāhmaṇā / ... khattiyo seṭṭho jane tasmiṃ ye gotta-paṭisārino ti /*, Ibid, p.86.
11. *cattāro me bho gotama vaṇṇā - khattiyā brāhmaṇā vessā suddā /*, Ibid, p. 80.
12. *jānāsi taṃ janapadakalyāṇiṃ khattiyī vā brāhmaṇī vā vessī vā suddī vā ti /*, *Poṭṭhapādasutta, Dīghanikāya*, Nalanda Edition, Vol. I, p. 160. Also *Tevijjasutta, Dīghanikāya*, Ibid, p. 204.
13. *Mahāparinibbānasutta, Dīghanikāya*, Nalanda Edition, Vol. II, p. 86.
14. *bhagavā pi khattiyo mayaṃ pi khattiyā, mayaṃ pi arahāma bhagavato sarīrānaṃ bhāgaṃ /*, Ibid, p. 126.
15. Franklin Edgerton (1953, vol. I, pp. 1-2) quotes passages from the Pāli canon, the Vinaya of the Mahīśāsakas, the Vinaya of the Dharmaguptakas and the *Vinayamātṛkā* on the early debates over the language of the Buddhist canon.
16. *na bodhisattvā hīna-kuleṣūpapadyante caṇḍāla-kuleṣu vā veṇukāra-kule vā rathakāra-kule vā puṣkasa-kule vā / atha tarhi kula-dvaye evopapadyante brāhmaṇa-kule kṣatriya-kule ca / tatra yadā brāhmaṇa-guruko loko bhavati, tadā brāhmaṇa-kule upapadyante / yadā kṣatriya-guruko bhavati tadā kṣatriya-kule upapadyante / etarhi bhikṣavaḥ kṣatriya-guruko lokaḥ / tasmād bodhisattvāḥ kṣatriya-kule upapadyante /*, *Lalitavistara* p. 14. The very same day the Bodhisattva was born, thousands of girls were also born to Kṣatriya and Brāhmaṇa householders: *tasyām eva rātryāṃ viṃśati-kanyā-sahasrāṇi kṣatriya-brāhmaṇa-naigama-gṛhapati-mahā-śāla-kuleṣu jātāḥ /*, Ibid, p. 83. Again notice the order. The Kṣatriyas come before the Brāhmaṇas, and there are no Vaiśyas or Śūdras.

17. *kauśala-kulaṃ mātaṅga-cyuty-upapannam na mātṛ-pitṛ-śuddham / ... tena na tat pratirūpam /, Lalitavistara*, p. 15.
18. *tatrogratejā nāma brahmakāyiko devaputraḥ ... evam āha - yathā brāhmaṇānāṃ mantra-veda-śāstra-pāṭheṣv āgacchati, tādṛśenaiva rūpeṇa bodhisattvo mātuḥ kukṣāv avakrāmitavyaḥ /, Lalitavistara*, Ibid, p. 29. This is of course balanced by the claim that the Buddhistic gods come down to the earth to teach Vedas to the Brāhmaṇas: *atha śuddhāvāsakāyikā devaputrā jambudvīpam āgatya divyaṃ varṇam antardhāpya brāhmaṇa-veṣeṇa brāhmaṇān vedān adhyāpayanti sma /*, Ibid, p. 11.
19. *Mahābhāṣya* (K), vol. 3, p. 174; *Manusmṛti*, 2.17-20; *Vāsiṣṭha-dharma-sūtra*, 8-9, 12-15. Also see: Romila Thapar (1973: 5), and Deshpande (1979a: 117).
20. *bhagavaṃ ca ṇaṃ addhamāgahīe bhāsāe dhammam ācikkhai / sā vi ya ṇaṃ addhamāgahī bhāsā bhāsijjamāṇī tesiṃ savvesiṃ āriyamaṇāriyāṇaṃ duppaya-caüppaya-miya-pasu-pakkhi-sarīsivāṇaṃ appappaṇo hiya-siva-suhadāya-bhāsattāe pariṇamai /, Samavāyaṅgasutta*, Āgamoddhārasamiti Edition, p. 60. Cited in L.B. Gandhi (1967: 85).
21. *addhamāgahāe bhāsāe bhāsai arihā dhammaṃ /*, Ovavāïyasutta, Āgamoddhārasamiti Edition, p. 34. *tae ṇaṃ samaṇe bhagavaṃ mahāvīre kūṇiassa bambhasāra-puttassa addhamāgahāe bhāsāe bhāsati /*, Ibid, p. 77. Cited in L.B. Gandhi (1967: 85)
22. *devā ṇaṃ bhante kayarāe bhāsāe bhāsanti ? kayarā vā bhāsā bhāsijjamāṇī visijjai? goyamā, devā ṇaṃ addhamāgahīe bhāsāe bhāsanti/ sā vi ya ṇaṃ addhamāgahī bhāsā bhāsijjamāṇī visijjai/, Bhagavaïsutta*, Āgamoddhārasamiti Edition, p. 231. Cited by L.B. Gandhi (1967: 86). Gandhi also cites an ancient verse quoted by Namisādhu: *ārisavayaṇe siddhaṃ devāṇaṃ addhamāgahī vāṇī/*
23. *Kathāsaritsāgara* passages in Lanman's *Sanskrit Reader*, p. 50ff.
24. *atha śabdānuśāsanam / ... keṣāṃ śabdānām / laukikānāṃ vaidikānāṃ ca / tatra laukikās tāvat - gaur aśvaḥ puruṣo hastī śakunir mṛgo brāhmaṇa iti / vaidikāḥ khalv api - śaṃ no devīr abhiṣṭaye / iṣe tvorje tvā / agnim īḷe purohitam / agna āyāhi vītaya iti /, Mahābhāṣya* (K), Vol. I, p. 1.
25. *loke viditā iti / atha vā bhavārthe ... ṭhañ / vede bhavāḥ vaidikāḥ / vaidikānām api laukikatve prādhānya-khyāpanāya pṛthag upādānam / atha vā bhāṣā-śabdānām eva laukikatvam iti bhedena nirdeśaḥ /, Pradīpa, Mahābhāṣya* (M), Vol. I, Pt. I, p. 6.
26. *siddhe śabdārtha-sambandhe lokato 'rtha-prayukte śāstreṇa dharma-niyamo yathā laukika-vaidikeṣu /, Vārttika* 1, *Mahābhāṣya* (K), Vol. I, pp. 6-8.
27. *mahān hi śabdasya prayoga-viṣayaḥ / sapta-dvīpā vasumatī / trayo lokāś catvāro vedāḥ sāṅgāḥ sa-rahasyā bahudhā vibhinnā eka-śatam adhvaryu-śākhāḥ sahasra-vartmā sāma-vedaḥ eka-viṃśatidhā bāhvṛcyaṃ navadhātharvaṇo vedo vākovākyam itihāsaḥ purāṇaṃ vaidyakam ity etāvān śabdasya prayoga-viṣayaḥ / etāvantaṃ śabdasya prayoga-viṣayam ananuniśamya santy aprayuktā iti vacanaṃ kevalaṃ sāhasa-mātram / etasmin ati-mahati śabdasya prayoga-viṣaye te te śabdās tatra tatra niyata-viṣayā dṛśyante / tad yathā / śavatir gati-karmā kambojeṣv eva bhāṣito bhavati vikāra enam āryā bhāṣante śava iti / hammatiḥ surāṣṭreṣu raṃhatiḥ prācya-madhyeṣu gamim eva tv āryāḥ prayuñjate / dātir lavanārthe prācyeṣu dātram udīcyeṣu / ye cāpy ete bhavato 'prayuktā abhimatāḥ śabdā eteṣām api prayogo dṛśyate / kva / vede/, Mahābhāṣya* (K), Vol. I, pp. 9-10.
28. *yady apy aprayuktā avaśyam dīrgha-satraval lakṣaṇenānuvidheyāḥ / tad yathā / dīrgha-satrāṇi vārṣaśatikāni vārṣa-sahasrikāṇi ca na cādyatve kaścid api vyavaharati kevalam ṛṣi-sampradāyo dharma iti kṛtvā yājñikāḥ śāstreṇānuvidadhate/, Mahābhāṣya* (K), Vol. I, pp. 8-9.
29. *avaśyam khalv asmābhir idaṃ vaktavyaṃ bahulam anyatarasyām ubhayathā vā ekeṣām iti / sarva-pāriṣadaṃ hīdaṃ śāstram / tatra naikaḥ panthāḥ śakya āsthātum /, Mahābhāṣya* (K), Vol. I, p. 400.

30. *na hi cchandāṃsi kriyante nityāni cchandāṃsi* /, *Mahābhāṣya* (K), Vol. II, p. 315.
31. *dṛṣṭānuvidhiś ca chandasi bhavati* /, *Mahābhāṣya* (K), Vol.I, p. 55.
32. *bhāṣāyām api dṛṣṭam evānuvidhīyate siddhe śabdārtha-sambandhe iti nyāyāt / dṛṣṭasyaiva chandasy anuvidhānam ity arthaḥ, na cchandasy eva dṛṣṭānuvidhānam iti* /, *Pradīpa, Mahābhāṣya* (M), Vol. I, Pt. I, p. 142.
33. *bhāṣāyāṃ tu samprati prayoge 'dṛṣṭasyāpi vyākaraṇāntarānusāreṇa śiṣṭa-prayogādinā vāpy avagatasādhutvasyāpy anuvidhānam ity arthaḥ* /, *Uddyota, Mahābhāṣya* (M), Vol. I, Pt. I, p. 142.
34. For instance, the following *Vārttikas*: *lokavad dhalādi-śeṣe*, *Vārttika* 9 on P.6.1.2.and *tatrāvayave śāstrārtha-sampratyayo yathā loke*, *Vārttika* 4 on P.6.1.84. Also see Patañjali on these *Vārttikas*.
35. *naiva loke na ca vede 'kāro vivṛto 'sti* /, *Mahābhāṣya* (K), Vol. I, p. 15.
36. *chandogānāṃ khalv api sātyamugri-rāṇāyanīyā ardham ekāram ardham okāraṃ cādhīyate* / ... *pārṣada-kṛtir eṣā tatrabhavatām / naiva loke na cānyasmin vede 'rdha ekāro 'rdha okāro vāsti* /, *Mahābhāṣya* (K), Vol. I, p. 117.
37. *rakṣohāgama-laghv-asaṃdehāḥ prayojanam* /, *Mahābhāṣya* (K), Vol. I, p. 1.
38. *purākalpa etad āsīt / saṃskārottara-kālam brāhmaṇā vyākaraṇaṃ smādhīyate / tebhyas tatra sthānakaraṇānupradānajñebhyo vaidikāḥ śabdā upadiśyante / tad adyatve na tathā / vedam adhītya tvaritā vaktāro bhavanti / vedān no vaidikāḥ śabdāḥ siddhā lokāc ca laukikāḥ / anarthakaṃ vyākaraṇam iti* /, *Mahābhāṣya* (K), Vol. I, p. 5.
39. For a detailed discussion of these Mīmāṃsā and Nyāya arguments, see K.C. Chatterji (1934).
40. *ūhaḥ khalv api / na sarvair liṅgair na sarvābhir vibhaktibhir vede mantrā nigaditāḥ / te cāvaśyaṃ yajñagatena yathā-yathaṃ vipariṇamayitavyāḥ / tān nāvaiyākaraṇaḥ śaknoti yathā-yathaṃ vipariṇamayitum* /, *Mahābhāṣya* (K), Vol. I, p. 1.
41. *laghv-arthaṃ cādhyeyaṃ vyākaraṇam / brāhmaṇenāvaśyaṃ śabdā jñeyā iti / na cāntareṇa vyākaraṇaṃ laghunopāyena śabdāḥ śakyā jñātum* /, *Mahābhāṣya* (K), Vol. I, p. 1.
42. *asandehārthaṃ cādhyeyaṃ vyākaraṇam / yājñikāḥ paṭhanti / sthūla-pṛṣatīm āgni-vāruṇīm anadvāhīm ālabheteti / tasyāṃ sandehaḥ sthūlā cāsau pṛṣatī ca sthūla-spṛṣatī sthūlāni pṛṣanti yasyāḥ sā sthūlá-pṛṣatīti / tāṃ nāvaiyākaraṇaḥ svarato 'dhyavasyati / yadi pūrva-pada-prakṛti-svaratvaṃ tato bahuvrīhiḥ / athāntodāttatvaṃ tatas tatpuruṣa iti* /, *Mahābhāṣya* (K), Vol. I, pp. 1-2.
43. *duṣṭaḥ śabdaḥ svarato varṇato vā mithyā-prayukto na tam artham āha / sa vāg-vajro yajamānaṃ hinasti yathendraśatruḥ svarato 'parādhāt* //, *Mahābhāṣya* (K), Vol. I, p. 2.
44. *evaṃ hi dṛśyate loke ya udātte kartavye 'nudāttaṃ karoti khaṇḍikopādhyāyas tasmai capeṭāṃ dadāti anyatvaṃ karoṣīti* /, *Mahābhāṣya* (K), Vol. I, p. 41.
45. *yad adhītam avijñātaṃ nigadenaiva śabdyate / anagnāv iva śuṣkaidho na taj jvalati karhicit // tasmād anarthakam mādhigīṣmahīty adhyeyaṃ vyākaraṇam* /, *Mahābhāṣya* (K), Vol.I, p. 2.
46. *avidvāṃsaḥ pratyabhivāde nāmno ye na plutiṃ viduḥ / kāmaṃ teṣu tu viproṣya strīṣv ivāyam ahaṃ vadet // abhivāde strīvan mā bhūmety adhyeyaṃ vyākaraṇam* /, *Mahābhāṣya* (K), Vol. I, p. 3.
47. *sarvaḥ plutaḥ sāhasam anicchatā vibhāṣā vaktavyaḥ* /, *Mahābhāṣya* (K), Vol. III, p. 420.
48. *yājñikāḥ paṭhanti / daśamy-uttara-kālam putrasya jātasya nāma vidadhyād ghoṣavad-ādy antar-antaḥstham a-vṛddhaṃ tri-puruṣānūkam an-ari-pratiṣṭhitaṃ tad dhi pratiṣṭhitatamaṃ bhavati dvy-akṣaraṃ catur-akṣaraṃ vā nāma kṛtaṃ kuryān na*

taddhitam iti / na cāntareṇa vyākaraṇaṃ kṛtas taddhitā vā śakyā vijñātum /, *Mahābhāṣya* (K), Vol. I, p. 4. This passage is important in that it shows the use of grammatical and phonetic terminology in the supposedly priestly usage.

49. *yājñikāḥ paṭhanti / āhitāgnir apaśabdaṃ prayujya prāyaścittīyāṃ sārasvatīm iṣṭiṃ nirvaped iti /*, *Mahābhāṣya* (K), Vol. I, p. 4.

50. *Mahābhāṣya*, Vol. I, p. 5. On some occasions, Patañjali himself raises the question as to how those who do not know grammar use the language properly. For instance: *idaṃ tāvad ayaṃ praṣṭavyaḥ / yady api tāvad vaiyākaraṇā vibhakti-lopam ārabhamāṇā a-vibhaktikān śabdān prayuñjate / ye tv ete vaiyākaraṇebhyo 'nye manuṣyāḥ kathaṃ te 'vibhaktikān sabdān prayuñjate / abhijñāś ca punar laukikā ekatvādīnām arthānām /*, *Mahābhāṣya* (K), Vol. I, p. 95. Also: *ghaṭena kāryaṃ kariṣyan kumbhakāra-kulaṃ gatvāha kuru ghaṭaṃ kāryam anena kariṣyāmīti / na tadvac chabdān prayokṣyamāṇo vaiyākaraṇa-kulaṃ gatvāha kuru śabdān prayokṣya iti / tāvaty evārtham artham upādāya śabdān prayuñjate /*, *Mahābhāṣya* (K), Vol. I, pp. 7-8.

51. *yad apy ucyate ācāre niyama iti yājñe karmaṇi sa niyamaḥ /*, *Mahābhāṣya* (K), Vol. I, p. 11.

52. *yarvāṇas tarvāṇo nāmarṣayo babhūvuḥ pratyakṣadharmāṇaḥ parāparajñā vidita-veditavyā adhigatayāthātathyāḥ / te tatra-bhavanto yad vā nas tad vā na iti prayoktavye yarvāṇas tarvāṇa iti prayuñjate yājñe karmaṇi punar nāpabhāṣante / taiḥ punar asurair yājñe karmaṇy apabhāṣitaṃ tatas te parābhūtāḥ /*, *Mahābhāṣya* (K), Vol. I, p. 11.

53. *ḷkāropadeśo 'śaktijānukaraṇa-pluty-ādy-arthaḥ*, *Vārttika* / *aśaktyā kayācid brāhmaṇyā ṛtaka iti prayoktavye ḷtaka iti prayuktam /*, *Mahābhāṣya* (K), Vol. I, p. 19.

54. *te 'surā helayo helaya iti kurvantaḥ parābabhūvuḥ /*, *Mahābhāṣya* (K), Vol. I, p. 2.

55. *Mahābhāṣya* (K), Vol. I, p. 2, and p. 10-11.

56. *bhūyāṃso 'paśabdā alpīyāṃsaḥ śabdāḥ / ekaikasya śabdasya bahavo 'pabhraṃśāḥ / tad yathā / gaur ity asya gāvī goṇī gotā gopotalikety evam-ādayo 'pabhraṃśāḥ /*, *Mahābhāṣya* (K), Vol. I, p. 10.

57. *bhūvādipāṭhaḥ prātipadikāṇapayaty-ādi-nivṛttyarthaḥ* *Vārttika*, *ke punar āṇapayaty-ādayaḥ / āṇapayati vaṭṭati vaḍḍhatīti /*, *Mahābhāṣya* (K), Vol. I, p. 259.

58. *loke hi kṛṣy-arthe kasim prayuñjate dṛśy-arthe ca disim /*, *Mahābhāṣya* (K), Vol. I, p. 259.

59. *bhūyasa eva grahaṇāni bhaviṣyanti / tad yathā / brāhmaṇa-grāma ānīyatām ity ucyate tatra cāvarataḥ pañcakārukī bhavati /*, *Mahābhāṣya* (K), Vol. I, p. 118.

60. *evaṃ hi kañcit kaścit pṛcchati / anantare ete brāhmaṇa-kule iti / sa āha / nānantare vṛṣala-kulam anayor antareti /*, *Mahābhāṣya* (K), Vol. I, p. 59.

61. *Mahābhāṣya* (K) on P.2.4.10 (*śūdrāṇām aniravasitānām*), Vol. I, p. 475.

62. *āpiśalam adhīte brāhmaṇī āpiśalā brāhmaṇī /*, *Mahābhāṣya (K), Vol. II, p. 205.* Also: *kāśakṛtsnena proktā mīmāṃsā kāśakṛtsnī tām adhīte kāśakṛtsnā brāhmaṇī /*, *Mahābhāṣya* (K), Vol. II, p. 325.

63. *kathaṃ strī nāma sabhāyāṃ sādhvī syāt /*, *Mahābhāṣya* (K), Vol. II, p. 208.

64. For example, see *Ṛgvedaprātiśākhya*, Chapter 14.

65. *eteṣām api svara-varṇānupūrvī-jñānārtha upadeśaḥ kartavyaḥ / śaśaḥ ṣaṣa iti mā bhūt / palāśaḥ palāṣa iti mā bhūt / mañcakaḥ mañjaka iti mā bhūt /*, *Mahābhāṣya* (K), Vol. I, p. 14.

66. *ke punaḥ śiṣṭāḥ / vaiyākaraṇāḥ / kuta etat / śāstra-pūrvikā hi śiṣṭir vaiyākaraṇāś ca śāstrajñāḥ / yadi tarhi śāstra-pūrvikā śiṣṭiḥ śiṣṭi-pūrvakaṃ ca śāstraṃ tad etad itaretarāśrayaṃ bhavati / itaretarāśrayāṇi ca na prakalpante / evaṃ tarhi nivāsata ācārataś ca / sa cācāra āryāvarta eva / kaḥ punar āryāvartaḥ / prāg ādarśāt pratyak kālaka-vanād dakṣiṇena himavantam uttareṇa pāriyātram / etasminn āryanivāse ye*

brāhmaṇāḥ kumbhī-dhānyā alolupā agṛhyamāṇakāraṇāḥ kiñcid antareṇa kasyāścid vidyāyāḥ pāragās tatrabhavantaḥ śiṣṭāḥ / yadi tarhi śiṣṭāḥ śabdeṣu pramāṇaṃ kim aṣṭādhyāyyā kriyate / śiṣṭa-parijñānārthāṣṭādhyāyī / kathaṃ punar aṣṭādhyāyyā śiṣṭāḥ śakyā vijñātum / aṣṭādhyāyīm adhīyāno 'nyaṃ paśyaty anadhīyānaṃ ye 'tra vihitāḥ śabdās tān prayuñjānam / sa paśyati / nūnam asya daivānugrahaḥ svabhāvo vā yo 'yaṃ na cāṣṭādhyāyīm adhīte ye cātra vihitāḥ śabdās tāṃś ca prayuṅkte / ayaṃ nūnam anyān api jānāti / evam eṣā śiṣṭa-parijñānārthāṣṭādhyāyī /, Mahābhāṣya (K), Vol. III, p. 174.

67. *evaṃ hi kaścid vaiyākaraṇa āha / ko 'sya rathasya praveteti / sūta āha / āyuṣmann aham prājiteti / vaiyākaraṇa āha apaśabda iti / sūta āha / prāptijño devānām priyo na tv iṣṭijña iṣyata etad rūpam iti /, Mahābhāṣya* (K), Vol. I, p. 488.
68. *akac-svarau tu kartavyau pratyaṅgam mukta-saṃsayam / tvakatpitṛko makatpitṛka ity eva bhavitavyam iti /, Mahābhāṣya* (K), Vol.I, p. 91. On this passage, Kaiyaṭa says that this is a rejection of Pāṇini's own rule and that the view of Patañjali, as a later grammarian, supersedes that of Pāṇini: *sūtra-pratyākhyānam etat / yathottaraṃ hi munitrayasya prāmāṇyam /, Pradīpa, Mahābhāṣya* (M), Vol. I, Pt. I, p. 217. Thus Kaiyaṭa is willing to accept a historically non-Pāṇinian form as a current standard Sanskrit form and additionally claim that the historically Pāṇinian form is no longer valid. This is a good example of a Pāṇinian form becoming a non-*śiṣṭa* form in later times.
69. For a detailed discussion of this question, see: Maurice Bloomfield (1929).
70. *dṛśyate khalv api viprayogaḥ / tad yathā - "akṣīṇi me darśanīyāni", "pādā me sukumārā" iti /, Mahābhāṣya* (K), Vol. I, p. 322.
71. *akṣīṇīti / dvitve 'pi loke bahuvacanaṃ dṛśyate ity arthaḥ /, Pradīpa; bhāṣye niyamārtham iti / akṣīṇītyāder asādhutvam iti bhāvaḥ /, Uddyota, Mahābhāṣya* (M), Vol. I, Pt. II, p. 238.
72. *śāstra-pūrvake prayoge 'bhyudayas tat tulyaṃ veda-śabdena /, Vārttika* 9, *Mahābhāṣya* (K), Vol. I, p. 10.
73. Bronkhorst (1981: 5) says: "There is one passage in the Nirukta which indicates that Yāska did not consider the Vedic language a precursor in time of Classical Sanskrit. In *Nir 2.2.* we read that certain 'Vedic primary nouns are derived from roots of Classical Sanskrit' (*bhāṣikebhyo dhātubhyo naigamāḥ kṛto bhāṣyante*). ... He continues: 'and also nouns of Classical Sanskrit from Vedic roots' (*athāpi naigamebhyo bhāṣikāḥ*). I consider these statements clear evidence that Yāska did not conceive of Vedic and Classical Sanskrit as being ordered in time." On p. 6, he says: "The conclusion we have to draw is that Yāska considered the Vedic and Classical languages somehow contemporaneous." For him, they are like the domains of eastern and northern dialects. While Śabara consistently justifies the Mīmāṃsā doctrine of the eternal Vedas, and of the uncreated self-existing relationship between words and meanings in Sanskrit (e.g. *Mīmāṃsādarśana*, Vol. I, p. 41, 91), he declares in the beginning of his *Bhāṣya*: "The words of the sūtras are, so far as possible, to be understood in that same sense which they are known to convey in common parlance" (*Mīmāṃsādarśana*, Vol. I, pp. 1-2). Thus the assumption of the various phases of Sanskrit being the same language is maintained as far as possible.
74. See: Note 72
75. For details, see Kiparsky (1979) and Deshpande (1978).
76. For details, see Deshpande (1978: 79ff).
77. *Pradīpa* on *Mahābhāṣya* (M), Vol. I, Sec. I, p. 243.
78. Siddheshwar Varma (1963: 5-15). For similar criticisms of Yāska, see the discussion in Bronkhorst (1981: 1-3). Bronkhorst defends Yāska against these criticisms

by pointing out that in his ideology Yāska had no time sequence for Vedic and Classical Sanskrit, and that for this reason, he had no historical intentions.

79. Francis G. Hutchins (1967).
80. *Vārttikas* 15-18 on P.1.1.44, *Mahābhāṣya* (K), Vol. I, pp. 102-5.
81. *Vārttika* 14 on P.1.1.44, *Mahābhāṣya* (K), Vol. I, p. 104.
82. See: Note 26.
83. See: Note 72.
84. *Mahābhāṣya* (K), Vol. I, p. 8.
85. Joshi-Roodbergen (1969: 6-7) say that what Kātyāyana calls *loka* '(Sanskrit speaking) people' has become restricted in Patañjali's time to a particular community called *śiṣṭas*. In Deshpande (1978: 99), I agreed with this conclusion. However, now I hold a slightly different view, which is presented later in this paper.
86. *Mahābhāṣya* on P.6.3.109, *Mahābhāṣya* (K), Vol. III, p. 174.
87. *Manusmṛti* (2.17-18); *Vāsiṣṭhadharmaśāstra* (1.4-13) For further discussion on these socio-geographical conceptions, see: Deshpande (1979a: 47ff); Deshpande (1982: 313ff).
88. *Mīmāṃsākoṣa*, Vol. 7, pp. 3925ff.
89. See: Note 26.
90. See: Note 40. Also see: *Mīmāṃsākoṣa*, Vol. III, pp. 1223ff.
91. Mīmāṃsakas like Kumārila do not accept the necessity of knowing grammar to be able to perform *ūha*. They argue that an intuitive knowledge of the language and a knowledge of the ritual logic through Mīmāṃsā are sufficient for this purpose. See: *Mīmāṃsākoṣa*, Vol. III, p. 1232.
92. See: Note 37.
93. See: Note 51.
94. *Mahābhāṣya* (K), Vol. I, p. 488.
95. *sarve deśāntare*, *Vārttika* 5, Introductory *Vārttikas*; *sarve khalv apy ete śabdāḥ deśāntare prayujyante / na caiva upalabhyante / upalabdhau yatnaḥ kriyatām /*, *Mahābhāṣya* (K), Vol. I, p. 9.
96. *Mahābhāṣya-Dīpikā*, p. 108.
97. Renou (1971: 248-9). On p. 249, Renou also remarks: "Quite far from having marked the fixation of a 'new language' emerging little by little from the *chandas*, Pāṇini mixes in a sort of bold syncretism the *chandas* and the *bhāṣā*; isolating the *chandas* only where there are peculiarities decidedly abolished or (more often) licences not lending themselves to a defined doctrine; isolating the *bhāṣā* only where the exigencies of the system led to upset a sūtra of the *chandas*." Actually, if one looks at the model adopted in the Dharmaśāstras, then one may not find Pāṇini's model so bold. Also, we must keep in mind that it is 'syncretism' only from our modern point of view. Indian grammarians did not subscribe to any notion of linguistic history, and from their point of view, their model was neither bold nor syncretistic. It was routine.
98. There is some question whether P.1.4.81-2 were originally *Vārttikas* which later got incorporated into the text of the *Aṣṭādhyāyī*. See: Böhtlingk (1887: 40)
99. This was the claim of the grammarians, while others, including Mīmāṃsakas claimed that they could learn the Vedic language from the Vedas and the colloquial language from the worldly usage, without the intervention of grammar. For this debate, see: *Mahābhāṣya* (K), Vol. I, p. 5. Also: K.C. Chatterji (1934). Also see: Note 91.
100. *rakṣohāgama-laghv-asandehāḥ prayojanam / ... na cāntareṇa vyākaraṇaṃ laghunopāyena śabdāḥ śakyā jñātum /*, *Mahābhāṣya* (K), Vol. I, p. 1. Also: *kiñcit sāmānya-viśeṣaval lakṣaṇaṃ pravartyaṃ yenālpena yatnena mahato mahataḥ śabdaughān pratipadyeran / kiṃ punas tat / utsargāpavādau /*, Ibid, p. 6. The

abstracted common usage and the restricted domains of *chandas* etc. are another example of *utsarga* "general rule" and *apavāda* "exception rule". This is one of the main principles of achieving economy of description in Pāṇini. But this notion of economy is also inherent in the Dharmaśāstra model.

101. *sādhuprayogānumitāṃś ca śiṣṭān na veda yo vyākaraṇaṃ na veda*, Quotation in *Vṛtti* on *Vākyapadīya* I. 12, p. 43. Also see *Vākyapadīya* I. 43 and *Vṛtti* on it, pp. 99-100: *tasmād apauruṣeyam anatiśaṅkanīyam puruṣahitopadeśāya pravṛttam āmnāyam pramāṇīkṛtya pṛṣodarādivac ca sādhu-śabda-prayogeṣu śiṣṭācaritam avicchinna-pāramparyaṃ sva-caraṇa-samācāram parigṛhya, virodhe ca sthita-vikalpāni utsargāpavādavanti pūrveṣāṃ ṛṣīṇāṃ smṛti-śāstrāṇi pratikālaṃ dṛṣṭa-śabda-svarūpa-vyabhicārāṇi pramāṇīkṛtyedam ācāryaiḥ śabdānuśāsanam prakrāntam anugamyate* / Interestingly, the *Vṛtti* glosses the word *śiṣṭaiḥ* in the verse I. 43 with *ācāryaiḥ*. This again creates the problem of the circular definition of *śiṣṭa* as a grammarian, which Patañjali tries to avoid.

102. For the notion of *ākṛti-gaṇa*, see: Renou (1942: 78-9). Laddu (1974: 26) refers to the "indefinite composition of the *ākṛti-gaṇas*" and says: "We cannot be sure here that their member forms could be taken as intended by him (= Pāṇini)." However, one may see in this procedure Pāṇini's intention to keep his grammar open-ended.

103. On P.6.3.109 (*pṛṣodarādīni yathopadiṣṭam*), Patañjali says: *atha kim upadiṣṭānīti / uccāritāni / kaiḥ ... / śiṣṭaiḥ /*, *Mahābhāṣya* (K), Vol. III, p. 174.

104. See: Devasthali (1962); Kielhorn (1887); Deshpande (1972: 251-3) and Cardona (1980).

105. For a discussion of this issue, see: Wujastyk (1982).

106. *Vākyapadīya* I. 148. Also see: Deshpande (1985a).

107. For details, see: Deshpande, "Changing Conception of the Vedas: From Speech-acts to Magical Sounds" (forthcoming in *Brahmavidyā, Adyar Library Bulletin*).

108. For the notions of "paradigm" and "paradigm-change" in the context of evolution of scientific theories, see: Thomas Kuhn (1962).

109. *prāg-udañcau vibhajate haṃsaḥ kṣīrodake yathā / viduṣāṃ śabda-siddhy-arthaṃ sā naḥ pātu śarāvatī //*, *Kāśikāvṛtti* on P.1.1.75.

110. Since the *Kāśikāvṛtti* refers to Śarāvatī, it most likely cannot be the mythical river Sarasvatī. V.S. Agrawala (1953: 38) says that "it may probably be identified with the Dṛṣadvatī or Chitāṅg flowing through Ambala district." It seems likely that it is the same as Satlaj.

111. *Mahābhāṣya* (K), Vol. I, pp. 9-10 and the parallel passage in *Nirukta*, Vol. I, pp. 127-128.

112. *Mahābhāṣya* (K) on P.6.3.109.

113. *atropavarṣa-varṣāv iha pāṇini-piṅgalāv iha vyāḍiḥ / vararuci-patañjalī iha parīkṣitāḥ khyātim upajagmuḥ /*, *KM*, p. 55.

114. Deshpande (1979b: 267) shows that the Śākalya tradition of the *Ṛgveda* was most probably from the eastern regions of India and that Yāska shared many linguistic features with this eastern tradition such as the existence of medial retroflex *Ḷ* and *Ḷh* for *ḍ* and *ḍh* respectively.

115. *Mahābhāṣya* (K), on P.6.3.109.

116. See: Deshpande (1979b: 265), Deshpande (1982b: 313-314), and Deshpande (1985c).

117. *etad-deśa-prasūtasya sakāśād agrajanmanaḥ / svaṃ svaṃ caritraṃ śikṣeran pṛthivyāṃ sarva-mānavāḥ //*, *Manusmṛti*, 2.20.

118. For details, compare the maps of the Śuṅga empire given in Joseph Schwartzberg (1978: 20).

119. *Samavāyāṅgasutta*, Āgamoddhārasamiti edition, p. 60.

120. Schwartzberg (1978: 162-165). For a similar approach concerning various north-Indian rivers marking different stages of Aryan advancement, see: Saloman (1978). Also: Deshpande (1978) and D.R. Bhandarkar (1931).
121. Deshpande (1979a: 44) shows that even Jainas considered Yavanas, Śakas etc. to be Mlecchas "barbarians". For their fallen status according to the Brahmanical traditions, see: *Manusmṛti* 10.43ff. Also see: Deshpande (1979a: 117, fn. 155) and Deshpande (1979b: 18).
122. *gauraḥ śucy-ācāraḥ piṅgalaḥ kapila-keśaḥ ity etān apy ābhyantarān brāhmaṇye guṇān kurvanti / ... na hy ayaṃ kālaṃ māṣa-rāśi-varṇaṃ āpaṇa āsīnaṃ dṛṣṭvādhyavasyati brāhmaṇo 'yam iti /, Mahābhāṣya* (K), pp. 411-2. This passage clearly shows that Brāhmaṇas were viewed as being *gaura* "white, fair", in contrast with the darker non-Brāhmaṇas. The color-prejudice is also seen from texts like the *Vāsiṣṭhadharmaśāstra* (18. 18): *kṛṣṇa-varṇā yā rāmā ramaṇāyaiva na dharmāya na dharmāyeti /*, "The woman who is of dark color, she may be used only for pleasure, but never for religious activities, never for religious activities."
123. *brāhmaṇāḥ kṣatriyāḥ vaiśyāḥ śūdrā varṇās trayo dvijāḥ / yuge yuge sthitāḥ sarve kalāv ādy-antayoḥ sthitiḥ //*, from *Śūdrakamalākara*, quoted by D. R. Bhandarkar (1911: 7).
124. In Bengal, for instance, the Brāhmaṇas considered the rest of the people to be Śūdras, who were subdivided into good and bad Śūdras.
125. *KM*, pp. 93ff. Also see: S.B. Chaudhuri (1948).
126. *śakāś ca yavanāś caiva pallavā bāhlikādayaḥ / prāyeṇa gaurāḥ kartavyā uttarāṃ ye śritā diśam //, Nāṭyaśāstra* (Nirnayasagara Press Edition), XXX, 89-90.
127. D.R. Bhandarkar (1911: 37) and R.G. Bhandarkar (1933, vol. I, pp. 624ff). On p. 637, R.G. Bhandarkar says: "The foreigners who came here before the Mahomedans were absorbed so quickly and on such a large scale in the Hindu social organisation, that in the modern society of India any attempt to decide who is an Aryan and who is a non-Aryan would be quite futile."
128. For the anthropological complexities, see: D.N. Majumdar, C. Radhakrishna Rao and P.C. Mahalnobis (1960: 106ff), P.C. Mahalnobis (1927) and S.K. Chatterji (1950: 190ff).
129. For the burning of the Khāṇḍava forest by the Pāṇḍavas and the destruction of its inhabitants, see: *Critical Text of the Mahābhārata*, 4 Volume edition, Bhandarkar Oriental Research Institute, Pune, 1971, Vol. I, pp. 274ff.
130. A commentator such as Nāgesabhaṭṭa on the *Mahābhāṣya* could not take Patañjali's description of Brāhmaṇas as being *gaura* "fair" seriously. He says that these are not invariable qualities, and gives a Dharmaśāstra interpretation of the word *gaura*: *aṣṭa-varṣā tu yā dattā śruta-śīla-samanvite / sā gaurī tat-suto yas tu sa gauraḥ parikīrtitaḥ //*, see *Uddyota* on *Mahābhāṣya*, Nirnayasagara edition, Vol. II, ed. by Shivadatta Kuddala, Bombay, 1912, p. 428. It is clear that Patañjali is contrasting *gaura* "fair" with *kāla* "dark, black", and has no ritual meaning in his mind.
131. Iravati Karve (1953: 17ff); Trautman (1979).
132. S.B. Joshi (1951) and (1952); Southworth (1971).
133. Emeneau (1954) and (1956); Kamil Zvelebil (1972); Southworth (1974) and (1979); and David McAlpin (1979).
134. Rājaśekhara *KM*, pp. 96-7) refers to *pāṇḍu* "white, fair" cheeks of the Yavana women and points out that in poetry there is not much difference between *gaura* and *pāṇḍu*.
135. *siddhe śabdārtha-sambandhe lokato 'rtha-prayukte śāstreṇa dharma-niyamo yathā laukika-vaidekeṣu /, Vārttika* 1 on the *Aṣṭādhyāyī, Mahābhāṣya* (K), Vol. I, p. 6.

136. *priya-taddhitā dākṣiṇātyā yathā loke vede ceti prayoktavye laukika-vaidikeṣv iti prayuñjate /, Mahābhāṣya* (K), Vol. I, p. 8.
137. Preference for long compounds in Bengal is evidenced in the Navya-Nyāya literature which developed there. For some other features, see: *dātir lavanārthe prācyeṣu dātram udīcyeṣu /, Mahābhāṣya* (K), Vol. I, p. 9. Also *Nirukta*, Vol. I, pp. 127-8.
138. *Kuvalayamālā*, pp. 152-3; Deshpande (1979a: 36ff).
139. For a discussion of the hateful attitude of some Jaina writers toward Sanskrit, see: Deshpande (1979a: 35-6, 55-6, 59-60).
140. In Sanskrit poetics, the Pāñcālī style of poetry is particularly viewed as being sweet and delicate, though perhaps to the extreme. Therefore, the Vaidarbhī style which has all the qualities without any one of them dominating over others is considered to be the best of the poetic styles. Vāmana's *Kāvyālaṃkārasūtra* 2.13 (*mādhurya-saukumāryopapannā pāñcālī*) and 2.11 (*samagra-guṇā vaidarbhī*). For details, see: V. Raghavan (1973: 147ff).
141. P.K. Atre's *Marāṭhā* was the leading newspaper in this campaign. The use of patriotic ballads was a prominent feature of this movement and several new ballads on the history of Maharashtra became popular during these years.
142. *Manusmṛti* 2.20 and *Vāsiṣṭha-Dharma-Śāstra* 1.1.10.
143. The upper-layer homogeneity and the lower-layer diversity as shown here are comparable to the distinction between the Great Tradition and the Little Tradition discussed by Milton Singer. For a discussion of the processes such as Sanskritization, Persianization and Anglicization, see: Deshpande (1979a), and Srinivas (1966, 1967).
144. For an examination of Karvé's theories, see: R.K. Gulati (1970) and Amitab Basu (1969).
145. Tulpule (1973: 23-4) and A.N. Deshpande (1966: 170ff, 187ff).
146. *Ekanāthī-Bhāgavat* 1.121ff. The same phenomenon of a Brāhmaṇa poet praising older poets including non-Brāhmaṇa ones is seen in Moropant's *Kavistava* and Mahīpati's *Bhaktavijaya*. See: *Rasataraṅgiṇī*, pp. 239-241, and *Navanīt*, pp. 296ff.
147. This is a controversial term, see: S.G. Tulpule (1973: 100ff, 350). Tukārām (*Tukārām-Gāthā, Abhaṅga* 163, p. 58) says that if a Kānaḍī (Kannada-speaking) woman marries a Marathi man, they do not understand each other. He asks Lord Viṭṭhal not to let the same thing happen in his relation with Tukārām.
148. *Dāsbodh*, 18th *Daśaka*, 6th *Samāsa*; 19th *Daśaka*, 9th *Samāsa*. For a detailed study of Rāmadās's nationalistic political and religious conception, see: G.B. Sardar (1969) and G.S. Deo (1943).
149. Quoted in N.B. Pawagi (1901: 350).
150. From *Journal of the Anthropological Society*, Bombay, Vol. 2, No. 4, quoted in N.B. Pawagi (1901: 419).
151. The Bengalis in particular have very bitter memories of the Maratha expeditions into Bengal. They use the name of the Marathas, like the mention of a bogeyman, to scare a child. Also see Veṅkaṭādhvari's *Viśvaguṇādarśacampū* (p. 83ff) for the reactions of the southerners to Marathas. In the battle of Panipat, several north-Indian Hindus fought on the side of the Afghan adversary, Ahmed Shah Abdali, who defeated the Marathas. Rajputs and Jats could not willingly accept the Maratha domination of the north.
152. V.K. Rajwade (1958: 189).
153. Particularly noteworthy are the attacks on Pune by Yashwantrao Holkar. Even Raghunathrao Peshwa asked the British to help him fight against his nephew who was the ruling Peshwa. We are also told that Malharrao Holkar declined to fight with

Najibkhan who was the adversary of the Marathas and an ally of Ahmad Shah Abdali on the fateful battlefield of Panipat.

154. This view is particularly prominent in the works of V.D. Savarkar. For a similar point of view, see Balraj Madhok (1970).

155. It may be noted that the word *rāṣṭra* in the word *mahārāṣṭra* is understood in Marathi in the sense of "nation", and hence the term came to mean a "great nation". It may be noted that the word *nāḍu* in the name Tamilnadu was expressly intended by the Tamil leaders to express their idea that their region is a "nation", while other states of India were simply *pradeśa* "regions". That the name "Maharashtra" was interpreted as "great nation" is quite clear. Even the Gujarati political leaders interpreted the name "Maharashtra" in this manner, and created the analogous name "Mahagujarat" for their region. Of course, this term also referred to the notion of Gujarat proper enlarged with Saurashtra and Kaccha. However, it is an analogical formation.

156. Emeneau (1967: 159). For details of the convergence theory, see Southworth and Apte (1974), Southworth (1974), and Hock (1975).

157. Introduction to *Śāṅkhāyana-Āraṇyaka*, Ānandāśrama Sanskrit Series, No. 90, Pune, 1922.

158. "The passage may indicate [cf. also *Śāṅkhāyana-Śrauta-Sūtra*, 4.10.3, where Śākalya is younger apparently than Māṇḍūkeya] that the Māṇḍūkeya Śākhā had its Saṃhitā text before Śākalya produced the Pada-Pāṭha, which is quite likely" (Keith, *Aitareya-Āraṇyaka*, p. 257, fn. 9).

159. Also see: Bloch (1970: 2).

160. See: Dandekar (1961: II, 3-4).

161. S.B. Pandit (*Atharvaveda*, Bombay, 1895, Vol. 1, Introduction, p. 6) records an informative account of his dealings with an *AV* reciter: "He was more shocked that the several MSS of that Veda ... exhibited numerous varieties of reading, and still more horrified when he found that the text he knew by heart ... was the worse for the improvements. His great anxiety at first was that the text I was going to publish should not show that his pāṭha was incorrect ... though he little hoped the Vaidikas would exchange their corruptions for our corrections."

162. Uvaṭa on *RPR* 13.10. On *RPR* 10.7, he says that some reciters pronounce *ṅ* in the place of an *anusvāra*.

163. *RPR* 1.2 refers to *anusvāra* as an unvoiced spirant, but 13.3 excludes it from spirants, and 13.5 considers it to be a voiced nasal sound; see: Deshpande (1976).

164. Also see James Bare (1976: 26-27).

165. Hannes Sköld (1926: 44ff.) refers to Vedamitra's view and say that if Vedamitra's description of *ḍ* and *ḍh* as palato-velars is correct, then their intervocalic replacements, namely *Ḷ* and *Ḷh*, could not be retroflexes. "But the description in all points coincides with that of that *l* of Lithuanian, of the Turkish and Slav languages, which is described as a 'guttural *l*' and the existence of which can be traced in Latin and Old Armenian" (p. 45). Sköld (p. 45) argues that the *ḍ/Ḷ* and *ḍh/Ḷh* alternation as upheld by Vedamitra and by Śākalya's text was not accepted by the *RPR* itself. His conclusion (p. 46) is interesting: "The development of *Ḷ* is posterior to the *Saṃhitā* text ... Is the *Ḷ* introduced by the Śākalas?" He points out that for the word *vīḍvagam* in *RV* 1.118.9, the word-text of Śākalya gives *vīḶu-agam*. Also see section 6.11 of this paper.

166. The Prakrit word *goṇī* for Skt. *gauḥ* is found in *MB* (M), Vol. I, Sec. I, p. 42. Other expressions noted by Patañjali are: *yarvāṇa* and *tarvāṇa* (Ibid., p. 56), *āṇavayati*, *vaṭṭati* and *vaḍḍhayati* (Vol. I, Sec. II, p. 125), and *diṇṇa* (Ibid., Vol. I, Sec. I, p. 74).

167. The *Samayasāra* of Kundakunda, ed. by J.L. Jaini, Lucknow, 1930. Verse 1.3 has *hodi*, while the verse 1.13 has *havadi*. Metrically both the forms are of equal quantity. This makes one wonder if one of these forms was not a scribal error for the other, or if in the oral tradition, the difference between *hodi* and *havadi* was simply metrically irrelevant.

168. *Pañcāstikāya*, Rāyacandra Jaina Śāstramālā, 3rd ed. (1967), Vol. 7.

169. Another example (*Vedic Variants*, Vol. II, p. 152) is the *Sāmaveda* variation of *made suśipram* with *madeṣu śipram*. On the variation *āpṛṇo 'si / āpṛṇoṣi*, Bloomfield and Edgerton (*Vedic Variants*, Vol. II, p. 152) remark: "The latter is corrupt." For similar spontaneous variation of *s/ṣ*, see: *Vedic Variants*, Vol. II, pp. 149ff.

170. The *VPR* (8.45) explicitly says that the Mādhyandina recension of the *YV* does not have the sounds *Ḷ* and *Ḷh* and that only the Kāṇva recension has these sounds. While the former is a North Indian tradition, the latter is a South Indian tradition. The commentaries of Uvaṭa and Anantabhaṭṭa on *VPR* (3.87; 3.91, etc.) make it quite clear that the Kāṇva recension has decidedly more retroflexion than the Mādhyandina recension.

171. The *RPR* (1.8, 10) classifies *ṛ* as a *jihvāmūlīya* 'produced at the root of the tongue', and *r* as either *dantamūlīya* 'produced at the root of teeth' or *barsvya* 'alveolar'. The *VPR* (1.65, 68) classifies *ṛ* as a tongue-root sound and *r* as a dental. The *SCA* (1.20, 28) holds the same view. For the *TPR* (2.18, 41), *ṛ* and *r* are both alveolars.

172. The only favorable references are to some political alliances made by the Aryan enemies of the king Sudās with non-Aryans (*RV* 7.18-19), and a reference to the non-Aryan king Bṛbu who gave gifts to Aryan poets (*RV* 6.45.31-33).

173. *RV* 1.51.5-6, 1.103.4, 10.95.7, 10.99.7, and 10.105.11. It is extremely important to recognize that all of these references to *dasyu-hattyā* are found in those parts of the *RV* which are traditionally regarded to be late parts of this text. This would most probably mean that even by the time of the late parts of the *RV*, the attitudes of the Vedic Aryans towards non-Aryan Dasyus had not significantly changed, and they still regarded dasyus as those who deserve to be killed by Indra.

174. Other important descriptions are *ayajyavaḥ* 'non-sacrificers' and *anindrāḥ* 'those who do not believe in Indra'.

175. Burrow (1967: 311) refers to twenty-five Dravidian loans in the *RV* and says that "it is not many, compared with the number in later Sanskrit." Kuiper (1955) lists many more non-Aryan loans in the *RV*, but many of these are debatable.

176. Vaidyanathan (1971). The rules of Tamilization of Sanskrit words are found in *Tolkāppiyam-Collatikāram*. For general rules for the Tamilization of Sanskrit words, see Vaidyanathan (1958), and Ganeshasundaram and Vaidyanathan (1958).

177. Bloch (1965: 58) thinks that *kāṭá-* is derived from *kartá-*. Referring to Bartholomae's attempt to connect *kāṭá-* and *kartá-*, Burrow (1972: 544) comments: "The connection of *kāṭá-* with *kartá-* is anything but certain, it could have a spontaneous cerebral and be connected with *kātu-* 'hole' along with which it is listed in *Nighaṇṭu* 3, 23."

178. W.J. Gedney, *Indic Loan-Words in Spoken Thai*, (Ph.D. dissertation, Yale University, 1947).

179. I refer to the following Sanskrit words, claimed to be Dravidian loanwords in the RV by Southworth (1979: 194):

Skt. *phala-* 'fruit' < DED 3299 *paẓu* 'ripen'
Skt. *kulpha-* 'ankle' < DED 1519 Ta. *kuḶampu* 'hoof'
Skt. *kulāya-* 'nest' < DED 1563 Ta. *kūṭu* 'nest'
Skt. *bila-* 'hole, cave' < DED 4459 Ta. *viḶ* 'open out'
Skt. *kula-* 'herd, flock' < DED 1513 Ta. *kuẓu* 'assembly',
or < DED 1562 Ta. *kūṭi* 'come together'

180. For a religio-historical perspective, see Dandekar (1967: 29ff). Emeneau (1974) discusses Sanskrit caste terminology and its bearing on borrowing from the Dravidian social structure. Also see Srinivas (1966: 1-45) and Chatterji (1962).

181. Chatterji (1962: 70-71). Also see Nilakanta Sastri (1967: 48ff). Burrow (*Collected Papers*, 1968: 312) points out "that the great majority (of Dravidian words in Sanskrit) have become established by the time of the epic poems, *Mahābhārata* and *Rāmāyaṇa*, and of these a large proportion are first quoted from these texts." Evidence gathered by Emeneau (1974: 112) for social convergence on the basis of caste terminology also begins with lists of caste terms in the *Mahābhārata*. Also see Hart (1975: 277ff).

182. *Śāṅkhāyana-Āraṇyaka* 7.13 refers to the views of Madhyama Māṇḍūkeya Magadhavāsin Prātibodhīputra. He is the middle Māṇḍūkeya residing in Magadha. For other early Brahmanic traditions in the east, see Chakladar (1928).

183. *Kauṣītaki-Brāhmaṇa* (7.6). See Keith, *Ṛgveda-Brāhmaṇas*, Harvard Oriental Series, no. 25 (1920): 387. Also see Chatterji (1960: 50).

184. Macdonell (1916: 14, 22-23) shows that where Śākalya's recension of the *RV* shows a merging of two vowels and a resulting loss of a syllable needed by the meter, we must restore the two original vowels. The *Aitareya-Āraṇyaka* (3.1.5) gives indications that the text of the Māṇḍūkeya recension in fact kept these vowels separate and was thus closer to the original than Śākalya's text. See Keith's note on the *Aitareya-Āraṇyaka*, p. 244.

185. For a more comprehensive study, see Rakshit (1966).

186. Oldenberg (1890, 1882: 9). He also points out (pp. 10-11) that the river Sadānīrā was the dividing line between the Vedic Aryans and the outlandic Aryans. The sacrificial fire had not crossed to the east of the river Sadānīrā.

187. Oldenberg (1890, 1882: 394) says: "Thus we have here a distinction between those stocks, who felt themselves to be qualified champions of Aryan culture, and those who were Aryans, it is true, but were not regarded as equally accredited partakers in this culture. Momenta of many kinds may have co-operated to bring about and enhance this difference. Association with non-Aryan elements, to which the stocks that had migrated to the greatest distances were especially exposed, may have been at the same time in play."

188. See: Hannes Sköld (1926: 44ff).

189. *atha vāg itihāsa-purāṇaṃ yac cānyat kiñcid brāhmīkṛtyevādhīyīta, tad apy evam eva vidyāt /, Śāṅkhāyana-Āraṇyaka* (8.11).

190. This process is called *abhūta-tad-bhāva* in Sanskrit grammar.

191. *Aitareya-Āraṇyaka* 3.2.3 uses the word *akṣarasamāmnāya* and says: "That which we call the person of the meters is the collection of letters. Its essence is the letter *a*." In 2.3.8, we have the assertion *a iti brahma* 'Brahman is named a '. In 2.3.6, *a* is said to represent the speech as a whole. This clarifies the relation between the concepts of *vāk*, *brahman*, and *akṣara-samāmnāya*.

192. *VPR* 8.1.32 refers to *varṇa-samāmnāya* and calls it *brahma-rāśi*; also *RT* 1.4. and *MB* (M), Vol. I, Sec. I, p. 102.

193. Chatterji (1956: 24-27). On page 26, he says: "Such a state of things is nothing new or remarkable in the history of literature - viz., of literary composition in one form, and an earlier one, and preservation and transmission in another and a later form of the language. The Vedas were probably compiled in the 10th century B.C., but some at least of the Vedic hymns were composed several centuries earlier and were continued from generation to generation by oral tradition, and these were unquestionally first composed in an older form of the speech than what we find in the compiled text, which is our received text."

194. Chatterji (1960: 52-54) doubts the Phoenician origin of the Brāhmī script and suggests that it was adopted from the ancient Sindh-Punjab script of the non-Aryans. However, we know nothing about such a Sindh-Punjab script, unless it refers to the Indus Valley script which still remains hopelessly undeciphered. Dani (1963) has reasserted Bühler's theory, and it has also been adopted by Mahadevan (1960 and 1970), who shows that Brāhmī was later adapted for Tamil.

195. Bühler (1895: 2-3). Though Cunningham thought that the Brāhmī script was of purely Indian origin, he remarks: "Similarly, the series of cerebral letters, which was also wanting originally in Tibetan, was afterwards supplied by the invention of new letters, which are simply the five dental letters reversed. This was not exactly the case with the cerebral letters of the Ariano-Pāli alphabet, but their forms differ so slightly from those of the dentals, that it seems highly probable that they must have been a late addition to the original alphabetical scheme" (*Corpus Inscriptionum Indicarum*, Vol. 1, Introduction, p. 49. Reprinted by Indological Book House, Banaras, 1961).

196. "In the lingual *Ḷa*, derived from the round *ḍ* a small semi-circle has been added to indicate the change of the phonetic value. Here also, I believe, we may recognize the influence of the grammarians or phoneticians. For the sound *ḍa* and *Ḷa* are frequently interchanged in the same word. Thus we find already in the Vedas regularly a *Ḷa* for *ḍa* between two vowels, as in *īḶe* for *īḍe*" (Bühler (1895: 77)).

197. "The absence of first two nasals *ṅ*, *ñ* and 'retroflex' or 'cerebral' consonants, namely *ṭ*, *ṭh*, *ḍ*, *ḍh* and *ṇ*, and the presence of ***g***, ***th***, ***d*** and ***b***, which do not occur in Tamil, clearly show that the Late Harappan language is closer to the Indo-European than to the Dravidian group of languages" (S.R. Rao, 1972-73: 9).

198. P.6.1.64 (*dhātv-ādeḥ ṣaḥ saḥ*) and P.6.1.65 (*ṇo naḥ*). The rules P.8.3.56ff. and P.8.4.14ff. indicate the complexity of the problem. Referring to the question of unclear morpheme boundaries, Brough points out that we can have "*pūrvāhṇaḥ*, but *durahnaḥ*, without option, whereas in other examples the option may be permitted: *surāpāṇam*, *surāpānam*. In spite of the struggle to reduce this complicated situation to a series of rules, the junction of *upasarga*s seems to have been particularly resistant to systematic formulation." With respect to P.8.4.1ff., he adds: "Many of the rules were doubtless valid, but it may be suspected that some of them are useful to the same extent as the advice given to schoolboys in elementary textbooks of Latin, that 'most names of rivers and many names of mountains are masculine'" (Brough, 1962: 107).

199. *MB M*, on P.6.1.64-65, Vol. II, p. 715. Patañjali provides partial generalizations for *ṣopadeśa* and *ṇopadeśa* categories, with lists of additions and exceptions. All *n*-initial verbs are *ṇopadeśa* verbs, except, *nṛt*, *nand*, *nard*, *nakk*, *nāṭ*, *nāth*, *nādh*, and *nṛ*. All *s*-initial verbs, with a post-initial vowel or a dental consonant, are *ṣopadeśa* verbs, except *sṛp*, *sṛj*, *stṛ*, *styā*, *sek*, and *sṛ*, but including *smi*, *svad*, *svid*, *svañj*, and *svap*.

200. In practice, we do not find a word-final *ś* followed by a word-initial *s*. The final *ś* changes either to *k* or *ṭ*. For development of the final *ś*, see Kuiper (1967a).

201. *RV* 1.173.12. Bloomfield's *Vedic Concordance* (p. 723) provides many more occurrences of *mo ṣu* in different texts. Other examples are *āsu ṣmā ṇaḥ* (*RV* 6.44.18), and *parīto ṣiñcata* (*RV* 9. 107.1). Abhyankar (1974: 55) calls the change of *sma* to *ṣma* in the above passage an irregular change.

202. P.8.3.101 (*yuṣmat-tat-tatakṣuṣv antaḥpādam*) has the condition *antaḥpādam* 'within the same metrical foot', and several following rules are governed by this condition. See the *Kāśikāvṛtti* on these rules for Vedic examples.

203. This refers to the precodification period, when the Vedic hymns were a floating oral literature. Esteller (1969: 9) says: "This will appear all the more convincing and decisive if we recollect that we are dealing with compositions in an archaic-literary

style of a language that is beginning a period of rapid evolution - owing to a swift expansion and the influence of a pre-Aryan linguistic substratum." Also see Chatterji (1960: 52). For a possible explanation of unevenness in these developments, see Lovins (1974: 242).

204. The *Kāśikāvṛtti* on P.8.3.102ff. quotes important examples of irregular retroflexion in the *Taittirīya-Saṃhitā*: *agniṣṭat* (1.1.14.5) and *agnistat* (3.2.5.4). Abhyankar (1974: 35) notes that the Taittirīya reciters occasionally pronounce *ṇ* in the place of *n* without any reason: *enāḥ/eṇāḥ*, and *agniḥ/agṇiḥ*. He also points out that this practice is already noticed by Bhartṛhari (about 400 A.D.). Kuiper (1965: 77ff.) notes the development of similar secondary retroflex variants from dentals in Munda. Hoffmann (1960: 176-77) refers to the variation in the Maitrāyaṇī and Kaṭha versions of the *Yajurveda*.

205. *AB - Aitareya-Brāhmaṇa; ApS - Āpastamba-Śrautasūtra; AV - Atharvaveda; HG - Hiraṇyakeśī-Gṛhyasūtra; KS - Kāṭhaka-Saṃhitā; MS - Maitrāyaṇī-Saṃhitā; RV - Ṛgveda; SV - Sāmaveda; TA - Taittirīya-Āraṇyaka; TB - Taittirīya-Brāhmaṇa; TS - Taittirīya-Saṃhitā; VS - Vājasaneyī-Saṃhitā.*

206. P.8.4.2 (*aṭ-ku-pv-āṅ-num-vyavāye 'pi*) gives the conditions for noncontiguous application of the retroflexion rule. For a recent study of the noncontiguous aspect of this process, see Dasgupta (1972: 118ff).

207. *raśruter laśrutir bhavati, MB* (M), Vol. I, Sec. I, p. 84. For details, see Deshpande (1975b: 22-26).

208. This compares well with Emeneau's suggestion (1974: 93) concerning the "backed" allophones of dentals which he suggests were later interpreted in terms of retroflexes by the mixed speakers.

209. Also see Eric Hamp (1976: 351-61), who has an insightful discussion of the *iti* problem, where the role of the inherited item and the role of the *Sprachbund* have been presented in a balanced manner.

210. Also see Weinreich, Labov, and Herzog (1968); Hoijer (1948); and Dell Hymes (1964) and (1971).

211. I am indebted to Professor William Gedney for information on Cambodian and Siamese treatment of Indic loanwords.

212. J.A. Stewart, *Manual of Colloquial Burmese*, London, 1955, p. 6.

213. Banikanta Kakati, *Assamese, Its Formation and Development* (Gauhati, 1941), revised edition in 1962 by G.C. Goswami. On p. 199, note 9, Goswami says: "The O.I.A. dental and cerebral series lost their original sound values and became alveolars, i.e., the point of articulation for the dentals is pushed back and for the cerebrals pushed forward" due to the Tibeto-Burman influence which had this levelling effect. See also P.C. Bhattacharya (1975: 242); Southworth (1971: 261) and (1974: 206, 214-5).

214. The origin of retroflexion in Javanese is controversial, and the influence of Sanskrit and/or the existence of retroflexes *ṭ* and *ḍ* in Proto-Austronesian are hotly debated issues. See *Proto-Austronesian* by Otto C. Dahl (Lund, 1973), pp. 55ff.; and "Problems of Austronesian Comparative Philology", by André G. Haudricourt, in *Indo-Pacific Linguistic Studies*, pt. 1., edited by Milner-Henderson (Amsterdam, 1965). It is very difficult to say that Javanese "developed" retroflexion due to Sanskrit influence. It would be more appropriate to say that the Sanskrit influence strengthened the allophonic variation between dentals and alveolars, a variation which may have been originally stylistic or dialectal and which was also influenced by Malay loanwords with apical stops which were pronounced further back than the Javanese apical stops. Despite the use of the word "retroflex" with respect to

Javanese *ḍ* and *ṭ* and **ṭ* and **ḍ* in Proto-Austronesian by Haudricourt and Dahl, there is actually no Sanskrit-like retroflexion in Javanese, but, rather, a contrast between dentals and alveolars. The retroflex signs in writing are due to the influence of Sanskrit, but have no corresponding phonetic value. The Sanskrit sounds have been definitely assimilated into the native phonology, e.g., the aspirate stops *ṭh* and *ḍh* are de-aspirated and assimilated into alveolar *ṭ* and *ḍ*. Similarly, the nasal retroflex *ṇ* and sibilant *ṣ* of Sanskrit are assimilated into dental *n* and *s* respectively. Thus, we cannot look at Javanese as being very different from the normal pattern of assimilation of foreign sounds into components of the native phonology. I am thankful to Professor Alton Becker for clarifying the relationship between Sanskrit and Javanese.

215. Georg Morgenstierne, "Neu-Iranische Sprachen", in *Handbuch der Orientalistik, Iranistik*, (Leiden-Köln, 1958: 169).
216. Emeneau (1974); K.A. Nilakanta Sastri (1967: 48ff.); Srinivas (1966: 1-45); Chatterji (1962: 82ff.) and (1965: 46ff.).
217. Skt. *vaṇij* 'merchant' and *paṇya-* 'merchandise' are related to Vedic *paṇi*, the name of a non-Aryan trading tribe.
218. For instance, the *Bhagavadgītā* (15.15) mentions Kṛṣṇa's claim that he is to be known from all the Vedas. Such statements can be found in almost all the Purāṇas. This kind of syncretism has been a hallmark of classical Hinduism.

BIBLIOGRAPHY

Abbott, Justine E. (1927). *Eknāth, A Translation from Bhaktalīlāmṛta, The Poet Saints of Maharashtra*, no. 2. Pune: Scottish Mission Industries Co. Ltd.

———. (1932). *Rāmdās, A Translation from Santavijaya, The Poet Saints of Maharashtra*, no. 8. Pune: Scottish Mission Industries Co. Ltd.

Abhyankar, K.V. (1974). *Veda-pada-pāṭha-carcā*. Post-Graduate and Research Department Series, no. 10. Pune: Bhandarkar Oriental Research Institute.

———. (1969). "Accents in Sanskrit." *Annals of the Bhandarkar Oriental Research Institute*, vol. 50, pp. 41-55.

Acharya, K.C. (1971). "Linguistic Remarks on Some Words in the 1st Kāṇḍa of the Paippalāda Saṃhitā of Atharvaveda." *Proceedings of the First All India Conference of Linguists*, pp. 96-99. Pune: Linguistic Society of India.

Agrawala, V.S. (1953). *India as Known to Pāṇini*. Lucknow: University of Lucknow.

Aitareya-Āraṇyaka. Edited and translated with notes, with parts of the *Śāṅkhāyana-Āraṇyaka*, by A.B. Keith. 1909. Reprinted in 1969. Oxford: Oxford University Press.

Allen, W. Sidney. (1951). *Phonetics in Ancient India*. London Oriental Series, no. 1. London: Oxford University Press.

Ananthanarayana, H.S. (1970). "Prakrits and Dravidian Languages." *Proceedings of the Seminar in Prakrit Studies*, pp. 65-75. Pune: University of Poona.

Andersen, Henning. (1968). "IE *s after i, u, r, k in Baltic and Slavic." *Acta Linguistica Hafniensia*, vol. 11, pp. 171-90.

———. (1973). "Abductive and Deductive Change." *Language*, vol. 49, pp. 765-793.

Andronov, M.S. (1963). "Lexico-Statistic Analysis of the Chronology of Disintegration of Proto-Dravidian." *Indo-Iranian Journal*, vol. 7, pp. 170-186.

———. (1970). *Dravidian Languages*. Moscow: Nauka Publishing House.

Āpastamba-dharma-sūtra. Edited by Georg Bühler. 1868. Bombay.

Āpiśali-śikṣā-sūtrāṇi. Edited by Yudhishthir Mimamsak. Ajmer, Saṃvat 2024.

Aṣṭādaśa-Upaniṣadaḥ. Edited by V.P. Limaye and R.D. Wadekar. 1958. Pune: Vaidika Saṃśodhana MaṇḍaḶa.

Bailey, C.J.N., and M.L. Gardens. (1974). "Naturalness in Historical Reconstruction and Changes that are not Natural." In *Natural Phonology*, pp. 13-20. Chicago: Chicago Linguistic Society.

Bailey, Grahame T. (1938). "The Development of English *t, d* in North-Indian Languages." In *Studies in North Indian Languages.* London.

Bajpai, Shiva G. (1979). "Greek *Praisoi* and Sanskrit *Prācya*: Problems of Identification and its Historical Significance." *Summaries of Papers presented at the Fourth World Sanskrit Conference*, pp. 79-82. Berlin: Humboldt University, Institute of Asian Studies.

Banerjea, A.C. (1963). *Studies in the Brāhmaṇas.* Delhi: Motilal Banarsidass.

Banerji Shastri, A. (1936-37). "The Nāgas." *Annals of the Bhandarkar Oriental Research Institute*, vol. XVIII, pp. 338-350.

Bare, James. (1976). *Phonetics and Phonology in Pāṇini.* Natural Language Studies, no. 21. Ann Arbor: Phonetics Laboratory, University of Michigan.

Basu, Amitabh. (1969). "A Prospectus for Population-Biological Study of Indian Castes." *Journal of the Indian Anthropological Society*, vol. IV, pp. 89-98.

Baudhāyanadharmaśāstra. Edited by E. Hultzsch. 1884. Leipzig.

Bendrey, V.S. (1943). Ed. Keśava Paṇḍita's *Daṇḍanītiprakaraṇam.* Pune: Bhārat Itihās Saṃśodhak MaṇḍaḶ.

Bhandarkar, D.R. (1911). "Foreign Elements in the Hindu Population." *Indian Antiquary*, pp. 7-37.

———. (1931). "Aryan Immigration into Eastern India." *Annals of the Bhandarkar Oriental Research Institute*, vol. XII, pt. II, pp. 103-116.

Bhandarkar, R.G. (1933). *Collected Works.* In three volumes. Edited by N.B. Utgikar. *Government Oriental Series.* Pune: Bhandarkar Oriental Research Institute.

Bhattacharya, Bishnupada. (1958). *Yāska's Nirukta and the Science of Etymology.* Calcutta.

Bhattacharya, P.C. (1975). "Sino-Tibetan (Boro), Assamese, Bengali and Indic Languages." *Indian Linguistics*, vol. 36, no. 3, pp. 240-246.

Bhave, V.L., and Tulpule, S.G. (1963). *Mahārāṣṭra-Sārasvata* by Bhave, with an Appendix by Tulpule. Bombay: Popular Prakashan.

Bhise, Usha R. (1980). "The Influence of Marathi Idiom on 20th Century Sanskrit Plays." *Bhāratīya Vidyā*, vol. XL, nos. 2-3, pp. 76-83.

Bloch, Jules. (1934, 1965). *Indo-Aryan, From the Vedas to Modern Times.* French original published in Paris, 1934; revised by the author and translated by Alfred Master, Paris, 1965.

———. (1920, 1970). *The Formation of the Marāṭhī Language.* French original published in Paris, 1920; translated into English by Dev Raj Chanana. 1970. Delhi.

Bloomfield, Maurice. (1906). *Vedic Concordance.* Cambridge: Harvard University Press.

———. (1929). "On Diminutive Pronouns in Jaina Sanskrit." *Indian Studies in Honor of Charles Rockwell Lanman*, pp. 7- 25. Cambridge, MA: Harvard University Press.

Bloomfield, Maurice, and Franklin Edgerton. (1932). *Vedic Variants*, vol. 2. Philadelphia.

Böhtlingk, Otto. (1887). *Pāṇinis Grammatik.* Leipzig: Verlag von H. Haessel.

Bṛhadāraṇyaka-Upaniṣad. Eighteen Principal Upaniṣads. Edited by V.P. Limaye and R.D. Wadekar. 1958. Pune: Vaidika Saṃśodhana MaṇḍaLa.

Bronkhorst, Johannes. (1981). "Nirukta and Aṣṭādhyāyī: Their Shared Presuppositions." *Indo-Iranian Journal*, vol. 23, pp. 1-14.

Brough, John. (1953). *The Early Brahmanical System of Gotra and Pravara.* Cambridge: Cambridge University Press.

———. (1962). *The Gāndhārī Dharmapada.* London Oriental Series 7. London: Oxford University Press.

Brown, Norman. (1953). *The United States and India and Pakistan.* Cambridge: Harvard University Press.

Bühler, Georg. (1895). *On the Origin of the Indian Brāhma Alphabet.* London.

———. (1898). *The Sacred Laws of the Āryas as taught in the Schools of Āpastamba, Gautama, Vasiṣṭha and Baudhāyana. Sacred Books of the East*, vol. II. New York.

Burrow, Thomas. (1936). "The Dialectical Position of the Niya Prakrit." In *Indian and Iranian Studies*, presented to George A. Grierson, pp. 419-435. London: University of London.

———. (1955). *The Sanskrit Language.* London: Faber and Faber.

———. (1968). *Collected Papers on Dravidian Linguistics.* Department of Linguistics publication no. 13. Annamalainagar: Annamalai University.

———. (1971). "Spontaneous Cerebrals in Sanskrit." *Bulletin of the School of Oriental and African Studies*, vol. 34, pp. 538-559.

———. (1972). "A Reconsideration of Fortunatov's Law." *Bulletin of the School of Oriental and African Studies*, vol. 35, pp. 531-545.

Burrow, Thomas, and M.B. Emeneau. (1961). *A Dravidian Etymological Dictionary*. Oxford: Oxford University Press.

Cardona, George. (1976). *Pāṇini: A Survey of Research*. The Hague, Paris: Mouton.

———. (1977). Review of Laddu (1974). *Language*, vol. 53, pp. 221-224.

———. (1980). "On the Paribhāṣā *upapadavibhakteḥ kārakavibhaktir balīyasī*." *Studien zur Indologie und Iranistik*, Heft 5/6, pp. 27-48.

Chakladar, H.C. (1928). "Eastern India and Āryāvarta." *Indian Historical Quarterly*, vol. 4, no. 1, pp. 84-101.

———. (1961-62). "Aryan Occupation of Eastern India." *Indian Studies, Past and Present*, 3. Calcutta.

Chanda, Ramaprasad. (1916). *The Indo-Aryan Races*. Rajshahi; reprinted in *Indian Studies, Past and Present*, Calcutta, 1969.

Chatterjee, K.C. (1934). "The Critics of Sanskrit Grammar." *Journal of the Department of Letters*, vol. 24, pp. 1-21. Calcutta: University of Calcutta.

Chatterji, S.K. (1936). "Purāṇa Legends and the Prakrit Tradition in New Indo-Aryan." In *Indian and Iranian Studies*, presented to George A. Grierson, pp. 457-466 London: University of London.

———. (1950). "*Kirātajanakṛti*, The Indo-Mongoloids, Their Contribution to the History and Culture of India." *Journal of the Royal Asiatic Society of Bengal, Letters*, vol. XVI, no. 2, pp. 143-235.

———. (1951). "Race-Movements and Pre-historic Culture." In *The Vedic Age*, pp. 143-171. Bombay: Bharatiya Vidya Bhavana.

———. (1956). "Old Tamil, Ancient Tamil and Primitive Dravidian." *Tamil Culture*, vol. 5, no. 2, pp. 1-28.

———. (1958). "Indianism and Sanskrit." *Annals of the Bhandarkar Oriental Research Institute*, vol. 38, pts. 1-2, pp. 1-33.

———. (1960). *Indo-Aryan and Hindi*. Calcutta: Firma K.L. Mukhopadhyaya.

———. (1960a). "The Pronunciation of Sanskrit." *Indian Linguistics*, vol. 21, pp. 61-82.

———. (1962). *Indianism and the Indian Synthesis*. Calcutta: University of Calcutta.

———. (1965). *Dravidian.* Annamalainagar: Annamalai University.

Chattopadhyaya, K.C. (1974). "Did Pāṇini Envisage 'A' as a Close Vowel?" *Charudeva Shastri Felicitation Volume*, pp. 194-205. Delhi.

Chaudhuri, S.B. (1948). "Regional Divisions of Ancient India." *Annals of the Bhandarkar Oriental Research Institute*, vol. XXIX, pp. 123-146.

Converse, H.S. (1974). "The Agnicayana Rite: Indigenous Origin?" *History of Religions*, vol. 14, no. 2, pp. 81-95.

Damsteegt, Th. (1978). *Epigraphical Hybrid Sanskrit.* Leiden: E.J. Brill.

Dandekar, R.N. (1961). *Vedic Bibliography*, vol. 2. Poona.

———. (1967). *Some Aspects of the History of Hinduism.* Pune: University of Poona.

Dani, A.H. (1963). *Indian Paleography.* Oxford: Oxford University Press.

Dāsabodh. By Rāmadās. Edited by N.R. Phatak. Bombay: Surekha Prakashan, 1966.

Daśarūpaka. By Dhanañjaya. With the commentary *Avaloka* by Dhanika and *Laghuṭīkā* by Bhaṭṭanṛsiṃha. Edited by T. Venkatacharya. *Adyar Library Series*, 97. Madras: Adyar Library, 1969.

Das Gupta, Jyotirindra. (1970). *Language Conflict and National Development.* Berkeley & Los Angeles: University of California Press.

Dasgupta, Probal. (1972). "Coronality, Old Indo-Aryan Palatals, and Ṇatva." *Indian Linguistics*, vol. 33, no. 2, pp. 99-122.

Deb, H.K. (1922). "India and Elam." *Journal of the American Oriental Society*, vol. 42, pp. 194-197.

———. (1925). "Rājaśekhara on Śiśunāga." *Journal of the American Oriental Society*, vol. 45, pp. 72-75.

Deo, G.S. (1943). *Satkāryottejak Sabhā Suvarṇamahotsav Granth, Rāmadās āṇi Rāmadāsī*, pt. 50. Dhulia: Satkāryottejak Sabhā.

Deshpande, A.N. (1966). *Prācīn Marāṭhī Vāṅmayācā Itihās*, pt. 1. Pune: Venus Prakashan.

Deshpande, Madhav M. (1972). "Pāṇinian Procedure of *Tapara-karaṇa*: A Historical Investigation." *Zeitschrift für vergleichende Sprachforschung*, Band 86, Heft 2, pp. 207-254.

———. (1975a). "Phonetics of *V* in Pāṇini." *Annals of the Bhandarkar Oriental Research Institute*, vol. 56, pp. 45-65.

———. (1975b). *Critical Studies in Indian Grammarians, I, The Theory of Homogeneity.* The Michigan Series in South and Southeast Asian Languages and Linguistics, no. 2. Ann Arbor: Center for South and Southeast Asian Studies, The University of Michigan.

———. (1975c). "Phonetics of Short *A* in Sanskrit." *Indo-Iranian Journal*, vol. 17, pp. 195-209.

———. (1976). "On the *Ṛk-Prātiśākhya* 13.5-6." *Indian Linguistics*, vol. 37, pp. 171-181.

———. (1977-78). "Some Aspects of Pre-historic Indo-Aryan." *Diamond Jubilee Volume, Annals of the Bhandarkar Oriental Research Institute.* Pp. 121-128.

———. (1978). "Pāṇinian Grammarians on Dialectal Variation." *Brahmavidya, Adyar Library Bulletin*, vol. 42, pp. 61-114.

———. (1979). "History, Change and Permanence: A Classical Indian Perspective." In *Contributions to South Asian Studies I.* Edited by Gopal Krishna. Pp. 1-28. Delhi: Oxford University Press.

———. (1979a). *Sociolinguistic Attitudes in India: A Historical Reconstruction.* Ann Arbor: Karoma Publishers, Inc.

———. (1979b). "Genesis of Ṛgvedic Retroflexion, A Historical and Sociolinguistic Investigation." In Deshpande-Hook (1979), pp. 235-315.

———. (1980). *Evolution of Syntactic Theory in Sanskrit Grammar: Syntax of the Sanskrit Infinitive -tumUN.* Ann Arbor: Karoma Publishers, Inc.

———. (1981). "Pāṇini and the Vedic Evidence: A Peep into the 'Past'." *Golden Jubilee Volume*, pp. 52-65. Pune: Vaidika Saṃśodhan MaṇḍaLa.

———. (1982a). "Linguistic Presuppositions of Pāṇini 8.3.26-27." *Proceedings of the International Seminar on Pāṇini*, pp. 23-42. Pune: Centre of Advanced Study in Sanskrit, University of Poona.

———. (1982b). "Rājaśekhara on Ethnic and Linguistic Geography of India." In *Dr. D.N. Shastri Felicitation Volume: Indological Studies*, pp. 312-327. Ghaziabad: Vimal Prakashan.

———. (1983a). "Nation and Region: A Sociolinguistic Perspective on Maharashtra." In *National Unity: The South Asian Experience.* Edited by Milton Israel. Pp. 111-134. Delhi: Promilla & Co., Publishers.

———. (1983b). "Pāṇini as a Frontier Grammarian." *CLS 19, Papers from the 19th Regional Meeting*, pp. 110-116. Chicago: Chicago Linguistic Society.

———. (1985a). "Sanskrit Grammarians on Diglossia." In *South Asian Languages: Structure, Convergence and Diglossia.* Edited by Bh. Krishnamurti. Pp. 312-321. Delhi: Motilal Banarsidass.

———. (1985b). "Sanskrit Grammarians: Differing Perspectives in Cultural Geography." *Aligarh Journal of Oriental Studies,* vol. II, nos. 1-2, pp. 57-68.

———. (1985c). "Historical Change and the Theology of Eternal Sanskrit." *Zeitschrift für vergleichende Sprachforschung,* vol. 98, no. 1, pp. 122-149.

———. (1987). "Sanskrit and Prakrit: Some Sociolinguistic Issues." In *Select Papers from SALA-7* (South Asian Languages Analysis Roundtable Conference, held in Ann Arbor, May 17-19, 1985). Edited by Elena Bashir, Madhav M. Deshpande, and Peter E. Hook. Pp. 76-93. Bloomington: Indiana University Linguistics Club.

———. (1988). "Pāṇini and the Northwestern dialect: Some suggestions on Sūtra 3.3.10." In *Languages and Cultures, Studies in Honor of Edgar C. Polomé.* Pp. 111-122. Berlin: Mouton de Gruyter.

———. (Forthcoming). "Vedas in Ancient India: From Speech-acts to Magical Sounds." In *Word in the Religious Traditions of the World.* Edited by C. Jan Schwearingen. University of Arizona Press.

———. (In preparation) "Aryans, Non-Aryans and Brahmins: A Study in Sociolinguistic History."

Deshpande, Madhav M., & Hook, Peter Edwin. (1979). Editors. *Aryan and Non-Aryan in India.* Ann Arbor: Karoma Publishers, Inc. & Center for South and Southeast Asian Studies, the University of Michigan.

Devasthali, G.V. (1962). "The Aim of the Vārttikas of Kātyāyana." In *Munshi Felicitation Volume,* pp. 52-63. Bombay: Bharatiya Vidya Bhavana.

Dīghanikāya. In 3 Volumes. *Nālandā Devanāgarī Pali Series.* 1958. Nalanda: Pali Publication Board, Bihar Government.

Ebert, R.P. (1976). Introduction to *Diachronic Syntax.* Chicago: Chicago Linguistic Society.

Edgerton, Franklin. (1936). "The Prakrit Underlying Buddhistic Hybrid Sanskrit." In *Indian and Iranian Studies,* presented to George Grierson. London: University of London.

———. (1953). *Buddhist Hybrid Sanskrit Grammar and Dictionary.* vol. I, *Grammar*; vol. II. *Dictionary.* New Haven: Yale University Press.

Emeneau, M.B. (1954). "Linguistic Prehistory of India." *Proceedings of the American Philosophical Society*, vol. 98, pp. 282-292.

———. (1956). "India as a Linguistic Area." *Language*, vol. 32, pp. 3-16.

———. (1962a). "Bilingualism and Structural Borrowing." *Proceedings of the American Philosophical Society*, vol. 106, no. 4, pp. 430-42.

———. (1962b). *Brahui and Dravidian Comparative Grammar*. Berkeley: University of California.

———. (1967). *Collected Papers on Dravidian Linguistics, Ethnology and Folktales*. Annamalainagar: Annamalai University.

———. (1971). "Dravidian and Indo-Aryan: The Indian Linguistic Area." *Symposium on Dravidian Civilization*, pp. 33-68. Austin, Texas: University of Texas.

———. (1974). "Indian Linguistic Area Revisited." *International Journal of Dravidian Linguistics*, vol. III, no. 1, pp. 92-134.

Emeneau, M.B., and Thomas Burrow. (1962). *Dravidian Borrowings from Indo-Aryan*. Berkeley and Los Angeles: University of California Press.

Esteller, A. (1968). "Problems in the Text-Critical Reconstruction of the Ṛgveda-Palimpsest." *Annals of the Bhandarkar Oriental Research Institute*, vols. 48-49, pp. 1-16.

———. (1969). "The Quest for the Original Ṛgveda." *Annals of the Bhandarkar Oriental Research Institute*, vol. 50, pp. 1-40.

Fortunatov, Ph. (1881). "L + Dental im Altindischen." *Beiträge zur Kunde der Indo-Germanischen Sprachen* (Göttingen), vol. 6, pp. 215-220.

Gandhi, L.B. (1967). *Three Apabhraṃśa Works of Jinadattasūri*. Baroda: Oriental Institute.

Ganeshan, S.N. (1971). "Phonological Pattern of Tamil and Homonymy Due to Loanwords from Sanskrit." *Proceedings of the First All-India Conference of Linguists*, pp. 152-157. Pune: Linguistic Society of India.

Ganeshsundaram, P.C., and S. Vaidyanathan. (1958). "An Evaluation of Sanskrit Loan-words in Tamil from the Point of View of Nannūl." *Turner Jubilee Volume. Indian Linguistics*, vol. 1, pp. 63-70.

Gaüḍavaho, by Vākpatirāja. Originally edited by S.B. Pandit. Re-edited by N.R. Utgikar. *Bombay Sanskrit and Prakrit Series*, no. 34. Pune, 1927.

Gautama-dharma-śāstra. Edited by A.F. Stenzler. 1876. London: Sanskrit Text Society.

Geiger, W., and E. Kuhn. (1895-1901). *Grundriss der Iranischen Philologie,* vol. 1. Strassburg.

Gharpure, J.R. (1946). English translation of *Smṛticandrikā, Āhnikakāṇḍa. The Collection of Hindu Law Texts,* vol. XXVIII. Bombay.

Ghatage, A.M. (1941). *Introduction to Ardhamāgadhī.* Kolhapur: School and College Bookstall.

———. (1962). *Historical Linguistics and Indo-Aryan Languages.* Bombay: University of Bombay.

Ghosh, Batakrishna. (1951). "Vedic Literature - General View." In *The Vedic Age,* pp. 229-244. Bombay: Bharatiya Vidya Bhavana.

Ghosh, Manomohan. (1934). "The Date of the Bharata Nāṭyaśāstra." *Journal of the Department of Letters,* University of Calcutta, vol. XXV, pp. 1-54.

Gīrvāṇavāṅmañjarī, by Dhuṇḍirāja Kavi. Edited by U.P. Shah. *The M.S. University Oriental Series,* no. 4. Baroda: Oriental Institute, 1960.

Gode, P.K. (1954). *Studies in Indian Literary History.* vol. II. Bombay, 1954.

———. (1956). *Studies in Indian Literary History.* vol. III. Pune, 1956.

Gramopadhye, G.B. (1941). *Peśave Daptarātīl Marāṭhī Bhāṣece Svarūp.* Pune: B.M. Nerlekar.

Grierson, George Abraham. (1906). *The Piśāca Languages of North Western India.* London.

———. (1929). "The Language of the Mahānayaprakāśa." *Memoirs of the Asiatic Society of Bengal,* vol. 11, no. 2.

———. (1931). "On the Modern Indo-Aryan Vernaculars." *Indian Antiquary,* vol. lx-lxii, supplement, pp. 6-52.

Gulati, R.K. (1970). "Biological and Cultural Affinities, An Interpretation." *The Eastern Anthropologist,* vol. XXIII, no. 3, pp. 235-242.

Hamp, Eric P. (1976). "Why Syntax Needs Phonology." In *Papers from the Parasession on Diachronic Syntax.* Chicago: Chicago Linguistic Society.

Hart, George L. (1975). *The Poems of Ancient Tamil.* Berkeley: University of California Press.

Hertel, Johannes (1921). Ed. *Bharaṭakadvātriṃśikā. Sächsische Forschungsinstitut für Indogermanistik. Indische Abteilung.* Nr. 2. Leipzig, 1921.

———. (1922). *On the Literature of the Śvetāmbaras of Gujarat. Sächsische Forschungsinstitut für Indogermanistik. Indische Abteilung.* Nr. 1. Leipzig.

Hock, Hans Henrich. (1975). "Substratum Influence on (Ṛgvedic) Sanskrit?" *Studies in the Linguistic Sciences*, vol. 5, no. 2, pp. 76-125. Urbana: University of Illinois.

Hock, Hans Henrich, and Rajeshwari Pandharipande. (1976). "The sociolinguistic position of Sanskrit in pre-Muslim India." In *Studies in Language Learning*, vol. 11, pp. 105-138. Urbana: University of Illinois.

Hoffmann, Karl. (1960). "Review of Wackernagel's *Altindische Grammatik*." *Zeitschrift der Deutschen Morganländischen Gesellschaft*, vol. 110, pp. 175-182.

Hoijer, Harry. (1948). "Linguistic and Cultural Change." *Language*, vol. 24, no. 4, pp. 335-345.

Hutchins, Francis G. (1967). *The Illusion of Permanence: British Imperialism in India.* Princeton: Princeton University Press.

Hymes, Dell, ed. (1964). *Language in Culture and Society.* New York: Harper and Row.

———. (1971). *Pidginization and Creolization of Languages.* London: Cambridge University Press.

Ivanov, V.V., and V.N. Toporov. (1968). *Sanskrit.* Moscow: Nauka Publishing House.

Jha, Vivekanand. (1970). "Varṇasaṃkara in the Dharmasūtras." *Journal of the Economic and Social History of the Orient*, vol. XIII, pp. 273-288.

Jñāneśvarī. By Jñāneśvar. Edited by S.V. Dandekar. 4th edition. Pune: Prasad Prakashan. 1967.

Joshi, S.B. (1951). "Etymology of Place-Names Paṭṭi-Haṭṭi, Some Observations on the History of Maharashtra and Karnataka." *Annals of the Bhandarkar Oriental Research Institute*, vol. 32, pp. 41-56.

———. (1952). *Marhāṭī Saṃskṛtī, Kāhī Samasyā.* Pune: Antar Bharati Prakashan.

Joshi, S.D., and Roodbergen, J.A.F. (1969). *Patañjali's Vyākaraṇa-Mahābhāṣya, Avyayībhāva-Tatpuruṣāhnika.* Edited and translated with introduction and notes. Pune: Centre of Advanced Study in Sanskrit, University of Poona.

Kantor, R.N., and R.J. Jeffers. (1984). "*A History of the Sanskrit Gerund.*" *Indogermanische Forschungen*, Band 89, pp. 89-103.

Karvé, Irawati. (1953). *Kinship Organisation in India. Deccan College Monograph Series* 11. Pune: Deccan College.

———. (1968). *Hindu Society - An Interpretation.* 2nd revised edition. Pune: Deshmukh Prakashan.

Kāśikāvṛtti. By Vāmana and Jayāditya. With *Padamañjarī* by Haradatta and *Nyāsa* by Jinendrabuddhi. Six volumes. *Prācya Bhāratī Series*. 1965-67. Banaras: Tara Publications.

Kathāsaritsāgara. By Somadeva. Edited by Jagadishlal Sastri. 1970. Delhi: Motilal Banarsidass.

Katre, S.M. (1944). *Some Problems of Historical Linguistics in Indo-Aryan*. Bombay: University of Bombay. Reprinted by Deccan College, Pune, 1965.

Kāvyādarśa. By Daṇḍin. Edited by Rangacharya Raddi Shastri. 1938. *Government Oriental Series*, Class A, no. 4. Poona: Bhandarkar Oriental Research Institute.

Kāvyālaṃkārasūtra. By Vāmana. Edited by Narayana Rama Acharya. 4th edition. 1953. Bombay: Nirnaya Sagara Press.

Kāvyamīmāṃsā. By Rājaśekhara. Edited by C.D. Dalal and R.A. Sastry. Revised and enlarged by K.S. Ramaswami Sastri. *Gaekwad's Oriental Series*, no. 1. 1934. Baroda: Oriental Institute.

Keith, A.B. (1909). See *Aitareya-Āraṇyaka*.

Kielhorn, Franz. (1887). "Notes on the Mahābhāṣya, 7, Some Devices of Indian Grammarians." *Indian Antiquary*, vol. 16, pp. 244-252.

Kimura, Ryukan. (1927). *A Historical Study of the Terms Hīnayāna and Mahāyāna, and the Origins of Mahāyāna Buddhism*. Calcutta: University of Calcutta.

Kiparsky, Paul. (1979). *Pāṇini as a Variationist*. Cambridge: MIT Press & Poona University Press.

KM See: *Kāvyamīmāṃsā*.

Konow, Sten. (1929). *Kharoṣṭhī Inscriptions. Corpus Inscriptionum Indicarum*, vol. 2, pt. 1. Calcutta.

———. (1936). "Note on the Ancient North-Western Prakrit." In *Indian and Iranian Studies*, presented to George Grierson, pp. 603-612. London: University of London.

Kosambi, D.D. (1947). "Early Brahmins and Brahmanism." *Journal of the Bombay Branch of the Royal Asiatic Society*, vol. 23, New Series, pp. 39-46.

———. (1950). "On the Origin of the Brahmin Gotras." *Journal of the Bombay Branch of the Royal Asiatic Society*, vol. 26, New Series, pp. 26-80.

———. (1965). *Ancient India*. New York: Meridian.

Kuhn, Thomas. (1962). *The Structure of Scientific Revolution*. 2nd edition. Chicago: Chicago University Press.

Kuiper, F.B.J. (1948). *Proto-Munda Words in Sanskrit.* Amsterdam.

———. (1955). "Ṛgvedic Loanwords." In *Festschrift für W. Kirfel, Studia Indologica, Bonner Orientalistische Studien,* Neue Serie, Band 3. Bonn.

——— (1958). "Ṛgvedic *Kīrín-* and *KrīḶí-*." *Indian Linguistics,* vol. 1, pp. 349-362.

———. (1965). "Consonant Variation in Munda." In *Indo-Pacific Studies,* pt. 1. Edited by Milner-Henderson. Amsterdam.

———. (1967). "The Genesis of a Linguistic Area." *Indo-Iranian Journal,* vol. 10, pp. 81-102.

———. (1967a). "The Sanskrit Nominative Singular *Víṭ.*" *Indo- Iranian Journal,* vol. 10, pp. 103-125.

Kuvalayamālā. By Uddyotanasūri. Edited by A.N. Upadhye. *Singhi Jaina Granthamālā,* no. 45. 1959. Bombay: Bharatiya Vidya Bhavana.

Laddu, S.D. (1974). *Evolution of the Sanskrit Language from Pāṇini to Patañjali.* Pune: Poona University Press.

Lalitavistara. Edited by P.L. Vaidya. *Buddhist Sanskrit Text Series I.* Darbhanga, Bihar: Mithila Institute, 1958.

Law, B.C. (1933). *A History of Pali Literature.* Vols. I-II. Calcutta: University of Calcutta.

Lovins, J.B. (1974). "Why Loan Phonology is Natural Phonology?" In *Natural Phonology,* pp. 240-250. Chicago: Chicago Linguistic Society.

Macdonell, A.A. (1916). *A Vedic Grammar for Students.* Oxford: Oxford University Press. Reprinted in 1971.

Madhok, Balraj. (1970). *Indianisation.* New Delhi: S. Chand & Co.

Mahābhāṣya (K). By Patañjali. Edited by Franz Kielhorn in three volumes, 1880-1885. 3rd revised edition by K.V. Abhyankar. 1962-1972. Poona: Bhandarkar Oriental Research Institute.

Mahābhāṣya (M) of Patañjali. With the commentary *Pradīpa* by Kaiyaṭa, and *Uddyota* by Nāgeśabhaṭṭa. In three volumes. Delhi: Motilal Banarsidass, 1967.

Mahadevan, Iravatham. (1968). "Tamil-Brāhmī Inscriptions of the Sangam Age." *Second International Conference - Seminar of Tamil Studies,* pp. 73-106. Madras.

———. (1970). *Tamil-Brāhmī Inscriptions.* Madras: State Department of Archaeology, Government of Tamilnadu. Pp. 1-15.

Mahalnobis, P.C. (1927). "Analysis of Race-Mixture in Bengal." *Journal of the Asiatic Society of Bengal,* New Series, vol. XXIII, pp. 301-333.

Majumdar, D.N., C. Radhakrishna Rao, and P.C. Mahalnobis. (1960). *Race Elements in Bengal, A Quantitative Study. Indian Statistical Series*, no. 3. Calcutta: Indian Statistical Institute.

Manusmṛti. Edited by V.L. Panshikar. 1902. 3rd ed. Bombay: Nirnaya Sagara Press.

Martinet, André. (1966). *Elements of General Linguistics*. Chicago: University of Chicago Press.

Master, Alfred. (1960). "Initial Cerebrals in Indo-Aryan." In *P.K. Gode Commemorial Volume*, pp. 260-269. Pune: Oriental Book Agency.

———. (1964). *A Grammar of Old Marāṭhī*. Oxford: Oxford University Press.

MB See: *Mahābhāṣya*.

McAlpin, David. (1979). "Linguistic Prehistory." In Deshpande-Hook (1979), pp. 175-189.

Mehendale, M.A. (1948). *Historical Grammar of Inscriptional Prakrits*. Pune: Deccan College.

———. (1963). "Upaniṣadic Etymologies." In *Munshi Felicitation Volume*. Bombay: Bharatiya Vidya Bhavana.

———. (1965). "The Use of *Ḷ* in the Speech of Yāska." In *Nirukta Notes*, Series I, pp. 8-16. Pune: Deccan College.

———. (1968). *Some Aspects of Indo-Aryan Linguistics*. Bombay: University of Bombay.

———. (1975). "The Ṛgvedasaṃhitākāra and Father Esteller." *Bulletin of the Deccan College Research Institute*, vol. 35, nos. 1-2, pp. 97-116.

Meillet, Antoine. (1912-13). "Les Consonnes intervocaliques en Védique." *Indogermanische Forschungen*, vol. 31, pp. 120-125.

Mīmāṃsādarśana. By Jaimini. With Śabara's *Bhāṣya* and Kumārila's *Tantravārttika* and *Ṭupṭīkā*. In 6 parts. *Ānandāśrama Sanskrit Series*, Volume 97. Pune: Ānandāśrama.

Mīmāṃsākośa. Edited by Kevalānanda Sarasvatī. In 7 volumes. 1952. Vai: Prājña Pāṭhaśālā.

Miranda, Rocky V. (1977). "The Assimilation of Dravidian Loans to Konkani Phonological and Morphological Patterns." *Indo-Iranian Journal*, vol. 19, nos. 3-4.

Nadkarni, Mangesh V. (1975). "Bilingualism and Syntactic Change in Konkani." *Language*, vol. 51, pp. 672-683..

Nāṭyaśāstra. Ascribed to Bharata. Edited by Sivadatta and Kashinath Pandurang Parab. 1894. *Kāvyamālā Series*, no. 42. Bombay: Nirnaya Sagara Press.

Navanīt. A Collection of Marathi Poetry, prepared by Parashuram Pant Godbole, and revised by Shrikrishna Shastri Talekar and Ravaji Shastri Godbole. 1878. Bombay: Government Central Book Depot.

Nirukta. By Yāska. With Durga's commentary. *Ānandāśrama Sanskrit Series*, no. 88, pts. 1-2. 1921, 1926. Pune: Ānandāśrama.

Norman, K.R. (1980). *Pali Literature.* Wiesbaden: Otto Harrassowitz.

Oldenberg, Hermann. (1882, 1890). *Buddha; His Life, His Doctrine, His Order.* Original German published in Berlin, 1882. English translation by Hoey, London, 1890.

———. (1890, 1962). *Ancient India, Its Languages and Religions.* Originally published in *Deutsche Randschau*, Berlin, 1890; English edition, Calcutta, 1962.

———. (1896, 1973). *Vedic Research.* Original German published in *Zeitschrift der deutschen morgenländischen Gesellschaft*, vol. 50, 1986. Translated by V.G. Paranjpe, Pune, 1973.

Panikkar, K.M. (1961). *Hindu Society at Cross Roads.* Bombay: Asia Publishing House, 1955; 3rd revised edition, 1961.

Pāṇinīya-śikṣā. Critically edited in all its five recensions, with introduction, translation, and notes, by Manmohan Ghosh. Calcutta: University of Calcutta.

Paṇṇavaṇāsutta. Edited by Punyavijaya Muni and Dalsukh Malvania. 1969. *Jaina Āgama Series*, no. 9, Pts. 1-2. Bombay: Mahavira Jaina Vidyalaya.

Parpola, Asko. (1975). "Tasks, Methods and Results in the Study of the Indus Script." *Journal of the Royal Asiatic Society*, pp. 178-209.

Pawagi, N.B. (1901). *Prākṛt va Marāṭhī Bhāṣecā Itihās.* Pune.

Raghavan, V. (1973). *Studies on Some Concepts of the Alaṃkāra Śāstra. Adyar Library Series*, 33. Madras: Adyar Library.

Rahurkar, V.G. (1974). "Who Were the Paṇis?" *CASS Studies*, no. 2, pp. 43-50. Pune: University of Poona.

Rajwade, V.K. (1958). *Lekhasaṃgraha.* Edited by Lakshman Shastri Joshi. Delhi: Sahitya Akademi.

Rakshit, H.K. (1966). "The Brahmans of India, An Anthropometric Study." *Man in India*, vol. 46, pp. 33-58.

Rao, G. Subba. (1954). *Indian Words in English.* Oxford: Oxford University Press.

Rao, S.R. (1972-73). "The Indus People Begin to Speak." *Journal of the Andhra Historical Research Society*, vol. 33, pp. 1-34.

Rasataraṅgiṇī. A selection of Marathi poetry. Edited by S.V. Pendse. 3rd edition. Bombay: Macmillan & Company, 1923.

Rastogi, Moti Lal. (1957). "Śaunaka and Abhinihita Sandhi in Ṛgveda." *Indian Linguistics, Bagchi Memorial Volume*, pp. 21-29.

Renou, Louis. (1941). "The Valid Forms in Bhāṣā." *Indian Historical Quarterly*, Volume XVII, pp. 245-250.

———. (1941-42). "Connexions entre le Rituel et la Grammaire en Sanskrit." *Journal Asiatique*, vol. 233, pp. 105-165.

———. (1942). *Terminologie Grammaticale du Sanskrit*. In three volumes. Paris.

Ṛgveda-Prātiśākhya, pt. 1. Edited by M.D. Shastri. Banaras, 1959.

Risley, Herbert. (1915). *The People of India*. 2nd edition. London: W. Thacker & Co.

Ṛk-Prātiśākhya, pt. 1. Edited by M.D. Shastri, Banaras, 1959.

Ṛktantra. Ascribed to Śākaṭāyana. Edited by Surya Kanta. Lahore, 1939; reprinted in Delhi, 1971.

Rocher, Rosane. (1962). "The Hindu Grammarians and Linguistic Change." *Journal of the Oriental Institute*, Baroda, vol. II, p. 260-68.

———. (1975). "India." *Historiography of Linguistics, Current Trends in Linguistics*, vol. 13, pp. 3-67. The Hague, Paris: Mouton.

RPR See: *Ṛgveda-Prātiśākhya*

RT See: *Ṛktantra*.

Saloman, Richard. (1978). "The Three Cursed Rivers of the East and their Significance for the Historical Geography of Ancient India." *Adyar Library Bulletin*, vol. 42, pp. 32-60.

Śāṅkhāyana-Āraṇyaka. See *Aitareya-Āraṇyaka*.

Sardar, G.B. (1969). *The Saint Poets of Maharashtra*. Translated from Marathi into English by Kumud Mehta. Bombay: Orient Longmans.

Sardesai, G.S. (1957). "Blue Prints of Shivaji's Career - The Chatrapati's Titles." *Journal of the University of Bombay*, vol. XXV (New Series), pp. 17-21.

Sastri, Nilakanta K.A. (1967). *Cultural Contacts between Aryans and Dravidians*. Bombay: Manaktala and Sons.

Sastri, Subramanya P.S. (1930). *Tolkāppiyam*. Vol. 1. English translation. Madras.

———. (1934). *History of Grammatical Theories in Tamil*. Madras.

Śatapatha-Brāhmaṇa. Edited by Albrecht Weber. Berlin, 1849. Reprinted in Banaras: *Chowkhamba Sanskrit Series*, vol. 96, 1964.

Scharfe, Hartmut. (1961). *Die Logik im Mahābhāṣya*. Berlin.

———. (1977). *Grammatical Literature*. In *A History of Indian Literature*, vol. 5, Fasc. 2. Edited by Jan Gonda. Wiesbaden: Otto Harrassowitz.

Schwartzberg, Joseph E. (1978). Ed. *A Historical Atlas of South Asia.* Chicago: The University of Chicago Press.

Schwarzchild, L.A. 1973. "Initial Retroflex Consonants in Middle Indo-Aryan." *Journal of the American Oriental Society*, vol. 93, no. 4, pp. 482-487.

Sekasubhodaya, by Halāyudha Miśra. Edited with notes, introduction, and translated into English by Sukumar Sen. *Bibliotheca Indica*, no. 286. Calcutta: Asiatic Society, 1963.

Shapiro, Michael C., and Schiffman, Harold F. (1981). *Language and Society in South Asia.* Delhi: Motilal Banarsidass.

Sharma, U.C. (1973). "The Dāśarājña War." *CASS Studies*, no. 1, pp. 101-126. Poona: University of Poona.

Sircar, D.C. (1960). *Studies in the Geography of Ancient and Medieval India.* Delhi: Motilal Banarsidass.

Skold, Hannes. (1926). "Papers on Pāṇini and Indian Grammar in General." *Lunds Universitets Årsskrift* (Leipzig), N.F. Avd. 1, Band 21, N. 8.

Southworth, Franklin C. (1971). "Detecting Prior Creolization, An Analysis of the Historical Origins of Marathi." In *Pidginization and Creolization of Languages.* Edited by Dell Hymes. Pp. 255-273. Cambridge: Cambridge University Press.

———. (1974). "Linguistic Stratigraphy of North India." *International Journal of Dravidian Linguistics*, vol. III, no. 2, pp. 201-223.

———. (1979). "Lexical Evidence for Early Contact between Indo-Aryan and Dravidian." In Deshpande-Hook (1979), pp. 191-233.

———. (1981). Review of Deshpande 1979. *Language*, vol. 57, pp. 932-935.

Southworth, Franklin C., and Apte, Mahadev. (1974). "Introduction" to *International Journal of Dravidian Linguistics*, vol. III, no. 1, pp. 1-20.

Srinivas, M.N. (1966). *Social Change in Modern India.* Berkeley & Los Angeles: University of California Press.

———. (1967). "The Cohesive Role of Sanskritization." In *India and Ceylon: Unity and Diversity*, pp. 67-82. Edited by Philip Mason. Oxford: Oxford University Press.

Staal, J.F. (1967). *Word Order in Sanskrit and Universal Grammar.* Foundations of Language, Supplementary Series, no. 5. Amsterdam.

———. (1974). "The Origin and Development of Linguistics in India." In *Studies in the History of Linguistics, Traditions and Paradigms*, pp. 63-73. Edited by Dell Hymes. Bloomington: Indiana University Press.

———. (1975). "The Concept of Metalanguage and its Indian Background." In *Journal of Indian Philosophy*, vol. 3, pp. 315-354.

———. (1982). "Ritual, Grammar, and the Origins of Science in India." *Journal of Indian Philosophy*, vol. 10, pp. 3-35.

Subbiah, Rama. (1968). "Tolkāppiyam and Phonetics." *Indo-Iranian Journal*, vol. 10, pp. 251-260.

Taittirīya-Brāhmaṇa. *Ānandāśrama Sanskrit Series*, no. 37. In three parts. 1934, 1938 and 1942. Pune: Ānandāśrama.

Taittirīya-Prātiśākhya. Edited and translated by W.D. Whitney. New Haven, 1868.

Thapar, Romila. (1973). *The Past and Prejudice*. Delhi: Publications Division, Government of India.

Thieme, Paul. (1955). Review of Burrow's *The Sanskrit Language*. *Language*, vol. 31, no. 3, pp. 428-448.

TPR See: *Taittirīya-Prātiśākhya*.

Trautmann, Thomas. (1974). "Cross-Cousin Marriage in Ancient North India?" In *Kinship and History in South Asia*, Michigan Papers on South and Southeast Asia, no. 7, pp. 61-103. Ann Arbor: Center for South and Southeast Asian Studies, The University of Michigan.

———. (1979). "The Study of Dravidian Kinship." In Deshpande and Hook (1979), pp. 153-173.

Tukārām-Gāthā. Edited by A.V. Marathe. 1964. Bombay: Sāhitya Rasamālā.

Tulpule, S.G. (1960). *An Old Marathi Reader*. Pune: Venus Prakashan.

———. (1973). *Yādav Kālīn Marāṭhī Bhāṣā*. A revised edition of the 1942 original. Pune: Venus Prakashan.

Turner, R.L. (1924). "Cerebralization in Sindhi." *Journal of the Royal Asiatic Society*, vol. 3, pp. 555-84.

———. (1975). *Collected Papers*. London: Oxford University Press.

Vaidya, C.V. (1930). *History of Sanskrit Literature*. Pune.

Vaidyanathan, S. (1958). "A Study of the Semantics of Sanskrit Loanwords in Modern Tamil." *Indian Linguistics*, vol. 1, pp. 95-99.

———. (1971). *Indo-Aryan Loan-words in Old Tamil*. Madras.

Vājasaneyi-Prātiśākhya. Edited and translated by Indu Rastogi. Kashi Sanskrit Series, no. 179. 1967. Banaras.

Vākyapadīya. By Bhartṛhari. Edited by K.V. Abhyankar and V.P. Limaye. *University of Poona Sanskrit and Prakrit Series*, vol. 2. 1965. Pune: University of Poona.

Vākyapadīya. By Bhartṛhari. *Kāṇḍa* I, with the *Vṛtti* and *Paddhati* of Harivṛṣabha. Edited by K.A. Subramania Iyer. 1966. Pune: Deccan College.

Varma, Siddheshwar. (1963). "Scientific and Technical Presentation as Reflected in the Mahābhāṣya of Patañjali." *Vishveshvarananda Indological Journal*, vol. I, no. 1, pp. 1-36.

Vāsiṣṭhadharmaśāstra. Edited by A.A. Führer. *Bombay Sanskrit and Prakrit Series*, no. XXIII. 1916. Bombay.

Vedic Variants. See Bloomfield and Edgerton (1932).

Viśvaguṇādarśacampū. By Veṅkaṭādhvarin. Edited by B.G. Yogi. Revised by M.G. Bakre. 1923. Bombay: Nirnaya Sagara Press.

VPR See: *Vājasaneyiprātiśākhya*.

Walleser, Max. (192). "Zur Aussprache von Skr. *a*." *Zeitschrift für Indologie und Iranistik* (Leipzig), Band 5, pp. 193-202.

Weinreich, Uriel. (1953). *Languages in Contact*. 3rd printing, 1964. Paris: Mouton.

Weinreich, Uriel; William Labov; and Maurice Herzog. (1968). *Empirical Foundations for a Theory of Language Change*. Austin: University of Texas Press.

Wujastyk, Dominik. (1982). "Do Paribhāṣās wrongly immunize Pāṇini's theory against criticism?" *Proceedings of the International Seminar on Pāṇini*, pp. 97-103. Pune: University of Poona.

Zvelebil, Kamil. (1970). *Comparative Dravidian Phonology*. The Hague-Paris: Mouton.

———. (1972). "The Descent of the Dravidians." *International Journal of Dravidian Linguistics*, vol. I, no. 2, pp. 57-63.

Zvelebil, Kamil, and Svarny. (1955). "Remarks on the Articulation of the Cerebral Consonants." *Archiv Orientalní*, vol. 23, pt. 3.

Zwicky, Arnold. (1970). "Greek-Letter Variables and the Sanskrit *ruki*-Class." *Linguistic Inquiry*, vol. 1, pp. 549-55.